SEASONS OF WORSHIP

SEASONS OF WORSHIP

A Spiritual Calendar for the Church Today

STEVEN D. BROOKS

WIPF & STOCK · Eugene, Oregon

SEASONS OF WORSHIP
A Spiritual Calendar for the Church Today

Copyright © 2024 Steven D. Brooks. All rights reserved. Except for brief quotations in critical publications or reviews, no part of this book may be reproduced in any manner without prior written permission from the publisher. Write: Permissions, Wipf and Stock Publishers, 199 W. 8th Ave., Suite 3, Eugene, OR 97401.

Wipf & Stock
An Imprint of Wipf and Stock Publishers
199 W. 8th Ave., Suite 3
Eugene, OR 97401

www.wipfandstock.com

PAPERBACK ISBN: 978-1-6667-8454-1
HARDCOVER ISBN: 978-1-6667-8455-8
EBOOK ISBN: 978-1-6667-8456-5

01/08/24

All Scripture quotations, unless otherwise indicated, are from The ESV® Bible (The Holy Bible, English Standard Version®), copyright © 2001 by Crossway, a publishing ministry of Good News Publishers. Used by permission. All rights reserved.

Scripture quotations notated (NRSV) are from New Revised Standard Version Bible, copyright © 1989 National Council of the Churches of Christ in the United States of America. Used by permission. All rights reserved worldwide.

Any Internet addresses (websites, blogs, etc.) printed in this book are offered as a resource. They are not intended in any way to be or imply a full endorsement of the author, nor does the author vouch for the content of these sites for the life of this book.

Art by Minna Lim

To Brooke,
my wife, best friend, and ministry partner,
who has encouraged me with the importance of the Christian year

In memory of Dr. William Lock, mentor and friend,
who shared his notes regarding this manuscript

Be sure to check out Worship Quest Ministries

Encouraging worship renewal and spiritual formation for the global Christian church
worshipquest.net

CONTENTS

PREFACE | xi

INTRODUCTION | xv

Chapter 1	WHAT'S IN A SEASON?	1
Chapter 2	BIBLICAL, HISTORICAL, AND THEOLOGICAL FOUNDATIONS FOR KEEPING SACRED TIME	4
Chapter 3	A CALL FOR UNITY	10
Chapter 4	CHRISTIAN YEAR SPIRITUALITY	13
Chapter 5	SACRED TIME: The Day. The Week. The Year	18
Chapter 6	ADVENT	35

Overview | 39
Song List | 41
Worship Service Overview | 45

First Sunday of Advent
Worship Service | 47
Scripture Presentation | 52

Second Sunday of Advent
Worship Service | 55
Scripture Presentation | 60

Third Sunday of Advent
Worship Service | 62
Scripture Presentation | 66

Fourth Sunday of Advent
Worship Service | 69
Scripture Presentation | 74

	Christmas Eve
	Candlelight Service | 76
	Scripture Presentation | 80
CHAPTER 7	CHRISTMAS | 82
	Overview | 86
	Song List | 88
	Worship Service | 92
	Scripture Presentation | 95
Chapter 8	EPIPHANY AND AFTER EPIPHANY | 97
	Overview | 106
	Song List | 108
	Worship Service | 111
	Scripture Presentation | 116
Chapter 9	LENT | 121
	Ash Wednesday
	Overview | 128
	Song List | 130
	Worship Service | 132
	Scripture Presentation | 141
	Lent
	Overview | 144
	Song List | 146
	Worship Service | 149
	Scripture Presentation | 154
Chapter 10	HOLY WEEK AND THE GREAT TRIDUUM | 157
	Palm/Passion Sunday
	Overview | 163
	Song List | 165
	Worship Service | 168
	Scripture Presentation | 173
	Maundy Thursday
	Overview | 175
	Song List | 176
	Worship Service | 178
	Scripture Presentation | 181

	Good Friday
	Overview | 183
	Song List | 184
	Worship Service | 187
	Scripture Presentation | 195

Easter Saturday/Vigil
Overview | 198
Song List | 200
Reflective Worship Experience | 202
Scripture Presentation | 205

Chapter 11   EASTER | 208

Easter Sunday
Overview | 214
Song List | 216
Worship Service | 219
Scripture Presentation | 227

Ascension Sunday
Overview | 231
Song List | 233
Worship Service | 236
Scripture Presentation | 240

Pentecost Sunday
Overview | 242
Song List | 244
Worship Service | 246
Scripture Presentation | 251

Chapter 12   AFTER PENTECOST | 253

Trinity Sunday
Overview | 259
Song List | 260
Worship Service | 262
Scripture Presentation | 266

Reformation Sunday
Overview | 268
Song List | 269
Worship Service | 271
Scripture Presentation | 276

All Saints' Sunday
Overview | 279
Song List | 281
Worship Service | 283
Scripture Presentation | 288

Christ The King Sunday
Overview | 293
Song List | 295
Worship Service | 298
Scripture Presentation | 303

CONCLUSION | 305

POSTSCRIPT | 307

SUGGESTED RESOURCES FOR LEARNING MORE ABOUT THE CHRISTIAN YEAR | 308

ABOUT THE ARTWORK | 309

BIBLIOGRAPHY | 311

PREFACE

My spiritual journey began at a young age. Every week, my older brother and I eagerly boarded the big blue church bus, which navigated through our neighborhood picking up kids like us to go to the local conservative Baptist church. As time went on, our family grew more involved, and my parents and sister joined us in becoming an integral part of this tight-knit church community. My father took on responsibilities as a deacon and the church's sound technician, while my mother found her role as a dedicated Sunday School teacher and choir member. Sundays were synonymous with church. In fact, I can't remember a Sunday during my childhood when we were not in church. A typical Sunday entailed a morning worship service, fellowship over lunch with church friends, an afternoon choir practice, and the evening service. We also attended the Wednesday night AWANA[1] program. Church held a significant place in our lives, and it was during those years that I devoted myself to Christ.

Because our church did not follow any official sacred pattern of time in worship, I had no real sense or understanding of sacred time. In fact, I had never even heard the term "sacred time" until I attended college, where I first learned of the Christian year—a calendar of seasons for the church that focuses on the life of Christ and subsequent birth and growth of the church. The observance of these seasons of the Christian year has a long history in the life of the Christian faith uniting the global church in telling the story of God's redemptive work in the world.

When I first learned about the Christian year, my reaction wasn't entirely positive. I mistakenly believed it would lead to inauthentic worship or empty rituals. I didn't see how the Christian year could reveal Christ and honor his life, death, resurrection, and eventual return. Fortunately, over time, my understanding and appreciation for the Christian year have grown,

---

1. AWANA is a non-profit organization with a mission to develop children and their families through Bible study and ministry; www.awana.org.

and I'm grateful for this journey of change in perspective. I understand the apprehension some may have for following the Christian year because at one time I was hesitant to allow the Christian year a place in my worship.

Scripture does not explicitly mandate the observance of the Christian year calendar. The New Testament does not provide some equivalent to Leviticus twenty-five, where God laid out the major annual fasts and feasts for the people of Israel. So, although the Christian year is structured around the biblical story of Jesus, it is not commanded in Scripture the way the Jewish holidays are for the Jews. However, it is important to note that Christians aren't commanded to celebrate Easter or Christmas in the way we do either. The church year, therefore, is not something all Christians must observe, or must observe in the same way. In fact, Eastern Orthodox believers have a different pattern for yearly worship and even celebrate Christmas and Easter on a different day than those in the West. Nevertheless, I believe that engaging with the Christian year calendar can enhance our spiritual journey, fostering a sense of unity with the global church, and providing opportunities for communal worship, meditation, and growth in faith.

It is important to note that time has no sacredness of its own, but rather, serves as a tool to be redeemed and employed by humans in order to participate and celebrate the eternal. Time becomes sacred as it finds its completeness in God.

Theologian Robert Webber suggests that because we live in a time of cultural and spiritual transition, many Christians are searching for a deeper worship experience than the non-connected church[2] provides: "Many younger evangelicals and older ones as well are searching the past to find ways of spiritual formation that have deeply affected the spiritual lives of many generations."[3] I have seen this first-hand at one of the universities where I teach a theology of worship course. The university offers a chapel service called Liturgical Chapel, which employs prayers from the Book of Common Prayer, follows the Scripture reading schedule of the lectionary[4], and offers the Lord's Supper at every service. It is held in a room that seats

---

2. A non-connected church, also called a "free church," is a Christian church that holds no connection with the recognized mainline churches such as the Catholic, Presbyterian, Lutheran, or Methodist churches. One main difference between connected and non-connected churches is the ecclesiastical polity within the denomination or church structure.

3. Webber, *Ancient-Future Time*, 15.

4. The lectionary is a pre-selected collection of scriptural readings from the Bible that can be used for worship, study or other theological uses. Some congregations use the Revised Common Lectionary which follows the liturgical year in a three-year cycle (Years A, B, and C) and provides scriptural recommendations that complement the current season of the liturgical year.

over five-hundred people when filled, and it is regularly filled. Younger evangelicals are being drawn to ancient forms of liturgy. They are discovering the value of connecting with their past while moving toward the future and finding this experience to be both spiritually formative and unifying.

Author and preacher Francis Chan wrote an article whereas he cites his observations as to why young people are leaving their churches in large numbers. His opening paragraph concludes with questions that should cause the reader to consider the worship gatherings being offered within their own church. He writes that young people,

> . . . may like their initial visits, but soon enough they lose interest. They're enjoying church more than ever but often walk away unfulfilled. We've come up with some beautiful and creative elements to attract them, but somehow the water seems shallow. Believe it or not, people of all ages still go to church wanting to experience God. He's more exciting than what we can offer. They can get good music at concerts and entertainment at the movies. When they come to church, they want and expect something more. They want to see and encounter God. Our job is to create a sacred space, so He can reveal Himself. Could it be that, in our quest to creatively make Jesus cool to the younger generation, we've actually hidden Him? Do we plan meetings that are so busy and overproduced that we crowd Him out?[5]

As a result of the Protestant free church movement and its contemporary driven worship model, the Christian year is rarely, if ever, considered a relevant or effective worship component for free church worshipers. It certainly is not considered as an opportunity for spiritual growth through its use in worship. The book in your hands is an attempt to challenge this perspective and encourage a different way of thinking. Moreover, I propose that by integrating the Christian year into the worshiping life of the church, a deeper connection to the historical worship and unity of the church will be experienced and embraced.

The purpose of this book is threefold: first, to provide biblical, historical, and theological foundations for the Christian year; second, to encourage the adoption of the Christian year in modern worship settings as a means of spiritual formation; and third, to offer practical resources for the different seasons of the Christian year that can be used in various church settings.

We will begin with an introduction of sacred time and consider why it is important in the worshiping life of the church. Sacred time is not only

---

5. Chan, "Why Are They Leaving?," 22.

important in the corporate gathering, but also in the personal worship of each Christ follower.

The biblical, historical, and theological foundations of the Christian year are presented in chapter 2. The historical pattern of worship of the church forms the way in which we worship today. The past forms the present and guides the future. Contemporary churches too often discard the past which may result in a narrow view of worship. The church today should embrace historical patterns of worship in a way that makes it relevant for today's worshipers. There is much we can learn from the centuries of faithful worshipers that have gone before. We must be careful not to lose the fullness of our Christian heritage. Disregarding our past leaves us at risk of becoming theologically shallow, spiritually weak, and reliant upon the present culture.

Chapters 3–5 discuss the importance of the Christian year in the process of spiritual formation in the lives and hearts of worshipers. Our worship should form us spiritually.[6] Planned and purposeful observance of the Christian seasons and special days can become an important tool for spiritual formation through worship, as well as a means for spiritual growth, vitality, and true unity within the church.

Chapters 6–12 take the reader on a journey through the seasons of the Christian year discovering the origins for each season and how the worshiper is provided the opportunity to be formed spiritually through its observance. Each chapter includes practical tips on how to incorporate the Christian year into the worshiping life of the church—a resource guide providing a variety of resources and examples of worship opportunities for the seasons and special days of the Christian year. These resources encourage us to not just talk about the importance of the Christian year, but to transform our talk into action. It is within these resources that we find practical ideas for incorporating the Christian year into church worship services as they help us move from contemplation to practice. The resources for each season or day include: an overview, song lists, an example of a worship service, and a Scripture presentation. If you are a worship planner, leader, or pastor, you can use these examples exactly as they are, adapt them to fit your worship setting, or simply use them as a springboard to create your own worship opportunities based on the seasons of the Christian year. May God bless you as you plan and lead his Bride, the church, in worship.

Ultimately my hope is that this book will serve as a valuable resource for ministry leaders, students studying worship, and individuals seeking to deepen their personal relationship with the Lord through meaningful worship experiences.

6. For more on worship as spiritual formation, see my book *Worship Formation*.

INTRODUCTION

WHILE A DOCTORAL STUDENT focusing on worship theology and spiritual formation, I had the privilege of studying the Christian year and its impact on the church. Consequently, I have become a firm believer that our lives are spiritually formed through observing sacred time and living in the reflection of Christ's life, death, resurrection, and ultimate return. It is my hope and desire that churches not currently following a sacred pattern of time will consider the Christian year as an avenue of spiritual formation through worship.

The Christian year, also called the "church year" or "liturgical year," is the Christian way of marking time. It is a time-honored tradition observed by numerous Protestant churches around the world. Rooted in the history of Christianity, this calendar provides a structured framework for worship, reflection, and spiritual growth. Despite some criticisms and misunderstandings, the Christian year calendar holds immense value for Protestant churches, fostering a deeper understanding of the gospel, promoting unity among believers, and facilitating a meaningful connection to the broader Christian community.

Telling the fullness of God's story[1] throughout its seasons, the Christian year reflects upon the life of Christ as well as the birth and subsequent growth of the church. In corporate worship we come together to remember Christ's saving acts allowing them to affect the way we live and worship. The Christian year is "an instrument through which we may be shaped by God's saving events in Christ . . . it is not the Christian year that accomplishes our spiritual pilgrimage but Christ himself who is the very content and meaning of the Christian year."[2] The observance of the Christian year offers the worshiper

---

1. The story of God is comprised of *creation* (in the beginning, God made all things seen and unseen), *incarnation* (God sent his one and only Son, Jesus Christ, into a fallen creation to save and redeem), and *re-creation* (Christ the King will return at the end of time to once again redeem all things).

2. Webber, *Ancient-Future Time*, 24.

an opportunity to live in the pattern of Christ's life, death, and resurrection. Following this pattern reveals Christ as we remember the fullness of his story.

At the same time, care must be taken for the Christian year not to become ritualistic. The Christian year is a great resource, but like all elements of worship, it should be viewed as a vehicle to reveal the presence of God in order for his glory to be made palpable in our midst. Observing sacred time must not be a means unto itself. Following the Christian year is not about checking off a box so we can offer God true worship. It's not a mere obligation, but a meaningful way to engage with God and deepen our relationship with him.

I am reminded of Amos and God's response to the people's worship. The people of Israel were diligent in their worship practices. They were wholehearted in their duties and emotionally satisfied with their offerings to God. Yet their practice of worship did not guarantee engagement with God. In Amos chapter 5, God rebukes the people for their actions: "I hate, I despise your feasts! I cannot stand your burnt offerings and grain offerings . . ." (Amos 5:21a). This is a strong indictment against the worshipers of Amos' time. But before we judge them, we must admit that we too have the temptation of our worship being an empty offering. A healthy relationship with God is vital for positive spiritual formation to occur in our lives. The Christian year provides a foundation for authentic worship, approaching the throne of mercy with awe and reverence. It serves as a valuable tool to continually reorient our hearts and minds towards God's enduring love and the transformative power of Christ's message.

Before proceeding, we should also acknowledge the significance an emphasis on the Christian year has with Christians around the world and throughout history. Reflecting on the broader context helps the church understand its connection to a larger faith community. By observing sacred time and the various seasons of the church year, we join millions of Christ followers throughout history who have proclaimed God's mighty deeds of salvation. This sense of unity and continuity strengthens our faith journey and reminds us that we are part of a rich and diverse tradition that transcends time and geographical boundaries. Throughout the span from Advent to Pentecost, we unite with the global community of believers, as well as all of creation, in offering our worship to the Sovereign over all sovereigns . . . the Lamb seated on the throne!

> *And I heard every creature in heaven and on earth*
> *and under the earth and in the sea, and all that is in them, saying,*
> *"To him who sits on the throne and to the Lamb be blessing*
> *and honor and glory and might forever and ever!" (Rev 5:13)*

Chapter 1

WHAT'S IN A SEASON?

WORSHIP IS OUR RESPONSE to who God is, and empowered by the Holy Spirit, holds the transformative power to shape our inner beings spiritually. As followers of Jesus, we are privileged to engage in both personal and corporate worship. Through personal worship, we cultivate an intimate and profound relationship with God, as emphasized in Ephesians 3:14–19. In corporate worship gatherings, we find encouragement for spiritual growth and the opportunity to uplift and support one another through our worship. Therefore, intentional planning and effective leadership play a crucial role in creating worship services that facilitate spiritual transformation within the lives of worshipers. By crafting worship experiences that prompt individuals to become more Christ-like, we can foster a genuine connection with God and facilitate profound spiritual growth and transformation in the lives of worshipers:

> *And we all, with unveiled face, beholding the glory of the Lord, are being transformed into the same image from one degree of glory to another. For this comes from the Lord who is the Spirit.*
> (2 Cor 3:18)

To experience worship renewal, worshipers must actively seek opportunities that facilitate this type of transformative encounter with God. Embracing the telling of God's story is crucial to offer worship that truly honors and acknowledges his actions throughout history. The historical sacred calendar assists in rehearsing God's story and plays a central role within Christianity, influencing much of Christian worship, often without us realizing it. The significance of time in Christian worship tells us a great deal about following Christ and about the way in which we worship. Professor and author James F. White states,

> The centrality of time in Christianity is reflected in Christian worship. This worship, like the rest of life, is structured on recurring rhythms of the week, the day, and the year. In addition, there is a lifelong cycle. Far from trying to escape time Christian worship uses time as one of its essential structures. Our present time is used to place us in contact with God's acts in time past and future. Salvation, as we experience it in worship, is a reality based on temporal events through which God is given to us. The use of time enables Christians to commemorate and experience again those very acts in which salvation is grounded.[1]

The Christian year provides a meaningful way for Christ followers to mark time. However, within the Protestant free church movement, there has been a general lack of interest in the Christian year. In my years of full-time ministry in churches often characterized as "non-liturgical,"[2] I've observed that many church members are not familiar with the Christian year, and those who are often associate it with Roman Catholic practices, leading to strong resistance. I believe this resistance to the Christian year can be attributed to three main factors. Firstly, some individuals have a history with Roman Catholicism and left due to dissatisfaction with the "rote and ritual" of worship. When they encounter terms like *Advent* or *Lent*, it reminds them of what they left behind and the reasons for their departure. Secondly, many have family and friends attending less than dynamic Roman Catholic churches that seem to prioritize liturgy over the worship of God, reinforcing the negative perceptions. Lastly, fear of the unknown plays a role, as there are practices within the Roman Catholic church that Protestants may not understand or agree with, leading to criticism rather than seeking understanding. These negative responses have contributed to a culture of ignoring or avoiding the Christian year in Protestant free church settings. Further discussion on this resistance will be explored in chapter two.

Over the years, I have sensed that many within the Protestant free church movement desire a deeper form of worship than what the typical local church provides. In countless churches across the globe, the spiritual discipline of worship is highly misunderstood. When people think of

---

1. White, *Introduction to Christian Worship*, 48.
2. The American Journal of Theology states, "In popular speech 'non-liturgical churches' are those whose theory and practice of public worship do not involve a fixed and prescribed ritual of language and action, such as can be set down in a prayer-book or similar manual." Pratt, "The Liturgical Responsibilities," 641.

worship, most often, they think of music. Worship has regularly been perceived as synonymous with music. This misunderstanding of worship has led to people attending worship services unsure of the proper way to engage with God.

If worship includes, as I believe, a retelling of the Christ story, then keeping sacred time would enable the church to recall the story on a consistent basis throughout the year. The observance of the Christian year holds a significant place in the history of the Christian faith, representing the life of Christ and his ultimate purpose. By purposefully observing the seasons of the church year, we create a meaningful vehicle for spiritual growth and vitality within our congregation. By helping our congregations understand and embrace the Christian year, we may initiate a renewal of worship in both their personal and communal lives. Engaging in worship through the seasons of the Christian year deepens our grasp of theology (who is God?) and worship (our response to who God is) and allows us to embrace God's powerful acts of salvation with renewed enthusiasm and fresh perspectives.

Chapter 2

BIBLICAL, HISTORICAL, AND THEOLOGICAL FOUNDATIONS FOR KEEPING SACRED TIME

FOLLOWING THE CHRISTIAN YEAR can provide solid biblical and theological foundations infused with historical tradition that will encourage spiritual formation in our lives. Furthermore, following the Christian year has the potential to deepen the personal and corporate worship engagement of worshipers and bring unity to the worshiping community.

My desire is for God's people to embrace a form of worship that is spiritually meaningful and forming. Protestant free churches have historically been very good at evangelism and discipleship, but relatively weak on worship. Yet many worshipers today are seeking a deeper, more substantial time of congregational worship. While the traditional evangelical services may have served us well in the past, our churches need to re-evaluate our worship practices as we strive to encourage people toward a deeper relationship with God.

To develop a greater understanding of the Christian year we must first establish a biblical, historical, and theological foundation for such an emphasis. In this chapter I want to engage in a theological reflection of the Christian year while also reflecting upon biblical passages that offer examples and instructions for living according to the Christian year calendar. We will then have an opportunity to glean application principles for our worship. In addition to the biblical and theological reflections, I will offer a glimpse of history as to how the church has observed the Christian year over the years. I do so by weaving historical references and observations throughout my entire discussion.

A movement within worship today has reintroduced contemporary worshipers to ancient forms of worship, including a rediscovery of sacred time. There are signs that the observance of the Christian year as a way of keeping time is slowly making its way back into the worship of Protestant free churches. Though the Christian year has its origins in the ancient church, many are finding that it is still as applicable today as it was in previous centuries.

In the nineteenth century, ancient Christian documents were discovered that trace the observance of certain holy days back to the early church. The *Didache* from the first century, the *Apostolic Constitutions* from the third century, and the diaries of *Egeria* of the fourth century all give evidence of the celebration of special Christian days. In viewing the history of the church and observing the worship patterns of the early Christians it becomes clear that the Christian year had an important role in the foundation of all Christianity—the retelling of the Christ events.[3]

The Christian year traces its origins to the early centuries of the church, where it was developed as a way to commemorate and celebrate key events in the life of Christ. By following this sacred time calendar, churches continue a legacy that connects them to the historic Christian faith. Embracing the Christian year allows congregations to engage with the rich tapestry of church history, drawing inspiration from the saints and martyrs who have gone before.

As stated earlier, many Protestants continue to resist the incorporation of the observance of the Christian year in their worship practices because they correlate the Christian year with Roman Catholicism. This misperception is potentially a result of the Reformation period, in which many of the Protestant Reformers discarded holy days as man-made and not Scripture-derived. *Sola Scriptura* (Scripture alone) was one foundational doctrinal principle during the Protestant Reformation. According to the principle of *sola Scriptura*, liturgical worship, apostolic authority, etc., which were not specifically expressed in the Bible were to be abolished. Most early American Protestants strongly emphasized the Lord's Day, but otherwise their observance of the Christian year was largely limited to Easter and Christmas until the twentieth century. Even Christmas was not observed in most American Protestant churches until the nineteenth century.[4]

In contrast to Roman Catholics who find equal authority in Scripture and tradition, Protestants believe the Bible to be the ultimate authority in faith and practice. Reformers like Martin Luther insisted that the Bible alone serve as the Christian's rule with no higher authority in the church than God's Word. Yet it is important to recognize that the formulators of

---

3. Christ events include the birth, life, death, resurrection, ascension, and ultimate return of Jesus Christ.

4. Hickman, *The New Handbook of the Christian Year*, 26.

the principle of *sola Scriptura* did not intend it to be applied narrowly. For instance, Article VI of the Westminster Confession of Faith states:

> *The whole counsel of God, concerning all things necessary for His own glory, man's salvation, faith, and life, is either expressly set down in Scripture, or by good and necessary consequence may be deduced from Scripture; unto which nothing at any time is to be added, whether by new revelations of the Spirit, or traditions of men.*[5]

Early defenders of *sola Scriptura* realized that God intends for all believers to deduce principles from his Word and apply them to every area of practice. Scott Aniol states, "What Luther and the other Reformers intended with *sola Scriptura* is that the Bible must be the supreme authority for the Christian, not that it will be the only source of information utilized in the application of its authoritative principles. They recognized the necessity of using common sense and reason to apply Scripture's principles to life."[6]

Additionally, there are some Protestant free church Christians and denominations that strongly adhere to the Regulative Principle of worship, holding to the interpretation that worshipers should only follow that which Scripture dictates for corporate worship.[7] Since Scripture does not expressly mandate the observance of certain seasons and holy days of the Christian year, those that adhere to the Regulative Principle would claim that they should be avoided at all costs. The Regulative Principle can be better understood by considering the following statement from the Westminster Confession of Faith:

5. A Puritan's Mind, "The 1647 Westminster Confession of Faith: Chapter I, Article VI" https://www.apuritansmind.com/westminster-standards/chapter-1/

6. Aniol, *Worship in Song*, 7.

7. Due to the scope of this book, we can only provide a brief overview of the Regulative Principle of worship and its counterparts, the Inventive Principle and the Normative Principle. Here's a summary:
   a. The Regulative Principle: Whatever is not directed in Scripture is forbidden. This principle is often associated with certain Protestant traditions that strictly follow Scriptural commands in shaping their worship practices.
   b. The Inventive Principle: This is the opposite of the Regulative Principle and is associated with Roman Catholicism. Instead of Scripture guiding worship, the church is seen as the final authority, allowing for the invention of practices and methods deemed appropriate.
   c. The Normative Principle: Whatever is not expressly forbidden is permissible. Churches adhering to this principle have freedom in worship practices that do not contradict Scripture, within reasonable boundaries.

Both the Regulative and Normative Principles agree on the authority of Scripture in worship but differ in how they interpret and apply that authority practically in corporate worship.

> But the acceptable way of worshiping the true God is instituted by himself, and so limited by his own revealed will, that he may not be worshiped according to the imaginations and devices of men, or the suggestions of Satan, under any visible representation, or any other way not prescribed in the Holy Scripture.[8]

Likewise, Article 32 of the Belgic confession states:

> In the meantime we believe, though it is useful and beneficial that those who are rulers of the Church institute and establish certain ordinances among themselves for maintaining the body of the Church, yet that they ought studiously to take care that they do not depart from those things which Christ, our only Master, has instituted. And therefore we reject all human inventions, and all laws which man would introduce into the worship of God, thereby to bind and compel the conscience in any manner whatever.[9]

In essence, the Regulative Principle aims to guide the church in worshiping God according to the ways he has prescribed, not in our own ways.

However, this is not to say that every aspect of our worship is explicitly dictated by Scripture. Instead, it means that there must be Scriptural warrant for all that is done within a worship service. As with the conviction of *sola Scriptura*, we should include worship elements within our services which are not only prescribed in Scripture, such as singing, prayer, the reading of Scripture, preaching, and the observance of baptism and the Lord's Supper, but also those that may be logically deduced from general biblical principles.

While there is Scriptural merit for holding to the Regulative Principle, there are also a few difficulties with this view. For instance, there is no passage which explicitly states that we are to worship only according to what is found in Scripture. There is also uncertainty with how strict we ought to be with this principle. For example, should musical instruments be allowed in corporate worship? The New Testament does not mention the use of musical instruments in the church. In fact, some, including French theologian and reformer John Calvin, have argued that instruments should not be used in corporate worship. Yet instruments are widely accepted in most Protestant churches today.

---

8. A Puritan's Mind, "The 1647 Westminster Confession of Faith: Chapter XXI, Article I" https://www.apuritansmind.com/westminster-standards/chapter-21/

9. A Puritan's Mind, "The Belgic Confession Circa 1561 A.D.: Article XXXII" https://www.apuritansmind.com/creeds-and-confessions/the-belgic-confession-circa-1561-a-d/

So how are we to decide on the aspects of worship that the Scriptures are silent on (i.e. announcements, child dedications, etc.)? A response is once again found in the Westminster Confession of Faith:

> . . . there are some circumstances concerning the worship of God, and government of the Church, common to human actions and societies, which are to be ordered by the light of nature, and Christian prudence, according to the general rules of the word, which are always to be observed.[10]

In other words, church leadership is to use its best judgment in matters not explicitly mentioned or clearly mandated by Scripture. Churches are free to set the times for their service, to choose the form of music, include announcements, or other issues which do not violate Scripture—including the utilization of the Christian year within worship.

Interestingly, Catholics were the first to recognize that the Christian year was primarily Christocentric, revolving around the life, death, and resurrection of Jesus Christ. Recognizing that the celebration of pivotal events in Jesus' life formed the basis of the Christian year, Catholics were prompted to reshape the Christian year calendar. The most notable change was the removal of many saints' days from the calendar, allowing Advent, Christmas, Epiphany, Lent, Holy Week, Easter, and Pentecost to become more noticeable. This evangelical reform of the Christian year began to dismantle the wall built by Protestants, enabling them to recognize the Christocentric essence of the Christian year and its vital significance to the collective faith of the church.

Still, the conviction of *sola Scriptura* and a strict interpretation of the Regulative Principle from a fundamental viewpoint remain formal principles in many Protestant churches today, especially in denominations describing themselves as "Bible believing." And yet, many worship elements observed today in our Protestant churches are a result of traditions passed down from one generation to another. Moreover, many of these traditions do not find their origins in Scripture or the early church. Each generation is influenced by its culture, which has the potential of developing traditions passed down without biblical or theological foundations. The church has been notorious for accepting passed down traditions without questioning its biblical or theological reasoning leading to a style of worship dictated by culture rather than one that is founded on biblical principles. The result is worship that generally lacks spiritual maturity and depth.

---

10. A Puritan's Mind, "The 1647 Westminster Confession of Faith: Chapter I, Article VI" https://www.apuritansmind.com/westminster-standards/chapter-1/

Christian theologian Karl Barth states, "Christian worship is the most momentous, the most urgent, the most glorious action that can take place in human life."[11] Unfortunately, many Christians today rarely find this exhilarating worship experience described by Barth in public worship. If we are to address this issue forthrightly, we must consider a proper view of the purpose of the church and her worship.

The main calling of the church is to worship God, living in fellowship with Christ, and joining with him in enlarging his kingdom. The Westminster Catechism states the chief end of man is to glorify God and enjoy him forever. This declaration sums up God's plan for individual Christians as well as for "his body, that is, the church" (Col 1:24). The primary work of the church is worship. Evangelism, teaching, fellowship, discipleship, missions, and the healing of broken lives are all extremely important works of the church; but it is worship that is the foundation of all the others. When Jesus was questioned about which was the greatest command to follow, he answered, "love the Lord your God with all your heart and with all your soul and with all your mind and with all your strength" (Mark 12:30). The primary endeavor in which Christians should engage is to love God. Another way to say this is to worship God. Loving God is a response to who God is and how he has revealed himself. Responding to God's revelations properly is worship, therefore, it is appropriate to conclude that loving God is an act of worship. Jesus continued by saying we should follow loving God by loving one another (Mark 12:31). The church is called to be a worshipping community first and foremost. All the other functions of ministry flow out of the worship of the church.

Considering these observations about the formative strength and importance of Christian worship throughout the centuries, there is solid historical and biblical evidence to conclude that the Christian year is beneficial in the process of spiritually formative worship. By following the Christian year calendar, worshipers are invited to take an in-depth look at the life of Christ as well as the birth and subsequent growth of the church throughout the centuries. The fullness of God's story is remembered and anticipated through Christian year observation. This annual Christian year calendar observance may serve as a discipleship tool in our churches today. Moreover, following the Christian year not only invites the worshiper into biblical and historical events, but also calls for the church to be unified in its worship.

---

11. Barth, quoted in von Allmen, *Worship*, 13.

Chapter 3

A CALL FOR UNITY

THE NEW TESTAMENT DESCRIBES the church's inception as a passionate group of individuals, burning with fire in their hearts and fervor in their souls for Jesus Christ the risen Lord. These dedicated followers of Christ established the church—founded by Jesus, augmented by apostolic preaching and teaching, and spread through persecution and missionary zeal. Along with the spread of Christianity came diversity in worship—a natural by-product as various cultures, ages, and personalities joined together to worship. Sadly, all too often, diversity in worship is a cause for division rather than unity. Various approaches to worship have the potential to cause confusion and misunderstanding. God, however, has placed a high priority on unity within the church; moreover, he has made unity vital to worship.[12] Corporate worship is most powerful, most full, and most effective when we are unified with those we are worshiping alongside.

One way to encourage unity within the church is through the retelling of God's story in worship. In corporate worship, we should gather to remember Christ's saving acts. The Christian year is a resource that expresses the whole of God's story: from creation, to incarnation, and concluding with the re-creation of all things upon Christ's return. The utilization of the Christian year in our worship has the potential to bring worshipers together in unity deeply affecting the way we live and worship the triune God—Father, Son, and Holy Spirit. When we gather, we are to worship God appropriately by having a proper view of God as triune. Only then are we free to worship in light of the fullness of God's story allowing him to transform our lives and our worship.

---

12. see Romans 15:1–6

The gathered church is to be seen in a trinitarian perspective as well. Dale Moody states "the church is that fellowship of faith created by the living God as Father, Son, and Holy Spirit to the praise of his glory."[13] The church is unquestionably connected to all three members of the Godhead—worshipping the Father, serving the Son, filled with the Holy Spirit. As we worship the triune God we become as Paul states, and Moody reiterates, "the praise of his glory" (Eph 1:12). Just as the Father, Son, and Holy Spirit are unified, the church is to be unified in purpose and worship. Jesus prays specifically for this unity when he prays to his Father, "that they may be one, even as we are one" (John 17:11).

Once we have heard the call for unity and begin to understand its importance in offering worship to God, we must ask, "How then, should we worship?" Ralph Martin states, "One supreme way in which the people can gain enrichment from the worship is to give them an understanding that each facet of the public worship of God has meaning in which they are invited to contribute a significant activity—in praising, praying, giving, as in remembering, listening, confessing, believing, and acting out. These are all verbs of involvement and choice."[14] Worshipers within a congregation must be invited to participation while maintaining unity within the fellowship.

Over the years, worship, primarily music and the arts, has been a topic for debate in the church rather than a source of unity. The term "worship wars" has generally been used when strong disagreements arise, particularly in relation to musical style, within the church. Some disagreements have become so intense that churches have divided over this volatile issue. As author and professor of church music Donald Hustad states, "It has often puzzled me that music—which Martin Luther described as a 'noble, wholesome, and joyful creation,' a gift of God—should so frequently be a source of conflict in the church."[15] Battles have been waged based on a variety of issues: traditional versus contemporary; hymns versus praise choruses; organ versus piano versus guitar; drums versus no drums; too loud versus too soft, etc. Despite these challenges and concerns, we must understand that the task of the worshiper remains to approach God with sincerity and truth, offering heartfelt worship without regard to personal preferences or comfort.

Following the Christian calendar is one way in which worshipers can be the answer to Christ's prayer that we would be unified. The story of the Bible is found in the Christian year, and we join our hearts, minds, and lives in the remembrance of God's story. As we remember, we are brought

---

13. Moody, *Spirit of the Living God*, 442.
14. Martin, *The Worship of God*, 143.
15. Hustad, *Jubilate II*, xii.

together to proclaim, enact, and sing his saving deeds throughout history and we are encouraged to put aside our personal preferences, desires, and ideas to focus on Christ and his church.

Moreover, the Christian year calendar serves as a unifying force within the global church. By following the same calendar, believers around the world share a common rhythm of worship. This fosters a sense of unity and shared identity, transcending boundaries. The calendar also provides opportunities for ecumenical cooperation and collaboration, as different churches come together to celebrate and commemorate important events in the Christian story. Such unity and communal identity strengthen the bonds of fellowship and contribute to the broader witness of the church.

Through this annual cycle of observances, we can unite with Christians worldwide, sharing our common heritage and faith in Jesus Christ. Picture this scenario: five churches scattered across the globe, each weaving their worship around the rhythm of the Christian year. One congregation is in Kenya, another in London, a third in Belfast, the fourth in Seoul, and the last in the United States. Despite their vast differences in culture, ethnicity, and language, they all synchronize their worship with the Christian year calendar. The day is Pentecost Sunday. Across these five congregations, a shared theme resonates, as they read the same Scripture passages, offer similar prayers, and raise their voices in songs that celebrate the Holy Spirit's descent on that very day of Pentecost. It's a breathtaking image of the global church worshiping in harmony.

A unified sense of worship allows for spiritually formative worship to occur in our lives. We must remove the distractions that keep us from unity and prevent us from experiencing the fullness of God. Observing the Christian year will provide a foundation for the process of spiritual formation.

Chapter 4

CHRISTIAN YEAR SPIRITUALITY

CHRISTIAN YEAR SPIRITUALITY FORMS Christ followers around the story of redemption in Christ. It is not a step-by-step program or principles you follow to achieve spiritual growth. It is entirely Christ-centered and uses the biblical story to conform our lives to his. As Israel was formed by their story of slavery, redemption, covenant, and the promised land, so the church today is shaped by the story of God, forming us around the events of Jesus' birth, life, death, resurrection, ascension, outpouring of his Spirit, and ultimate return in glory. At every turn within the Christian year, we see and hear Jesus as we are encouraged to follow him.

Unfortunately, there is a culture of narcissism that has crept into our churches and our worship. A narcissistic preoccupation with the self has led to the development of issues concerning worship within the church. In such cases, worship is not primarily about God and what he has done, but becomes about us—what we like, what we want, and what we feel we deserve. A disregard for the incredible saving act of the One true and holy God and a denial of the fullness of the story of God has found its way into our worship. We have bypassed the Almighty, sovereign God, and have positioned our own unworthy selves as the focus of worship. Webber states, "The church's emphasis upon worship fits the *experience culture* in which we live. . . . Current popular phrases surrounding the worship experience seem oriented around personal perception. 'Did you *like* the worship? . . .' The more appropriate experiential question is 'Did God's story, which was proclaimed and enacted today, make a transformative impact on your life?' Or, 'How has the weekly rehearsal of the meaning of human life that is rooted in God's story changed the way you treat your family, your neighbors, the people with whom you work?'"[16] An indication of this self-centered perspective creeping into our worship services, whether intentionally or by conditioning, is evident when we structure our worship gatherings based on either the Hallmark or academic calendars.

When worship services are patterned after the Hallmark calendar, they revolve around holidays such as Mother's Day, Father's Day, Independence Day, Valentine's Day, etc. These greeting card occasions tend to set the tone for our worship services. However, the worship service of a church should be about remembering God's work done in our lives and anticipating the work he is yet to accomplish. This dual act of remembrance and anticipation should take center stage in any congregation. We may well honor moms on Mother's Day and dads on Father's Day, but the central focus of the worship service must be on worshiping the One who gave us our moms and dads.

Moreover, the academic school year at times guides our church calendar. Churches begin their serious studies in the fall when school is in session. Ministries take their annual hiatus during the summer, and church seems to enter maintenance mode until September when school starts up again and ministries resume meeting. This pattern oftentimes creates a lull in the expression of worship throughout the congregation during the summer months as they wait for everything to fall back into a familiar rhythm—as if God deserves any less of our enthusiastic, wholehearted worship during the summer months.

By aligning with either the Hallmark or academic calendar, churches may find themselves at risk of becoming weary in a faith that conforms to the cultural norms and societal expectations. There lies a potential danger in mimicking the world's patterns when it comes to our worship practices. The essence of worship isn't about commemorating cultural holidays or worldly events; rather, it's a profound celebration of God and a retelling of his magnificent narrative.

Due to the incomprehensible nature of God, both the Hallmark and academic calendars prove inadequate in guiding congregations towards a deeper form of worship. However, embracing the Christian year in our public worship endeavors allows us to emphasize and cultivate spiritual growth more effectively. The observance of the Christian year is a dynamic reliving of the paschal mysteries. It is a time for us to relive for ourselves the saving events of Christ. Too often we remember past events without allowing them to affect our worship today. James F. White states, "When we recall the past events of salvation, they come alive in their present power to save. Our acts of remembrance bring the original events back to us with all their meaning.

---

16. Webber, *The Divine Embrace*, 94.

And so, we continue to "proclaim the Lord's death until he comes" (1 Cor 11:26)."[17] The Christian year presents God's narrative in a profound manner, molding the way we engage in worship today. The significant events of Christ become intertwined with our own personal salvation history.

Biblical worship is never about me and my worship. Instead, biblical worship is about God and remembering his saving deeds throughout history. One Old Testament passage that lays a foundation for remembrance in our worship is found in the book of Deuteronomy. It is here where God instructs Moses on how to remember:

> *"When your son asks you in time to come, 'What is the meaning of the testimonies and the statutes and the rules that the Lord our God has commanded you?' then you shall say to your son, 'We were Pharaoh's slaves in Egypt. And the Lord brought us out of Egypt with a mighty hand. And the Lord showed signs and wonders, great and grievous, against Egypt and against Pharaoh and all his household, before our eyes. And he brought us out from there, that he might bring us in and give us the land that he swore to give to our fathers. And the Lord commanded us to do all these statutes, to fear the Lord our God, for our good always, that he might preserve us alive, as we are this day. And it will be righteousness for us, if we are careful to do all this commandment before the Lord our God, as he has commanded us.'* (Deut 6:20–25)

Later, Peter wrote to Christians under persecution encouraging them in their worship and reminding them not to forget all God had done for them:

> *But you are a chosen race, a royal priesthood, a holy nation, a people for his own possession, that you may proclaim the excellencies of him who called you out of darkness into his marvelous light. Once you were not a people, but now you are God's people; once you had not received mercy, but now you have received mercy.* (1 Pet 2:9–10)

In these passages we see there is power for our worship in remembering. When we remember God's saving deeds, we are inspired to worship him and grow in our spirituality.

The Greek word, *anamnesis*, literally meaning the drawing near of memory, encapsulates this idea of remembrance perfectly. *Anamnesis* is not just remembering an event that happened in the past but drawing it near to experience it once again. The present encounter with God through past events is the purpose behind the Christian year. In remembering the saving

---

17. White, *Introduction to Christian Worship*, 68.

events, we do not take a trip in a time machine into the past, nor drag the past into the present by repeating the ancient event through a mythic drama. These events are history, not myth. They are, as Taft says, "*ephapax*, once for all. There was one exodus from Egypt and one resurrection of Christ, and we can neither repeat them nor return to them. But that is not to say they are dead, static, over and done with. They created and manifested and remain the bearers of a new and permanent quality of existence called salvation, initiating a permanent dialectic of call and response between God and his people."[18] The events of the Christian year may be in the past, but their reality is ever present reaching to each new generation; after all, the promise was made "to you and to your descendants, forever."[19]

So, in remembering the past, we neither return to it nor do we recreate it in the present. Just as God is ever present, his past saving events are to be remembered as true for all time. The past, present, and future are always relevant in God's time. "Christmas is not just about the coming of Christ to Bethlehem, but about the coming of Christ to me, and about my going out to others. And Easter is not about the empty tomb in Jerusalem some 2000 years ago, but about the reawakening here and now of my baptismal death and resurrection in Christ."[20]

There is danger in not remembering all God has done for us as well as throughout all of history. Nehemiah 9:16–17a states, "But our ancestors acted arrogantly; they became stiff-necked and did not listen to Your commands. They refused to listen and did not remember Your wonders You performed among them. They became stiff-necked and appointed a leader to return to their slavery in Egypt."[21] It's crucial to recognize that worship past is connected to worship present. As followers of Christ, we are called to remember, and our worship becomes most impactful when we recall God's mighty deeds.

Remembrance informs our personal and corporate worship, which can be directed by the Christian year. Moreover, spiritual lives may be formed by Christian year observance and practice. The seasons of the Christian year focus on Jesus Christ and his church. Christian year spirituality invites us back to the life, death, and resurrection of Jesus Christ. As we enter the very life of Christ, his life imbues our lives, and we learn to live in the pattern of his life and death as we die to sin and rise to new life in Christ. Theologian

---

18. Taft, *Beyond East and West*, 17.
19. Genesis 13:15
20. Taft, *Beyond East and West*, 18.
21. Holman Christian Standard Bible ©1999, 2000, 2002, 2003, 2009 Holman Bible Publishers. Used by Permission.

Marva Dawn claims, "Our worship is made much richer when we let the nature of each particular season guide our choices of songs, accompaniments, texts, sermon themes, prayers, drama, art."[22] There is depth to the Christian year leading those that observe it to find spiritual formation for personal worship as well as valuable resources for corporate worship. A resurgence of sacred time in our worship can invite us into a life ready to embrace spiritual formation.

At the heart of the Christian year calendar is its emphasis on the events of the Christ story: his birth, life, death, resurrection, ascension, and imminent return. Participation in these events enhances the opportunity for spiritual formation as worshipers are invited to journey alongside Christ, deepening understanding of his redemptive work. The cyclical rhythm of remembrance helps worshipers grasp the significance of Christ's incarnation, sacrifice, and victory over sin and death. By being immersed in the Christian year, the church reaffirms the centrality of Christ in its worship. As the Christ story is continually recalled, it has the potential to shape the spiritual life of each worshiper. And though spiritual formation is not the primary function of worship, it is a wonderful by-product in the development of the spiritual life of the worshiper.

At this point you may be thinking, "You're giving too much power to the Christian year. There's no way that following the Christian year calendar can accomplish so much for my spirituality." These statements hold validity if we consider the Christian year to be the ultimate goal. However, we should view the Christian year as a tool that shapes us through God's redemptive events in Christ. With this perspective, we understand that the Christian year does not independently foster spirituality; rather, Christ himself embodies the true content and significance of the Christian year.

The early Christians believed all time found its meaning in the death and resurrection of Jesus Christ. They allowed their lives to be shaped by the saving events of Christ. They epitomized Paul's words: "For me to live is Christ" (Phil 1:21) and they demonstrated how lives can be ordered through the discipline of keeping sacred time.

Observing sacred time is a practical way of being more truly formed into the likeness of Christ. It provides spiritual refreshment by giving order to our lives. Believers will naturally take on a different perspective as their lives are ordered around the life of Christ, bringing unity with Christ and with one another.

---

22. Dawn, *How Shall We Worship?*, 33.

Chapter 5

SACRED TIME

The Day. The Week. The Year

EMBRACING THE PRACTICE OF observing sacred time provides Christians with a profound opportunity to establish a rhythm in their lives that fosters a continuous sense of spirituality. This intentional rhythm, interwoven with the fabric of daily existence, ensures that moments of devotion and connection with the divine become an integral part of one's identity. Moreover, the significance of sacred time extends beyond individual spiritual growth, as it unifies worshipers globally in a harmonious symphony of adoration, echoing through time and space.

Sacred time is not confined to mere observances or rituals; it's a dynamic interplay between the eternal and the temporal. By engaging with these sacred rhythms, Christians find themselves not only drawn closer to the heart of God but also woven into the tapestry of a global community that spans cultures, languages, and continents. Thus, the practice of sacred time offers a pathway to spiritual depth, unity, and an unwavering connection to the timeless truths that underpin the Christian faith.

Delving into the concept of sacred time reveals a triadic structure comprising—the day, the week, and the year—that forms the very foundation of the Christian year. The day, as a unit of sacred time, invites believers to consecrate each dawn with gratitude and purpose, while the week introduces a recurring cycle of rest and reflection, mirroring the divine order established at creation. These lay the groundwork for the grand tapestry of the year, which weaves together the profound narratives of Christ's birth, ministry, crucifixion, resurrection, and ascension. This panoramic view of sacred time creates an interconnected narrative that allows worshipers to walk in the footsteps of Christ, celebrating his life and reliving his transformative acts.

THE DAY

The liturgical day begins at sunset. Genesis 1:5 tells us, "And there was evening and there was morning, the first day." The day is divided by times of worship and prayer. Biblical texts suggest patterns of daily prayer for worshipers of Almighty God.

> *Now this is what you shall offer on the altar: two lambs a year old day by day regularly. One lamb you shall offer in the morning, and the other lamb you shall offer at twilight.* (Exod 29:38–39)
>
> *Evening and morning and at noon I utter my complaint and moan, and he hears my voice.* (Ps 55:17)
>
> *Now Peter and John were going up to the temple at the hour of prayer, the ninth hour.* (Acts 3:1)

The roots for the rhythm of daily time lie in the Jewish worship tradition. This rhythm was translated into a Christian experience of the day. Disciplines for times of prayer developed early. For instance, the *Didache*, from the late first century, states,

> *You must not pray like the hypocrites, but "pray as follows" as the Lord bids us in his gospel:*
>
> *"Our Father in heaven, hallowed be your name; your Kingdom come; your will be done on earth as it is in heaven; give us today our bread for the morrow; and forgive us our debts as we forgive our debtors. And do not lead us into temptation, but save us from the evil one, for yours is the power and the glory forever."*
>
> *You should pray in this way three times a day.*

Today, Scot McKnight claims there are two types of praying that occur among worshipers at church—praying *in* the church when individuals pray only what's on their hearts and minds and praying *with* the church when the congregation prays set prayers creating a rhythm of unified prayer with all those praying around the globe.

Christians use various terms for the practice of praying with the church—liturgical prayer, the Divine Office, fixed-hour prayers, the divine hours, the hours of prayer, or the *Opus Dei* (the "work of God"). McKnight asserts, "No matter what term we use, it is what we are doing that is important: We are joining hands and hearts with millions of other Christians to say the same thing at the same time. By doing this, we are creating in our lives a sacred rhythm of prayer"[23] with the purpose of learning to engage God together, not simply alone in the church, but with the church. Praying together unites the church as we come into union with God. The closer we come to God, the closer we come to God's people who are gathered around the heart of God.

Praying with the church is to follow Jesus' example by praying through the Psalms. McKnight observes Jesus as a master of the Psalms:

> "Whenever he heard them, in the synagogue and at the temple, he took them to heart, for the Psalms spilled constantly from his lips. Because of this, anyone who follows Jesus into the church to pray will quickly learn that praying with Jesus means using the Psalms: His entire life was bathed with psalms."[24]

The church has structured the reading of psalms by creating prayer books. These prayer books are finding their way into many churches and invite worshipers to pray in a way that Jesus himself modeled.

The Eastern Orthodox Church utilizes *The Manual for Eastern Orthodox Prayers*. A common prayer said by many Eastern Christians is the Jesus Prayer (see Figure 1). The history of the Jesus Prayer goes back, as far as we know, to the fifth century, with Diadochos (b. 400–d.500), who taught that repetition of the prayer leads to inner stillness. It is said to help to focus the mind exclusively on God with "no other thought" occupying the mind but the thought of God.

Benedict of Nursia (b.480–d.547) contributed greatly to sacred rhythm. He influenced Roman Catholic, Eastern Orthodox, and Protestant worshipers and reinforced the early Christian pattern of seven hours of prayer throughout the day and one at night; collectively they are known as "the Divine Office," or "the hours" (see Figure 2).

Hippolytus (b.170–d.235), in the *Apostolic Tradition*, written in the early part of the third century, wrote of three prayer times during the day: the third hour (9:00am) to meditate on the suffering of Christ for at that hour Christ was nailed to the tree; the sixth hour (12:00pm) to meditate on the suffering of Christ for at that hour all creation became dark; and the ninth hour (3:00pm) to meditate on the death of Christ for at that hour he died.[25]

---

23. McKnight, *Praying with the Church*, 2.
24. McKnight, *Praying with the Church*, 54.
25. Easton, *The Apostolic Tradition of Hippolytus*, 20.

Anglicans utilize *The Book of Common Prayer* which encourages a twice a day sacred rhythm, in the morning and the evening. Many find this morning and evening sacred rhythm to be a constant strength for life. Additionally, Phyllis Tickle wrote a modern comprehensive prayer book entitled *The Divine Hours*, which covers the entire day as well as the complete church calendar.

While praying with the church, throughout the course of a day, the Christian recollects the grand narrative of God. No matter the source used, the purpose of prayer is, as McKnight observes, "not to get good at it, but for the church to become good through it."[26]

The Christian day is a cycle of remembering Christ throughout one's daily efforts amid the concerns of the world. God's story is remembered, and we are being spiritually formed during our daily worship.

FIGURE 1
THE JESUS PRAYER

Jesus.
Lord Jesus.
Lord Jesus Christ.
Lord Jesus Christ, Son of God.
Lord Jesus Christ, Son of God, be merciful to me.
Lord, Jesus Christ, Son of God, be merciful to me, a sinner.
Lord Jesus Christ, be merciful to me a sinner.
Lord Jesus Christ, be merciful to me.
Lord Jesus Christ, be merciful.
Lord Jesus, be merciful.
Jesus, be merciful.

---

26. McKnight, *Praying with the Church*, 83.

FIGURE 2
THE DIVINE OFFICE

Traditional Name	Name of Office	Time (Today)
Vigils (or Matins)	Office of Readings	Midnight
Lauds	Morning Prayer	6AM—11AM
(Prime)	(No longer generally used)	(6AM—7AM)
Terce	Midmorning Prayer	9AM
Sext	Midday Prayer	12PM
None (rhymes with "tone")	Midafternoon Prayer	3PM
Vespers	Evening Prayer	3PM—6PM
Compline	Night Prayer	Before Bed

St. Benedict's Rule, chapter 16:[27]

"'Seven times in the day,' says the Prophet [psalmist], 'I have rendered praise to you.' Now that sacred number of seven will be fulfilled by us if we perform the offices of our service at the time of the morning office, of prime, of terce, of sext, of none, of vespers and of compline, since it was of these day hours that he said, 'Seven times in the day I have rendered praise to you.' For as to the night office the same Prophet says, 'In the middle of the night I arose to glorify you.'"

THE WEEK

All of creation follows a rhythm or cycle. The sun rises and sets; the ocean tides rise and fall; human beings wake and sleep; we rise, we lie down; we are born, we die. Our lives are a cycle, and one critically important aspect of that cycle is rest. Therefore, God developed a built-in pattern of rest for his people. He called it Sabbath.

The discovery of electricity and its widespread use as a power source has disrupted the natural rhythm of rest. Before electricity, people relied on the rising and setting of the sun to determine their work and rest cycles.

---

27. Butler, *Saint Benedict's Rule for Monasteries*, 36.

With electric light sources, we can now work continuously, blurring the boundaries of rest and work.

In God's design, he sanctifies places and things to bring honor to his name. The Ark of the Covenant and the Tabernacle were set apart as his dwelling place, and Jesus, his Son, was set apart as the new tabernacle (John 1:14).[28] Similarly, God set apart the Sabbath—a holy day dedicated to rest and honoring him.

The Sabbath held significant importance for both the Jewish community and early Christians. It was a sacred day of rest and worship, not meant for self-gain through work, but rather to direct all focus on God. God himself set apart this day as a holy time, making it significant to his followers. In the Ten Commandments, God commands, "Remember the Sabbath day, to keep it holy" (Exod 20:8), and he provided Sabbath regulations (Exod 23:10–12; Exod 31:12–17), which Moses conveyed to the Israelites (Exod 35:1–3). The roots of this holy day can be traced back to the creation narrative, where God rested after six days (Gen 2:2), and to Israel's deliverance from Egypt (Deut 5:15).

The command for keeping the Sabbath was so important to God that it is reiterated in Exodus, Leviticus, Numbers, and Deuteronomy. Its significance is also seen in the fact that the longest command in the Ten Commandments deals with this holy day. Why did God spend so much time on this command? John Durham suggests "the probable reason . . . is the difficulty the people of Israel had keeping it, a difficulty attested by the attack of Amos (Amos 8:4–8) on the greedy merchants fidgeting for the Sabbath to pass."[29] God knows the hearts of people—then and now.

The Jewish week was divided into seven days, of which the final day was set aside for the worship of God. This day, called "Sabbath," meaning "seventh," was the only day to have a name assigned to it, the rest being noted by numerals. This Sabbath day came to commemorate the seventh day of creation as seen in Genesis 2:2. Christians saw Jesus' resurrection as a renewal of the first creation, which had become ruined by sin causing alienation from the Creator. Easter began a new era of the new creation in Christ (2 Cor. 5:17; Gal. 6:15). As a result, the early church set aside a day, in addition to going to the synagogue on the seventh day, for the weekly

---

28. Most modern translations of John 1:14 obscure an important point captured by a more literal rendition: the Word "became flesh and tabernacled among us." John has taken the Greek word for tabernacle (*skéné*) and made it a verb (*skénoó*). The result presents a powerful image with deep roots in the Old Testament. Jesus is the tabernacle. Where Jesus is, there is God. When someone met Jesus, he or she was in the presence of God.

29. Durham, *Exodus*, 288.

remembrance of the living, dying, and rising of Christ and to anticipate his future kingdom. This *anamnesis* (remembrance) and *prolepsis* (anticipation) occurred on the first day of the week, which we call Sunday.

It is clear in Scripture that the Resurrection marked the beginning of a new week.

> *When the Sabbath was past, . . . very early on the first day of the week, when the sun had risen, they went to the tomb.* (Mark 16:1–2)

We see hints in the New Testament of the observance of the first day as the occasion for Christian worship (see 1 Cor 16:2; Acts 20:7, 11; Rev 1:10). Yet Saturday maintained some liturgical significance. The *Apostolic Constitutions* provide a beneficial overview of the importance for early Christians to observe both the Sabbath and Sunday worship:

> *But keep the Sabbath, and the Lord's Day festival; because the former is the memorial of the creation, and the latter of the resurrection. But there is one only Sabbath to be observed by you in the whole year, which is that of our Lord's burial, on which men ought to keep a fast, but not a festival. For inasmuch as the Creator was then under the earth, the sorrow for Him is more forcible than the joy for the creation; for the Creator is more honorable by nature and dignity than his own creatures.*[30]

The link between Sunday and Sabbath is complex. The Jewish Sabbath finds its life from the images found in the Old Testament, primarily Exodus[31] and Deuteronomy.[32] Yet there is no evidence to suggest that the early church saw Sunday as a Christian Sabbath. Among Christians, the first day of the week was a day to gather for worship; not a day to abstain from work. Early on in Christianity, there is evidence that Christian's reinterpreted the biblical Sabbath rest as an eschatological event awaiting fulfillment in the age to come. Mark Searle suggests, "Christians were to exercise their new-won freedom and celebrate the 'rest' of God after the new creation by their total life-style, seven days a week."[33] Sunday, then, may be seen as the liturgical center, or heart, of the Christian year. As the oldest element of the Christian year, it is the nucleus around and out of which all the feasts and seasons of the year revolve. Regarding Sunday, Mark Searle maintains:

---

30. Donaldson, *Apostolic Constitutions*, 469.
31. Exodus 20:8–11
32. Deuteronomy 5:12–15
33. Searle, "Sunday," 63.

Historically, it is the original Christian feast. Theologically, it encapsulates the whole economy of salvation. Pastorally, it is the day when the local church comes to realize itself as church and when all the faithful are called to find themselves within the whole story of God.[34]

Second-century apologist Justin Martyr (b.100–d.165) told his pagan audience that,

we all hold this common gathering on Sunday since it is the first day, on which God transforming darkness and matter made the universe, and Jesus Christ our Savior rose from the dead on the same day.[35]

Christians soon adopted the pagan term "Sunday" and compared Christ rising from the dead to the rising of the sun.

A rediscovered meaning of Sunday as the day for recalling Christ's saving actions has been applied in liturgical scholarship and is included in the Sacred Liturgy from Vatican II:

The church celebrates the paschal mystery every seventh day, which is appropriately called the Lord's Day or Sunday. For on this day Christ's faithful are bound to come together into one place. They should listen to the word of God and take part in the Eucharist, thus calling to mind the passion, resurrection, and glory of the Lord Jesus. . . . The Lord's Day is the original feast day, and it should be proposed to the faithful and taught to them so that it may become in fact a day of joy and of freedom from work. . . . Sunday . . . is the foundation and kernel of the whole liturgical year.[36]

Yet within the early church, language used to describe Sunday, or the Lord's Day, confirms that it was not simply a recollection or memorial of Christ's resurrection, but was an important weekly expression of the constant eschatological readiness for the return of Christ. This concentration on *parousia*[37] was intended to permeate the whole of the Christian's daily prayer and life.

---

34. Searle, "Sunday," 59.
35. Richardson, *Early Christian Fathers*, 287.
36. Flannery, "The Constitution on the Sacred Liturgy," 29–30.
37. The Greek term most frequently used in the New Testament for the second coming of Jesus.

In addition to the climactic weekly rhythm of Sunday, the week also included the rhythms of the fast days of Wednesdays and Fridays dating back to Apostolic times. The first century *Didache* (8:1) instructs the faithful:

> *Your fasts must not be identical with those of the hypocrites. They fast on Mondays and Thursdays; but you should fast on Wednesdays and Fridays.*

Followers of Christ were instructed to fast on Wednesday, the day when Christ was betrayed, and Friday, the day of his crucifixion.

The fasting referred to here was not simply an abstention from meat or dairy products. It was a complete abstention from both food and drink until sundown. The Protestant church would eventually transition this fasting rhythm to the season of Lent, which we will discuss in chapter nine.

Much like the day, the week witnesses to Jesus Christ, serving as a structure for commemoration. Sunday stands out above all other days as a weekly anniversary of Christ's resurrection and anticipation of his coming again. As the Lord's Day, every Sunday witnesses to the risen Lord, testifies to the resurrection faith, and declares the fullness of God's story.

THE YEAR

Just as the week and day pointed to Jesus Christ, so too, the year became a structure that commemorated the Lord. The Christian year was largely patterned after the Jewish religious calendar and can be traced back to the third century A.D. It tells of Christ's redemptive story replacing the exodus and Passover events of the Old Testament history.

Alfred Edersheim has provided a brief background on the names of the Hebrew months, summarized in the following: The present Hebrew names of the months are derived from the Chaldee, or from the Persian language. They do not appear before the return from Babylon. Before that, the months were named only after their numbers, or from the natural phenomena characteristic of the seasons, as *Abib*, "sprouting," "green ears," for the first (Exod 13:4; 23:15; Deut 16:1); *Ziv*, "splendor," "flowering," for the second (1 Kgs 6:1); *Bul*, "rain," for the eighth (1 Kgs 6:38); and *Ethanim*, "flowing rivers," for the seventh (1 Kgs 8:2). The year was divided into *ecclesiastical*, which commenced with the month *Nisan* (the end of March or beginning of April), or about the spring equinox, and *civil*, which commenced with the seventh month, or *Tishri*, corresponding to the autumn equinox, and has by many been supposed to have only originated after the return from Babylon. But the analogy of the twofold arrangement of weights, measures, and money into civil and sacred, seem against this view, and it is more likely that from the first the Jews distinguished the civil year, which began in *Tishri*, from the ecclesiastical, which commenced in *Nisan*, from which month, as the first, all the other months were counted. In addition to this twofold division the Rabbis maintained that the annual tithing of the herds and flocks were to be figured from *Elul* to *Elul*, and for taxing fruits often from *Shebat* to *Shebat*.[38]

A presentation of the Jewish feasts can be found in Leviticus chapter twenty-three. This speech of Moses is directed to the community of Israel and presents Israel's festal calendar. The speech introduces five annual "festivals with a religious purpose"[39]: Passover and Unleavened Bread (vv. 4–8), the Feast of Weeks (vv. 9–22), the Feast of Trumpets (vv. 23–25), the Day of Atonement (vv. 26–32), and the Feast of Tabernacles or Booths (vv. 33–36). The twenty-third chapter of Leviticus not only presents the festivals, but also establishes dates and gives specific commands to be followed for the festivals. John Hartley states,

> *The primary purpose of this text is to set the dates for the celebration of these five feasts. Sometimes the duration of the feast is given (vv. 5a, 34b, 39a). A secondary purpose is to provide some ritual prescriptions in order to expand and confirm the rituals of a given feast. Two genres are thus intertwined: calendrical fixations and ritual regulations. This kind of mixture is commonplace in an ancient calendar as the calendars from Babylon, Ugarit, and Egypt attest.*[40]

Passover (*Pesach*) is the first feast presented in the calendar and commemorates the Israelites' deliverance from Egypt. A special meal would be prepared consisting of a year-old lamb, roasted over a fire, and eaten with bitter herbs and unleavened bread. This meal commemorates Israel's last night in Egypt when the Israelites placed blood on the doorposts of their homes, in accordance with God's instructions, to spare the lives of their firstborn. The angel of death, seeing the blood on the doorposts, passed over their homes.

The Feast of Unleavened Bread (*Matzot*) follows Passover and gets its name because no leaven was to be used during this seven-day period. Often, Passover and the Feast of Unleavened Bread were celebrated as one festival, since both were celebrated at the time of the first full moon of the spring (in the month of Nisan).

The time of firstfruits is an important period that leads into the next festival, the Feast of Weeks (*Shavout*). Firstfruits stipulates that the offering

---

38. Edersheim, *The Temple*, 158.
39. Hartley, *Leviticus*, 384.
40. Hartley, *Leviticus*, 370.

of the first harvested item was to be given as an offering to Yahweh. The firstfruit offering signified giving the best of the harvest to God. The Feast of Weeks, commemorating the beginning of the barley harvest, would occur seven weeks after the firstfruits were offered, generally interpreted to be fifty days, which is why it is also called the Feast of Pentecost.

One may assume that the Feast of Trumpets (*Rosh Hashanah*), occurring on the first day of Tishri, was a day for celebration, but it was in fact a day set aside for solemn rest. It was announced by the blast of a trumpet (shofar) and was characterized by the term "memorial" as the people of Israel would remember their covenant with God, that they were a nation who had accepted the responsibilities of being God's people, and in turn would pray for God to remember his covenant with them. By doing so, the nation also prepared for the Day of Atonement, eight days later, when they would repent and find atonement for all that had been done to break this covenant.

The Day of Atonement (*Yom Kippur*) would occur eight days after the Feast of Trumpets (the tenth day of Tishri) and was to be celebrated from evening to evening. This is the only place in the calendar where the precise time for a holy day is set, indicating an extra measure of importance. This day was so important to God that the punishment for not observing it was rather severe—to be cut off from the community. As the most solemn day of the year, set aside for complete penitence and atonement from sins, the people were to fast and pray for a full day, abstaining from all earthly pleasures. Even after the destruction of the temple in 70 AD, which put an end to ritual sacrifices, Yom Kippur continued to be a very important day in the Jewish calendar. The days between the first and the tenth of Tishri were days of penance while the actual day of atonement was marked by a strict fast, prayers and readings, and repeated confessions of the people's sins.

The Feast of Tabernacles (*Sukkot*), also called the Feast of Booths, was the most joyous festival of the year, beginning on the fifteenth of the seventh month (Tishri) and lasting for seven days. This feast focused on thanksgiving for the harvest and was the most popular of the festivals, often called simply "the Feast." The people of Israel would make a pilgrimage to Jerusalem staying in temporary shelters, or booths, made from branches, which they would erect themselves. These booths symbolized the shelters the Israelites lived in during the wilderness journey. The shelters reminded them not of the hardships of the wilderness, but of the provisions of God during their time in the wilderness.

John Hartley states that observing the annual festivals helped bring unity to the people of Israel:

> *Yahweh is jealous that his people celebrate each of the festivals. Participation unites the community around the great deeds Yahweh has done for his people. It stimulates the growth of the community's trust in God. The rituals of this feast tie the people directly to their saving heritage. At the same time the people are thankful to God for the produce of the new harvest, and together they remember what God has done. Celebration stimulates the corporate memory, keeping alive what God has done to give birth to and to form the nation Israel. It enables each generation to participate in the formative events of the nation. This participation through memory keeps alive the benefits initiated in those great saving deeds. An active memory endows the distinct customs and practices of each feast with meaning. Through observance of these feasts, the people keep in force the divine purposes initiated in the mighty acts of God.*[41]

It is essential to clarify that merely going through the motions of the Christian year, repeating past practices or events, would miss the true essence of its spiritual significance. The purpose of celebrating the Christian year is to be transformed by Christ—to experience his death, resurrection, rebirth, and to live in the hope of his glorious resurrection and imminent return. It is about a profound spiritual formation that shapes our lives and draws us closer to the heart of Christ. Robert Webber shares,

> *For the Jew to commemorate the past is not merely to recall it as a past event but to commemorate it in such a way that it gives the present new meaning. Therefore, the Jew is called upon to commemorate the Passover as though it is happening now. At the same time the commemoration of the past event has a future reference. The Passover, for example, looks forward to the day when all will gather in Jerusalem. Consequently, the past and the future converge on the present in such a way that it makes a difference in the worshipers' experience now.*[42]

Robert Taft claims there is no ideal model of Christian feast or calendar, which we must *discover* and to which we must *return*. He states that

> *it is up to each generation to do what the Apostolic Church did in the very composition of the New Testament: apply the mystery and meaning of Christ to . . . today. A liturgy is successful not because of its fidelity to some past ideal, but because it builds up the Body of Christ into a spiritual temple and priesthood by forwarding the*

---

41. Hartley, *Leviticus*, 392–93.
42. Webber, *Ancient-Future Time*, 31–32

> aim of Christian life: the love and service of God and neighbor; death to self in order to live for others as did Christ.[43]

Not only was the liturgical calendar of incredible importance to the people of Israel, and to Jews today, but it is also important to the church today. Observing the Christian year calendar ushers us into the remembrance of the redemptive acts of God on our behalf. Whenever we celebrate these remarkable acts, we build memories within the worshiping community. The influence of worship that recalls God's redemptive actions and envisions his ultimate sovereignty over all creation organizes our spiritual encounter with Christ. Expressing gratitude for God's salvific work and eagerly anticipating the new heavens and earth constitutes the core essence of the Christian year pattern of worship.

An additional motivation for observing the Christian year in worship is that our lives are a pattern—a rhythm—a cycle. The question becomes, what, or better yet who, do you want at the center of that cycle? Spiritual formation is an inevitable realization as we embrace the story of God in our daily, weekly, and yearly worship. Our brief overview of the day, week, and year leads us to consider the Christian year itself as well as the belief that observing the Christian year challenges the believer to experience the spiritually transforming power of God.

THE CHRISTIAN YEAR

During the Christian year, the church makes its way through the extraordinary events of Jesus' life: His coming (Advent and Christmas), his life (Epiphany and Lent), his death (Holy Week), and his resurrection (Easter, Ascension, and Pentecost). This is the story of Jesus. But that is not the only story the Christian year tells. Worshipers are also taken through a journey of the birth and growth of the church through the season after Pentecost. This is our story—the story of the church.

The Christian year includes two main time periods—*Extraordinary Time*, the seasons that focus on the exceptional events of Jesus' life; and *Ordinary Time*, the times of the year that focus on the ministry of Jesus and the church. In *Extraordinary Time* there are seasons that shine a light on the arrival of the Light of the World (Seasons of Light), as well as seasons that breathe life into Jesus' time on earth (Seasons of Life). The Seasons of Light begin with the waiting during Advent and leads into the incarnational wonder of Christmas. These seasons illuminate for us the self-emptying of God as the Son became flesh. The Seasons of Life begin with the penitential

---

43. Taft, *Beyond East and West*, 28.

nature of Lent and ushers the worshiper into the resurrection reality of Easter.

The seasons of Advent and Lent are times of preparation and expectation; the seasons of Christmas and Easter are times of celebration and rejoicing; the feast of Epiphany and the season after Pentecost[44] are times to grow deeper in faith as manifested through Jesus Christ. This overview of the Christian year leads us to explore each season in greater detail as we engage in biblical, historical, and theological reflections and contemplate examples and instructions for living according to the Christian year calendar.[45]

---

44. The period between Pentecost and the beginning of Advent may be designated as the season after Pentecost or *Ordinary Time*.

45. An in-depth exploration of each season and festival is beyond the scope of this book. There are, however, many books written exploring this topic, some of which I recommend at the conclusion of this book.

SEASONS OF LIGHT

Chapter 6

ADVENT

THE CHRISTIAN YEAR BEGINS with the season of Advent, which starts four Sundays before Christmas Day. Tracing the origins of Advent leads to two primary locations: the regions of northern and western Europe where the church had sent missionaries, and to the city of Rome. Advent first appeared near the end of the fourth century in the areas where the missionaries had settled. Due to vast amounts of commerce along the Mediterranean, influences by the Eastern church led to the addition of a period of penitential preparation in connection with the baptismal festival taking place on Epiphany, January 6 (the date on which the Eastern church celebrated Christ's birth). During this preparation period, all the faithful engaged in profound spiritual discipline, while those being welcomed into the church on Epiphany through baptism underwent intense catechesis. This pre-Epiphany practice of fasting and penitence remained the norm until the sixth century when it transitioned into what we now know today as Lent—a season of spiritual preparation for the celebration of the resurrection of Jesus, which included baptism and initiation into the church on Easter Sunday. It was not until the sixth century that Advent was used in preparation for the celebration of nativity rather than the baptism on Epiphany.

    The term advent means "coming" or "arrival." In Advent, God provides us with the story of his coming. Because of its placement in the Christian year, immediately preceding Christmas, it has often been misunderstood to be an exclusive focus on the coming of the baby in Bethlehem. The primary focus of Advent, however, has been on what is popularly called "the second coming." For it is in the anticipation of Christ's return, or advent, that worshipers today participate in the waiting. Followers of old anticipated the coming of Jesus as Messiah. Today we anticipate the coming of Jesus as well.

This time, not as Messiah, for Messiah has already come. During our advent we anticipate Christ's coming as King of kings and Lord of lords. In Advent, we find the promise that God will bring an end to all the wickedness and evil that we know and bring judgment and ultimately peace to all who trust in him. It is a time to prepare hearts, minds, and lives for the arrival of the King. A time to look within and work toward being ready to meet Christ when he comes again.[46]

Advent must be looked at in light of Isaiah's message to Israel. Isaiah prepared the people of Israel for the coming of the Messiah—not only his birth, but also his eschatological reign at the end of history.

FIRST SUNDAY OF ADVENT

Traditionally, the first Sunday of Advent, four Sundays before Christmas Day, focuses on Jesus' eschatological teachings. His teachings are clear, yet elusive. God has a plan, but he employs surprises, for no one knows the day or the hour of his coming (see Matt 24:36). This elusiveness is true not only of his "second coming," but also for his arrival in Bethlehem. Messiah was born in a way that most people did not expect. If not for the angels' declaration to lowly shepherds, the birth of Jesus may have gone mostly unnoticed. Even still, we find the lowly acknowledged his birth while the elite slept. Within this facet we discover a good lesson for the church today; keep watch and be aware otherwise we may be lying in the dark, asleep when the bridegroom returns and carries away his bride.

The lectionary texts for the first Sunday of Advent also encompass a deep yearning for righteousness: "Come let us walk in the light of the LORD" (Isa 2:5, Year A); "[O Lord,] you meet those who gladly do right, those who remember you in your ways" (Isa 64:5, Year B); "May the Lord make you increase and abound in love for one another and for all" (1 Thess 3:12, Year C).

SECOND SUNDAY OF ADVENT

The second Sunday of Advent introduces John the Baptizer as he declares the message of promise, strength, and hope. His cry is constant and uninhibited. The Baptizer speaks of justice and righteousness, preparing the way for the Christ. The lectionary texts reiterate the promise that there will be

---

46. The season of Advent must be looked at in reverse—from the end to the beginning. The second coming of Christ explains his first coming as a babe in the Bethlehem manger. Jesus was made incarnate as a human baby in order to grow to adulthood, impart knowledge through his life, and become the sacrifice for all mankind. His death and resurrection prepare the way for eternal life for all who trust in him.

peace (Isa 11:1–10, Year A) and even the Gentiles will find their hope (Rom 15:4–13, Year A); God will come with power and might and create a new heavens and a new earth (2 Pet 3:10, 13, Year B); the messenger of the Lord arrives (Mal 3:1–4, Year C) and a new harvest is reaped (Phil 1:11, Year C).

THIRD SUNDAY OF ADVENT

The third Sunday of Advent continues with John the Baptizer. The texts vary each year and sometimes find John in prison while other times he is in the desert. Regardless of location, the Baptizer faithfully points ahead to the One who is to come. This Sunday is sometimes called "Gaudete Sunday" (*Gaudete* is a Latin imperative verb meaning "rejoice"). The focus of looking ahead for the coming of the King encourages the church to rejoice, thus the name and spirit of this Sunday. The break away from the penitential feeling of Advent to rejoicing is enhanced by the epistle reading of Year C (Phil 4:4), "Rejoice in the Lord always; again I will say, rejoice."

FOURTH SUNDAY OF ADVENT

It is not until the fourth Sunday of Advent, which may occur as late as December 24, that we begin the focus on the birth of Jesus in Bethlehem. For the first time in Advent, we hear that the promises declared on previous Sundays will find its way to the womb of Mary. The waiting that has been forced upon us over the past three Sundays is brought to fruition . . . or has it? For even on this fourth Sunday, we are reminded to anticipate Christ's return and God's future reign. The God who is now with us, Emmanuel, in our midst, waits just as we do. We join with him, in his presence, waiting for his future reign. In the meantime, the church prays:

> *Come, thou long-expected Jesus*
> *born to set thy people free*
> *from our fears and sins release us*
> *let us find our rest in thee*
> *Israel's strength and consolation*
> *hope of all the earth thou art*
> *dear desire of every nation*
> *joy of every longing heart*[47]

This prayer directs us to both the birth of Jesus and the return of Christ at the end of time.

---

47. Text by Charles Wesley, 1744.

The Hebrew people longed for the coming of Messiah. They placed their hope in one day seeing the Anointed One.[48] Waiting for the Messiah gave meaning to their existence. The Christian church today continues that hope. As we worship during Advent, our lives are shaped and our hearts are formed by the Advent hope that Christ has come and will come again.

INCORPORATING ADVENT

Consider utilizing an Advent wreath in your personal or corporate worship. The Advent wreath consists of five candles: traditionally, three are purple—weeks 1, 2, 4; one is pink—week 3, symbolizing joy; and one is white—the Christ candle that is lit on Christmas Eve/Day, symbolizing that Christ has come. Lighting the candles each week provides a visual symbol that the Light of the world is preparing to make his entrance.

Pair the lighting of the Advent candles with the reading of Scripture. The primary text utilized during Advent comes from the prophet Isaiah. See "Advent Overview" for Scripture recommendations. You could also consider combining the candle lighting with personal testimonies. Extend an invitation to individuals or families within your church to share moments when they experienced God as the ultimate source of hope, peace, joy, and love.

During this season of Advent, be sure to sing Advent songs that focus on the anticipation of Christ's coming, rather than Christmas songs about the baby already born. For example, "O Come, O Come Emmanuel" and "Come Thou Long Expected Jesus" are good Advent songs reinforcing the expectation that occurs during Advent. "Joy to the World" is also a good song for Advent. Did you know Isaac Watts wrote "Joy to the World" not with the birth of Christ in mind, but rather his second coming? Songs such as "Angels We Have Heard on High" and "Hark! the Herald Angels Sing" focus on the birth of Jesus in Bethlehem and should be sung during the season of Christmas (see chapter 7) or later in the season of Advent—the fourth Sunday of Advent and Christmas Eve.

---

48. The Greek word Christ means "Anointed One."

ADVENT

OVERVIEW

TIME

Begins four Sundays before Christmas. Includes all days until Christmas. Length varies according to the date of the first Sunday. It is the beginning of the Christian year.

THEMES

- *The coming of the Messiah*. Israel waited and longed for the coming of the Messiah. The Old Testament is filled with passages of the prophets expressing the longing for a new day.
- *The birth of Christ*, not only in Bethlehem but also in our hearts. A unique characteristic of Jesus is that he not only comes into history but also takes up residence within our hearts. Advent is a time to examine the presence of Jesus in our lives and to surrender our lives to him.
- *The coming of Jesus at the end of history*. The observance of Advent must be approached in reverse, starting with an expectation of the second coming of Jesus and then moving toward his first coming.

SPIRITUAL CHALLENGE

Repent and prepare for the second coming of Christ. Cultivate an eager longing for the coming of Jesus to be birthed in your heart.

SCRIPTURE

First Sunday of Advent

- Old Testament: Isa 2:1–5; Isa 64:1–9; Jer 33:14–16
- Psalm: Ps 25:1–10; Ps 80:1–7, 17–19; Ps 122
- New Testament: Rom 13:11–14; 1 Cor 1:3–9; 1 Thess 3:9–13

- Gospel: Matt 24:36–44; Mark 13:24–37; Luke 21:25–36

Second Sunday of Advent

- Old Testament: Isa 11:1–10; Isa 40:1–11; Mal 3:1–4
- Psalm: Ps 72:1–7, 18–19; Ps 85:1–2, 8–13
- New Testament: Rom 15:4–13; Phil 1:3–11; 2 Pet 3:8–15a
- Gospel: Matt 3:1–12; Mark 1:1–8; Luke 1:68–79; Luke 3:1–6

Third Sunday of Advent

- Old Testament: Isa 12:2–6; Isa 35:1–10; Isa 61:1–4, 8–11; Zeph 3:14–20
- Psalm: Ps 126; Ps 146:5–10
- New Testament: Phil 4:4–7; 1 Thess 5:16–24; James 5:7–10
- Gospel: Matt 11:2–11; Luke 1:46b–55; Luke 3:7–18; John 1:6–8, 19–28

Fourth Sunday of Advent

- Old Testament: 2 Sam 7:1–11, 16; Isa 7:10–16; Micah 5:2–5a
- Psalm: Ps 80:1–7, 17–19; Ps 89:1–4, 19–26
- New Testament: Rom 1:1–7; Rom 16:25–27; Heb 10:5–10
- Gospel: Matt 1:18–25; Luke 1:26–38; Luke 1:39–45, (46–55); Luke 1:46b–55

SYMBOLS

- Light
- Advent wreath

COLORS[49]

- Royal Blue
- Purple/Violet

---

49. The intentional use of colors in worship spaces can enliven and deepen worship, as well as add to the beauty of the experience. Colors can symbolize truth, move the heart, and stir emotions. They have symbolic significance and remind us of God and his plan of redemption. The colors of the Christian year are part of the richness of the sacred calendar.

ADVENT
SONG LIST

CONTEMPORARY

Advent Hymn Christy Nockels, 2016

All Glory Be to Christ Dustin Kensrue, 2012

All the Heavens Reuben Morgan, 2002

All Who Are Thirsty Brenton Brown and Glenn Robertson, 1998

Ancient of Days Michael Farren, Jesse Reeves, Jonny Robinson, and Rich Thompson, 2018

Behold Our God Jonathan Baird, Meghan Baird, Ryan Baird, and Stephen Altrogge, 2011

Creation Sings the Father's Song Keith Getty, Kristyn Getty, and Stuart Townend, 2008

Days of Elijah Robin Mark, 1996

Emmanuel Michael W. Smith, 1983

Even So Come Chris Tomlin, Jason Ingram, and Jess Cates, 2015

Everlasting God Brenton Brown and Ken Riley, 2005

God With Us Jason Ingram and Leslie Jordan, 2012

He Shall Reign Forevermore Chris Tomlin and Matt Maher, 2015

Hearts Waiting (Joy to the World) Beth Redman, Chris Tomlin, Jonas Myrin, and Matt Redman, 2016

Here I Am to Worship Tim Hughes, 2000

Holy (Jesus You Are) Jason Ingram, Jonas Myrin, and Matt Redman, 2011

Hope Has A Name Kristian Stanfill, Sean Curran, and Jacob Sooter, 2020

King of Kings Brooke Ligertwood, Jason Ingram, and Scott Ligertwood, 2018

Let God Arise Chris Tomlin, Ed Cash, and Jesse Reeves, 2006

Let It Rise Holland Davis, 1997

Let Us Adore Reuben Morgan, 2005

Light of the World Matt Redman, 1999

Lord, We Wait Stuart Townend and Keith Getty, 2004

On That Day Jonny Robinson, Michael Farren, Nigel Hendroff, Rich Thompson, and Scott Lavender, 2022

Prepare the Way Charlie Hall and Louie Giglio, 2002

Revelation Song Jennie Lee Riddle, 2004

Save Us Dave Lubben, 2001

Soon and Very Soon Andrae Crouch, 1971

This Is Our God Reuben Morgan, 2008

Unto Us Steven Brooks, 2009

Waiting Here for You Chris Tomlin, Jesse Reeves, and Martin Smith, 2011

You'll Come Brooke Ligertwood, 2011

Your Great Name Krissy Nordhoff and Michael Neale, 2008

TRADITIONAL

Christ Whose Glory Fills the Skies Charles Wesley, 1740

Come Thou Long Expected Jesus Charles Wesley, 1744

Creator of the Stars of Night Unknown, 9th century

Crown Him with Many Crowns Matthew Bridges, 1851

Jesus Shall Reign Where'er the Sun Isaac Watts, 1719

Joy to the World Isaac Watts, 1719

Joyful, Joyful We Adore Thee Henry Van Dyke, 1907

Let All Mortal Flesh Keep Silence Gerard Moultrie, 5th century; trans., 1864

Lo, He Comes with Clouds Descending Charles Wesley, 1758

Lo, How a Rose 'Ere Blooming Unknown, 15th century

O Come All Ye Faithful John Francis Wade, 1743; Frederick Oakeley, trans., 1841

O Come, Divine Messiah M. l'abbé Pellegrin, 17th century

O Come, O Come Emmanuel 12th century; Ancient Antiphons (Latin), versified in 18th century; John Mason Neale, trans., 1851

Of the Father's Love Begotten Aurelius Clemens Prudentius, 10th century

Wake, Awake, for Night is Flying Catherine Winkworth and Philipp Nicolai, 1599

What If It Were Today? Lelia Morris, 1912

PRESENTATIONAL

Come Light Our Hearts Sandra McCracken, 2015

Comfort, Comfort Now My People Latifah Phillips and David Wilton, 2013

Deliver Us Andrew Peterson, 2004

Gather 'Round, Ye Children, Come Andrew Peterson, 2005

Light of the World (Sing Hallelujah) Andrew Bergthold, Ed Cash, Franni Cash, Martin Cash, and Scott Cash, 2020

Restless Audrey Assad and Matt Maher, 2010

Shine On Us Deborah D. Smith and Michael W. Smith, 1996

Soon Brooke Ligertwood, 2009

You Bring Peace Sam Hargreaves, 2014

GLOBAL[50]

Antim Din (Last Day Is Near) Sam Shahu, 2022 (Nepal)

Бог з Нами (God Is with Us) Jonathan Markey and Yarina Vislotska, 2019 (Ukraine)

Dekho Dekho Koi Aa Raha Hai (Behold Someone Is Coming) Traditional (Pakistan)

---

50. The global songs presented in this book consist of non-English songs, primarily from non-Western countries. They are included because singing one another's songs is a powerful way for the international church family to demonstrate its unity in Christ.

Nyatakan Hadir–Nya (Declare His Presence) Daniel Banni and Julian Maynard Wurangian, 2021 (Indonesia)

Ososŏ (Come, Now O Prince of Peace) Kōn-Yong Yi, 1990 (South Korea)

Bereden Väg För Herran (Prepare the Way, O Zion) Frans M. Franzen, 1812 (Sweden)

Salaam (Peace) Manal Samir, 2002 (Egypt)

Siyahamba (We Are Marching) Andries Van Tonder, 1952 (South Africa)

Toda la Tierra (All the Earth Is Waiting) Alberto Taulé, 1972 (Spain)

Wait for the Lord Communauté de Taizé, 1991 (France)

ADVENT
WORSHIP SERVICE OVERVIEW

Each Sunday of the following Advent worship service examples includes:

- The Advent hymn "O Come, O Come Emmanuel" to keep a common Advent thread throughout the season.
- Scripture presentation—Schedule a Scripture presenter[51] for each of the four Sundays. Have them begin the presentation from different spots in the worship space (i.e., back of the room, within the congregation, etc.). Have them begin in their spot then walk toward the Advent candles at a pace that positions them at the candles at the conclusion of the Scripture presentation. When they conclude the Scripture presentation, they should light the designated candle. Another option is to have the candle lit by someone other than the Scripture presenter. The presenter, therefore, does not move during the presentation of Scripture. Regardless of movement, encourage the presenter to memorize the passage of Scripture. Presenting Scripture from memory provides a profoundly powerful moment of worship.
- Lighting of the Advent candle—The traditional Advent wreath consists of five candles—one for each of the four Sundays of Advent and the Christ candle. Generally, there are three purple or dark blue candles (the colors of Advent), one pink candle (symbolizing joy to be lit on the third Sunday of Advent) and a white candle (the Christ candle to be lit on Christmas Eve or Christmas Day).
- A Time of Stillness—This is a time for Christian meditation (to think deeply upon God just as the psalmist was encouraged to do—"I will meditate on your precepts and fix my eyes on your ways" Ps 119:15). Begin with twenty seconds of silence followed by a solo melody

---

51. Scripture presenter vs. Scripture reader: a Scripture presenter will often memorize the passage of Scripture and present it to the congregation in an artistic way. A Scripture reader reads the passage from the Bible.

instrument (potentially a different instrument each week) quietly playing "O Come, O Come Emmanuel" one time through.
- A Time for Prayer—An opportunity to acknowledge God and his work in our lives and throughout the world as we await his coming.
- Offering Prayer and Offertory—This time of worship goes beyond collecting monetary tithes and offerings. This is a time to encourage the congregation to offer not only their money, but their time and efforts as an act of worship.

FIRST SUNDAY OF ADVENT
WORSHIP SERVICE

CALL TO WORSHIP

Advent is a time for anticipating the coming of Christ. During this season we not only remember those who waited for the coming of the *Messiah* (his first coming), but we also anticipate when he will come again, this time as our reigning *King* (his second coming). Throughout our time together, let's express the hope we discover in Christ Jesus as we engage in worship.

INSTRUMENTAL PIANO: HYFRYDOL ("COME THOU LONG EXPECTED JESUS")

WAITING HERE FOR YOU

Words and Music by Chris Tomlin, Jesse Reeves, and Martin Smith
© 2011 Rising Springs Music; Smith United; Thankyou Music; Vamos Publishing; worshiptogether.com songs

OPENING PRAYER

Maranatha, come Lord, Jesus. God, we live in hope because we know that you are our living hope—in whom we live, and move, and have our being. Amen.

EVEN SO COME

Words and Music by Chris Tomlin, Jason Ingram, and Jess Cates
© 2015 S. D. G. Publishing, Twelve Lions Music, Worship Together Music, Open Hands Music, So Essential Tunes, Chrissamsongs Inc., Go Mia Music, Vistaville Music

SCRIPTURE PRESENTATION

Isaiah 2:1–5

The word that Isaiah the son of Amoz saw concerning Judah and Jerusalem. It shall come to pass in the latter days that the mountain of the house of the Lord shall be established as the highest of the mountains, and shall be lifted up above the hills; and all the nations shall flow to it, and many peoples shall come, and say:

"Come, let us go up to the mountain of the Lord, to the house of the God of Jacob, that he may teach us his ways and that we may walk in his paths."

For out of Zion shall go the law, and the word of the Lord from Jerusalem. He shall judge between the nations, and shall decide disputes for many peoples; and they shall beat their swords into plowshares, and their spears into pruning hooks; nation shall not lift up sword against nation, neither shall they learn war anymore. O house of Jacob, come, let us walk in the light of the Lord.

LIGHT ADVENT CANDLE #1

Today is the first Sunday of Advent. The word Advent means "coming" or "arrival." Just as those in the Old Testament awaited the arrival of the Messiah, we still have that sense of waiting today; that sense of anticipation for Christ's coming—his second coming. And so, we gather to worship as we wait. During this season the world seems to spin faster. It gets busier and sometimes it feels out of control. So, each Sunday during Advent we want to give you an opportunity to let go of all the things that so easily hinder us and to breathe deeply. Try that now: take a deep breath in . . . and let it out. We will have a time of quiet meditation. Meditation simply means to think upon. We want you to think upon the Lord; to turn your eyes upon Jesus; to focus on him and to practice what Psalm 46 instructs us to do—to be still and know that he is God.

A TIME OF STILLNESS

[Twenty seconds of silence]

INSTRUMENTAL SONG: VENI EMMANUEL ("O COME, O COME EMMANUEL")

[A solo melody instrument quietly playing "O Come, O Come Emmanuel" one time through.]

A TIME FOR PRAYER

Dear God, as we light the first candle on the Advent wreath, we are reminded of the promise of your coming and the hope you bring into our lives. We offer our praise and gratitude for your unfailing love and the boundless grace you bestow upon us. We pray that you will shine the light of your hope into our hearts and into our world. In the name of Jesus, our only hope, we pray, Amen.

HOPE HAS A NAME

Words and Music by Kristian Stanfill, Sean Curran, and Jacob Sooter
© 2020 Worshiptogether.com Songs, sixsteps Music, Kristian Stanfill Publishing Designee, sixsteps Songs, Capital CMG Paragon, Sounds of Jericho, So Essential Tunes, Just When Publishing

OFFERING PRAYER

Gracious and loving God, as we gather on this first Sunday of Advent, we come before you with open hearts and eager spirits. We thank you for the gift of this season of anticipation and hope. During this season, we seek your guidance and strength to prepare our hearts and minds for the celebration of the birth of our Savior, Jesus Christ. Help us to reflect on the true meaning of this season and to share your love with others through acts of kindness and compassion.

As we embark on this journey of Advent, may your light shine brightly within us, illuminating our path and guiding us closer to you. Bless our worship, our fellowship, our service to others, and these gifts that we give—that we may become beacons of your love in a world that longs for hope.

In Jesus' name, we pray. Amen.

OFFERTORY
CHRIST OUR HOPE IN LIFE AND DEATH

Words and Music by Keith Getty, Matt Boswell, Jordan Kauflin, Matthew Merker, and Matt Papa
© 2020 Getty Music Publishing, Messenger Hymns, Jordan Kauflin Music, Matthew Merker Music, Getty Music Hymns and Songs, Love Your Enemies Publishing

PRAYER OF ILLUMINATION

Eternal God, as we enter this season of Advent, we come before you with hearts full of anticipation, longing to receive the illuminating power of your presence.

As we prepare to hear your word, we seek your wisdom and understanding, that the words spoken may resonate deeply within us. Like the flickering flames of the Advent candles, may your light pierce through the darkness of our minds, revealing the path of righteousness and hope.

As we listen with eager hearts, we yearn to draw closer to you. Open our minds and hearts to receive the depth of your truth, and may your word take root and flourish within us. As we await the coming of your Son, our Savior, let this sermon be a beacon of hope and renewal, preparing our souls to welcome him with joy.

We pray with gratitude and expectation, trusting in your faithfulness and guidance, in the name of Jesus Christ, our Redeemer, Amen.

SERMON

[If observing the Lord's Supper, continue. If not, proceed to the next congregational song.]

THE LORD'S SUPPER INSTRUCTIONS AND INVITATION

[Instrumental music played or congregational singing.]

THE MYSTERY OF FAITH

And so, in remembrance of these your mighty acts in Jesus Christ, we offer ourselves in praise and thanksgiving as a holy and living sacrifice, in union with Christ's offering for us, as we proclaim the mystery of faith:

CONGREGATION:

Christ has died; Christ is risen; Christ will come again.

KING OF KINGS

Words and Music by Brooke Ligertwood, Jason Ingram, and Scott Ligertwood

© 2018 Hillsong Music Publishing, Fellow Ships Music, So Essential Tunes

BENEDICTION

In Advent hope, we wait. We wait in anticipation and hope for the coming of Christ the King. Let hope live in your heart and overflow from you to others through every circumstance you find yourself in. In this Advent season, we need to see, feel, and share hope. As you go out into the hopeless world, share hope with those you meet. Amen.

FIRST SUNDAY OF ADVENT
SCRIPTURE PRESENTATION

BENEDICTUS BY ZECHARIAH
Luke 1:5-23, 57-80

CAST:
Narrator
Zechariah
Angel Gabriel

NARRATOR:
In the days of Herod, king of Judea, there was a priest named Zechariah, of the division of Abijah. And he had a wife from the daughters of Aaron, and her name was Elizabeth. And they were both righteous before God, walking blamelessly in all the commandments and statutes of the Lord. But they had no child, because Elizabeth was barren, and both were advanced in years. Now while he was serving as priest before God when his division was on duty, according to the custom of the priesthood, he was chosen by lot to enter the temple of the Lord and burn incense. And the whole multitude of the people were praying outside at the hour of incense. And there appeared to him an angel of the Lord standing on the right side of the altar of incense. And Zechariah was troubled when he saw him, and fear fell upon him. But the angel said to him,

ANGEL GABRIEL:
"Do not be afraid, Zechariah, for your prayer has been heard, and your wife Elizabeth will bear you a son, and you shall call his name John. And you will have joy and gladness, and many will rejoice at his birth, for he will be great

before the Lord. And he must not drink wine or strong drink, and he will be filled with the Holy Spirit, even from his mother's womb. And he will turn many of the children of Israel to the Lord their God, and he will go before him in the spirit and power of Elijah, to turn the hearts of the fathers to the children, and the disobedient to the wisdom of the just, to make ready for the Lord a people prepared."

NARRATOR:

And Zechariah said to the angel,

ZECHARIAH:

"How shall I know this? For I am an old man, and my wife is advanced in years."

NARRATOR:

And the angel answered him,

ANGEL GABRIEL:

"I am Gabriel. I stand in the presence of God, and I was sent to speak to you and to bring you this good news. And behold, you will be silent and unable to speak until the day that these things take place, because you did not believe my words, which will be fulfilled in their time."

NARRATOR:

And the people were waiting for Zechariah, and they were wondering at his delay in the temple. And when he came out, he was unable to speak to them, and they realized that he had seen a vision in the temple. And he kept making signs to them and remained mute. And when his time of service was ended, he went to his home. Now the time came for Elizabeth to give birth, and she bore a son. And her neighbors and relatives heard that the Lord had shown great mercy to her, and they rejoiced with her. And on the eighth day they came to circumcise the child. And they would have called him Zechariah after his father, but his mother answered, "No; he shall be called John." And they said to her, "None of your relatives is called by this name." And they made signs to his father, inquiring what he wanted him to be called. And he asked for a writing tablet and wrote, "His name is John." And they all wondered. And immediately his mouth was opened and his tongue loosed, and he spoke, blessing God. And fear came on all their neighbors. And all these things were talked about through all the hill country of Judea, and all who heard them laid them up in their hearts, saying, "What then will this child be?" For the hand of the Lord was with him. And his father Zechariah was filled with the Holy Spirit and prophesied, saying,

ZECHARIAH:

"Blessed be the Lord God of Israel, for he has visited and redeemed his people and has raised up a horn of salvation for us in the house of his servant David, as he spoke by the mouth of his holy prophets from of old, that we should be saved from our enemies and from the hand of all who hate us; to show the mercy promised to our fathers and to remember his holy covenant, the oath that he swore to our father Abraham, to grant us that we, being delivered from the hand of our enemies, might serve him without fear, in holiness and righteousness before him all our days. And you, child, will be called the prophet of the Most High; for you will go before the Lord to prepare his ways, to give knowledge of salvation to his people in the forgiveness of their sins, because of the tender mercy of our God, whereby the sunrise shall visit us from on high to give light to those who sit in darkness and in the shadow of death, to guide our feet into the way of peace."

NARRATOR:

And the child grew and became strong in spirit, and he was in the wilderness until the day of his public appearance to Israel.

SECOND SUNDAY OF ADVENT

WORSHIP SERVICE

(Advent candle #1 is pre-lit before the service begins)

CALL TO WORSHIP

Today we continue our journey through the Advent season. In just a few moments we will be lighting the candle of peace. Only Jesus, the Prince of Peace, can offer us true peace.

INSTRUMENTAL PIANO: DIVINUM MYSTERIUM ("OF THE FATHER'S LOVE BEGOTTEN")

COME THOU LONG EXPECTED JESUS

Words by Charles Wesley, 1744; Music by Rowland Hugh Prichard, HYFRYDOL, 1830
Public Domain

OPENING PRAYER

Dear God, the only true peace in this world is the peace that you offer. Help us live in peace with ourselves and with others. Amen.

O HOLY NIGHT

Placide Cappeau, 1843; translated by John S. Dwight, 1855
Public Domain

SCRIPTURE PRESENTATION

Micah 5:2–5a
But you, O Bethlehem Ephrathah, who are too little to be among the clans of Judah, from you shall come forth for me one who is to be ruler in Israel, whose

coming forth is from of old, from ancient days. Therefore, he shall give them up until the time when she who is in labor has given birth then the rest of his brothers shall return to the people of Israel.

And he shall stand and shepherd his flock in the strength of the Lord, in the majesty of the name of the Lord his God. And they shall dwell secure, for now he shall be great to the ends of the earth. And he shall be their peace.

LIGHT ADVENT CANDLE #2

Today is the second Sunday of Advent. This season of Advent is a time for us to open our hands, and our hearts, and accept the hope, joy, love, and peace that God offers. I know sometimes it doesn't feel like we have any of those things. Maybe you're here today not feeling like you have hope; or maybe you feel unloved; lacking joy and in desperate need of peace. Maybe you feel like your world is spinning out of control, or maybe, because of your circumstances, you feel as though God is far away. But God is drawing near during this season of Advent as we await his coming. No matter what the circumstances, no matter what we're going through, this is a time when we are encouraged to pause, take a breath, and remember that Christ himself is our peace. We want to give you an opportunity to do that today; to focus your attention on God. He's the reason we are here. He's the reason we gather for worship. During this season of Advent, we remember that Christ is coming. Christ, the Prince of Peace has already come, and Christ the King of kings will come again. Let's focus our worship, and still our hearts, as we worship Christ, the King of kings.

A TIME OF STILLNESS

[Twenty seconds of silence]

INSTRUMENTAL SONG: VENI EMMANUEL ("O COME, O COME EMMANUEL")

[A solo melody instrument quietly playing "O Come, O Come Emmanuel" one time through.]

A TIME FOR PRAYER

Father, as we light the second candle on the Advent wreath, we are reminded of the peace that Christ offers to the world. We offer our worship and praise, knowing that you are the source of all peace and comfort in our lives. We thank you for sending your Son, the Prince of Peace. We desperately need his peace. We long not solely for peace on earth, but also, more deeply, for the peace of Christ; that *"peace that surpasses all understanding"* (Phil 4:7). Lord, help us open our hearts to peace and may the peace of Christ reign in our lives. Amen.

GOD WITH US

Words and Music by Jason Ingram and Leslie Jordan
© 2012 Open Hands Music; So Essential Tunes; Integrity's Praise! Music; Little Way Creative

OFFERING PRAYER

Loving and merciful God, as we gather on this second Sunday of Advent, we come before you with hearts filled with gratitude and anticipation. We thank you for the precious gift of your Son, Jesus Christ, who brings peace to our lives.

During this season of preparation, we seek your wisdom and guidance to help us grow in faith and deepen our relationship with you. May our offerings today be a reflection of our commitment to follow in the footsteps of Jesus, bringing peace and reconciliation to those around us.

As we give our tithes and offerings, we trust that you will use them for the advancement of your kingdom and the well-being of others. Bless these gifts and multiply them, so they may touch the lives of many.

In the name of Jesus, our Prince of Peace, we pray. Amen.

OFFERTORY
GLORY IN THE HIGHEST

Words and Music by Travis Cottrell, Ben Cantelon, and Jeff Pardo
© 2018 Great Revelation Music, Universal Music—Brentwood Benson Publishing, Ben Cantelon Designee, Capitol CMG Paragon, Da Bears Da Bears Da Bears Music, Meaux Jeaux Music

PRAYER OF ILLUMINATION

Eternal God, as we journey through this season of Advent, we come before you with hearts full of anticipation, longing to receive the illuminating power of your presence.

As we prepare to hear your word, we seek your wisdom and understanding, that the words spoken may resonate deeply within us. Like the flickering flames of the Advent candles, may your light pierce through the darkness of our minds, revealing the path of righteousness and hope.

As we listen with eager hearts, we yearn to draw closer to you. Open our minds and hearts to receive the depth of your truth, and may your word take root and flourish within us. As we await the coming of your Son, our Savior, let this sermon be a beacon of hope and renewal, preparing our souls to welcome him with joy.

We pray with gratitude and expectation, trusting in your faithfulness and guidance, in the name of Jesus Christ, our Redeemer, Amen.

SERMON

[If observing the Lord's Supper, continue. If not, proceed to the next congregational song.]

THE LORD'S SUPPER INSTRUCTIONS AND INVITATION

[Instrumental music played or congregational singing.]

THE MYSTERY OF FAITH

And so, in remembrance of these your mighty acts in Jesus Christ, we offer ourselves in praise and thanksgiving as a holy and living sacrifice, in union with Christ's offering for us, as we proclaim the mystery of faith:

CONGREGATION:

Christ has died; Christ is risen; Christ will come again.

HE SHALL REIGN FOREVERMORE

Words and Music by Chris Tomlin and Matt Maher
© 2015 S.D.G Publishing, Worship Together Music, sixsteps Songs, Be Essential Songs, I Am A Pilgrim Songs

BENEDICTION

In Advent peace, we wait. We wait in anticipation and peace for the coming of Christ the King. Let peace live in your heart and overflow from you to others through every circumstance you find yourself in. In this Advent season, we need to see, feel, and share peace. As you go out into the peaceless world, share peace with those you meet. Amen.

SECOND SUNDAY OF ADVENT

SCRIPTURE PRESENTATION

GOD WITH US
with Isaiah 41:10

CAST:
4 Voices

VOICE 1:
God with us.
God [pause] with [pause] us.
I wish I could tell you that this world is whole. That it's perfect and without any flaws. I wish I could tell you that this world brings nothing but peace and healing. But I can't.

VOICE 2:
Fear not, for I am with you; be not dismayed, for I am your God; I will strengthen you, I will help you, I will uphold you with my righteous right hand.

VOICE 3:
I wish I could tell you that if you're nice, people will be nice to you. That if you're kind, they'll be kind to you. I wish I could tell you that this world won't knock you down day after day after day. But I can't.

VOICE 2:

Fear not, for I am with you; be not dismayed, for I am your God; I will strengthen you, I will help you, I will uphold you with my righteous right hand.

VOICE 4:

Darkness overwhelms. Tension strangles. Brokenness corrupts. Sin entangles. Fear increases. Temptations scream to get our attention. Peace seems hidden.

VOICE 2:

Fear not, for I am with you; be not dismayed, for I am your God; I will strengthen you, I will help you, I will uphold you with my righteous right hand.

VOICE 1:

And just when it seems like we can't take anymore . . .

ALL VOICES:

Emmanuel . . . God with us!

THIRD SUNDAY OF ADVENT

WORSHIP SERVICE

(Advent candles #1 and 2 are pre-lit before the service begins)

CALL TO WORSHIP

As we gather for worship, we will be reminded that true joy only comes from the Father, by his Son, and through the Holy Spirit.

INSTRUMENTAL PIANO: HYMN TO JOY ("JOYFUL, JOYFUL, WE ADORE THEE")

ANGELS WE HAVE HEARD ON HIGH

English text by James Chadwick, 1862; GLORIA, Traditional French Carol
Public Domain

OPENING PRAYER

Dear God, give us joy in our hearts, now and forever. As we worship you, fill us with your joy. Amen.

JOY HAS DAWNED

Words and Music by Keith Getty and Stuart Townend
© 2004 Thankyou Music

SCRIPTURE PRESENTATION

Philippians 2:1–11

So, if there is any encouragement in Christ, any comfort from love, any participation in the Spirit, any affection and sympathy, complete my joy by being of the same mind, having the same love, being in full accord and of one mind. Do nothing from selfish ambition or conceit, but in humility count others more significant than yourselves. Let each of you look not only to his own interests, but also to the interests of others. Have this mind among yourselves, which is yours in Christ Jesus, who, though he was in the form of God, did not count equality with God a thing to be grasped, but emptied himself, by taking the form of a servant, being born in the likeness of men. And being found in human form, he humbled himself by becoming obedient to the point of death, even death on a cross. Therefore, God has highly exalted him and bestowed on him the name that is above every name, so that at the name of Jesus every knee should bow, in heaven and on earth and under the earth, and every tongue confess that Jesus Christ is Lord, to the glory of God the Father.

LIGHT ADVENT CANDLE #3

Today is the third Sunday of Advent. We focus on the joy found in Christ as we join with all of creation, confessing Christ as Lord and worshiping him in all his glory and splendor. During this season the world likes to get busier and sometimes we as Christians get caught up in that. Sometimes it's okay, but most of the time we forget that there's a sense of calmness in God. So, throughout this season of Advent we're offering a time of quiet meditation for you to loosen your grip on everything that's been going on this week. All the things that are attempting to pull you away from God. Let those things go. Let's focus our full attention on God and as Psalm 46 says, let us be still and know that he is God.

A TIME OF STILLNESS

[Twenty seconds of silence]

INSTRUMENTAL SONG: VENI EMMANUEL ("O COME, O COME EMMANUEL")

[A solo melody instrument quietly playing "O Come, O Come Emmanuel" one time through.]

A TIME FOR PRAYER

As we light the third candle on the Advent wreath, we are reminded of the joy that comes from knowing you are with us always. We offer our worship and praise, rejoicing in the hope that your presence brings to our lives. Speak to us, Lord. Speak to us in the waiting, the hoping, the longing, the sorrow, and the rejoicing. Speak to us by your Word during these days of Advent and walk with us until the day of your coming. Amen.

JOYFUL, JOYFUL, WE ADORE THEE

Words by Linda Lee Johnson; Music by Ludwig van Beethoven
Words © 1985, 1988 Lillenas Publishing Company

OFFERING PRAYER

Gracious and loving God, on this third Sunday of Advent, our hearts are filled with gratitude and awe for your unending grace and boundless love. We thank you for guiding us through this season of joyful anticipation. As we prepare to celebrate the birth of our Savior, Jesus Christ, may we be filled with the joy of his teachings and the promise of eternal life through him. May our actions and words reflect the joy that comes from knowing you and following your ways.

We offer our gifts and offerings today, not out of obligation, but out of joy and gratitude for all that you have done for us. Bless these offerings, and may they be used to spread joy and hope to those who are hurting and in need.

In the name of Jesus, the source of our true joy, we pray. Amen.

OFFERTORY

GOD REST YE MERRY GENTLEMEN

18th century traditional English carol
Public Domain

PRAYER OF ILLUMINATION

Eternal God, as we journey through this season of Advent, we come before you with hearts full of anticipation, longing to receive the illuminating power of your presence.

As we prepare to hear your word, we seek your wisdom and understanding, that the words spoken may resonate deeply within us. As we listen with eager hearts, we yearn to draw closer to you. Open our minds and hearts to receive the depth of your truth, and may your word take root and flourish within us. As we await the coming of your Son, our Savior, let this sermon be a beacon of hope and renewal, preparing our souls to welcome him with joy.

We pray with gratitude and expectation, trusting in your faithfulness and guidance, in the name of Jesus Christ, our Redeemer, Amen.

SERMON

[If observing the Lord's Supper, continue. If not, proceed to the next congregational song.]

THE LORD'S SUPPER INSTRUCTIONS AND INVITATION

[Instrumental music played or congregational singing.]

THE MYSTERY OF FAITH

And so, in remembrance of these your mighty acts in Jesus Christ, we offer ourselves in praise and thanksgiving as a holy and living sacrifice, in union with Christ's offering for us, as we proclaim the mystery of faith:

CONGREGATION:

Christ has died; Christ is risen; Christ will come again.

JOY TO THE WORLD

Words by Isaac Watts, 1719; Music by George F. Handel, ANTIOCH, 1742; adapted by Lowell Mason
Public Domain

BENEDICTION

In Advent joy, we wait. We wait in anticipation and joy for the coming of Christ the King. Let joy live in your heart and overflow from you to others through every circumstance you find yourself in. In this Advent season, we need to see, feel, and share joy. As you go out into what's often a joyless world, share joy with those you meet. Amen.

THIRD SUNDAY OF ADVENT

SCRIPTURE PRESENTATION

MARY'S MAGNIFICAT
Luke 1:39–55

CAST:
2 Voices

VOICE 1:
My soul magnifies the Lord, and my spirit rejoices in God my Savior, for he has looked on the humble estate of his servant. For behold, from now on all generations will call me blessed; for he who is mighty has done great things for me, and holy is his name.

Remember with me this portion of the gospel of Luke chapter 1.

BOTH:
In those days Mary arose and went with haste into the hill country, to a town in Judah,

VOICE 1:
and she entered the house of Zechariah

VOICE 2:
and greeted Elizabeth.

VOICE 1:
And when Elizabeth heard the greeting of Mary,

BOTH:

the baby leaped in her womb.

VOICE 1:

And Elizabeth was filled with the Holy Spirit,

VOICE 2:

and she exclaimed with a loud cry,

BOTH:

"Blessed are you among women, and blessed is the fruit of your womb!

VOICE 2:

And why is this granted to me

BOTH:

that the mother of my Lord should come to me?

VOICE 1:

For behold, when the sound of your greeting came to my ears,

BOTH:

the baby in my womb leaped for joy.

VOICE 2:

And blessed is she who believed that there would be a fulfillment of what was spoken to her from the Lord."

VOICE 1:

My soul magnifies the Lord, and my spirit rejoices in God my Savior, for he has looked on the humble estate of his servant. For behold, from now on all generations will call me blessed; for he who is mighty has done great things for me, and holy is his name.

VOICE 2:

"And his mercy is for those who fear him from generation to generation. He has shown strength with his arm; he has scattered the proud in the thoughts of their hearts;

VOICE 1:

he has brought down the mighty from their thrones and exalted those of humble estate; he has filled the hungry with good things, and the rich he has sent away empty.

VOICE 2:

He has helped his servant Israel, in remembrance of his mercy, as he spoke to our fathers, to Abraham and to his offspring forever."

VOICE 1:

This is the gospel of the Lord.

Optional: follow this Scripture presentation with one of the following songs:

MAGNIFICAT

Words and Music by Keith Getty, Kristyn Getty, and Stuart Townend
© 2008 Thankyou Music

MY SOUL DOTH MAGNIFY THE LORD

Words and Music by Don Marsh
© 1979 New Spring Music

MY SOUL MAGNIFIES THE LORD

Words and Music by Chris Tomlin and Daniel Carson
© 2009 Rising Springs Music, Vamos Publishing, worshiptogether.com songs

FOURTH SUNDAY OF ADVENT

WORSHIP SERVICE

(Advent candles #1, 2, and 3 are pre-lit before the service begins)

CALL TO WORSHIP

Today we will light the candle of love. In 1 John 4:7 we read, "Dear friends, let us love one another, for love comes from God. Everyone who loves has been born of God and knows God."

INSTRUMENTAL PIANO: CANTIQUE DE NOEL ("O HOLY NIGHT")

ANGELS FROM THE REALMS OF GLORY

Words by James Montgomery, 1816; Music by Henry T. Smart, REGENT SQUARE, 1867
Public Domain

OPENING PRAYER

Dear God, we love you because you loved us first. Jesus, you told us that no greater love exists than when someone lays down their life for someone else. We are amazed when we consider that you laid aside your heavenly glory to come to earth for us. And then you laid down your life for us. There is no greater love than what you have given to us. Help us follow your example by loving others and telling others about your love, Jesus. Amen.

SING WE THE SONG OF EMMANUEL

Words and Music by Keith Getty, Matt Boswell, Matt Papa, and Stuart Townend

© 2015 Getty Music Hymns and Songs, Getty Music Publishing, Love Your Enemies Publishing, Messenger Hymns, Townend Songs

SCRIPTURE PRESENTATION

Isaiah 52:7–10

How beautiful upon the mountains are the feet of him who brings good news, who publishes peace, who brings good news of happiness, who publishes salvation, who says to Zion, "Your God reigns." The voice of your watchmen—they lift up their voice; together they sing for joy; for eye to eye they see the return of the Lord to Zion. Break forth together into singing, you waste places of Jerusalem, for the Lord has comforted his people; he has redeemed Jerusalem. The Lord has bared his holy arm before the eyes of all the nations, and all the ends of the earth shall see the salvation of our God.

LIGHT ADVENT CANDLE #4

Today is the fourth Sunday of Advent. The birth of Christ as a baby in Bethlehem is near. We can sense it in the air. Something, or in this case, someone is coming. There's excitement all around and within us. We prepare for his arrival. We ready our hearts to worship the King. We don't want to miss him. We want to be like the shepherds who ran to find Jesus, not like the innkeeper who had no room for him. We don't want to pass up the opportunity to be in the presence of Almighty God. And so, we quiet ourselves . . . and worship the newborn King . . . born in a manger . . . born in our hearts.

A TIME OF STILLNESS

[Twenty seconds of silence]

INSTRUMENTAL SONG: VENI EMMANUEL ("O COME, O COME EMMANUEL")

[A solo melody instrument quietly playing "O Come, O Come Emmanuel" one time through.]

A TIME FOR PRAYER

God, who deeply wants to send abundant love into the world, we honor and rejoice in who you are—the one and only Savior. As we light the fourth candle on the Advent wreath, we are reminded of the love that brought forth the miracle of Christ's birth. We offer our adoration and praise, acknowledging you as the ultimate source of love and grace in our lives. As we prepare to celebrate "God with us," Emmanuel, we lift our voices to praise the one who first loved us.

INFANT HOLY, INFANT LOWLY

Piotrowi Skardze, 13th century; Paraphrased by Edith M. G. Reed, 1921; Traditional Polish carol, W ZLOBIE LEZY
Public Domain

LEADER:

The gospel of John tells us . . .

CONGREGATION:

The Word became flesh and dwelt among us, and we have seen his glory, glory as of the only Son from the Father, full of grace and truth. (John 1:14)

LEADER:

Matthew provides this wonderful reminder of the prophet Isaiah's words, *"Behold, the virgin shall conceive and bear a son, and they shall call his name Emmanuel"* which means,

CONGREGATION:

God with us. (Matthew 1:23)

EMMANUEL (GOD WITH US)

Words and Music by Chris Tomlin and Jason Ingram
© 2021 Capitol CMG Paragon, S. D. G. Publishing

OFFERING PRAYER

Heavenly Father, on this fourth Sunday of Advent, we come before you with hearts overflowing with thanksgiving and reverence. We are humbled by the profound love you have shown us throughout this Advent season. During these days of anticipation, we seek to draw nearer to the heart of the Christmas story. Help us to grasp the depth of your love for humanity, demonstrated through the gift of your Son, our Savior, Jesus Christ.

As we reflect on the humble manger scene, we recognize the immense sacrifice you made for us. May this profound love inspire us to show compassion and kindness to all those we encounter, reflecting your love to the world.

We offer our gifts and offerings with hearts full of love and dedication. May they be used to share the message of your love and salvation with those who have yet to experience your grace.

In this final stretch of Advent, prepare our hearts to welcome the Christ-child with joy and reverence. May we carry the spirit of this season throughout the year, continuously seeking to share your love with others.

In the precious name of Jesus, the embodiment of your love, we pray. Amen.

OFFERTORY

LIGHT OF THE WORLD (SING HALLELUJAH)

Words and Music by Andrew Bergthold, Ed Cash, Franni Cash, Martin Cash, and Scott Cash
© 2020 Angie Feel Good Songs, Bay19, Capitol CMG Genesis, Capitol CMG Paragon, Scott Cash Publishing Designee, We The Kingdom Music

PRAYER OF ILLUMINATION

Eternal God, as we near the end of this season of Advent, we come before you with hearts full of anticipation, longing to receive the illuminating power of your presence. As we prepare to hear your word, we seek your wisdom and understanding, that the words spoken may resonate deeply within us. Like the flickering flames of the Advent candles, may your light pierce through the darkness of our minds, revealing the path of righteousness and hope.

As we listen with eager hearts, we yearn to draw closer to you. Open our minds and hearts to receive the depth of your truth, and may your word take root and flourish within us.

We pray with gratitude and expectation, trusting in your faithfulness and guidance, in the name of Jesus Christ, our Redeemer, Amen.

SERMON

[If observing the Lord's Supper, continue. If not, proceed to the next congregational song.]

THE LORD'S SUPPER INSTRUCTIONS AND INVITATION

[Instrumental music played or congregational singing.]

THE MYSTERY OF FAITH

And so, in remembrance of these your mighty acts in Jesus Christ, we offer ourselves in praise and thanksgiving as a holy and living sacrifice, in union with Christ's offering for us, as we proclaim the mystery of faith:

CONGREGATION:

Christ has died; Christ is risen; Christ will come again.

HARK! THE HERALD ANGELS SING

Words by Charles Wesley, 1739; Music by Felix Mendelssohn, MENDELSSOHN, 1840
Public Domain

BENEDICTION

In Advent love, we wait. We wait in anticipation and love for the coming of Christ the King. Let love live in your heart and overflow from you to others through every circumstance you find yourself in. In this Advent season, we need to see, feel, and share love. As you go out into the loveless world, share love with those you meet. Amen.

FOURTH SUNDAY OF ADVENT

SCRIPTURE PRESENTATION

AN EVENT FOR EVERYONE

Luke 2:8–18 (from *THE MESSAGE*)[52]

CAST:

3 Voices
Group (3–5 voices)
Singer (humming; can choose any melodic tune on a major scale)
Percussionist (cajon)

VOICE 1:

There were shepherds camping in the neighborhood. They had set night watches over their sheep. Suddenly, *[percussionist and singer begin]* God's angel stood among them and God's glory blazed around them. They were terrified. The angel said,

VOICE 2:

"Don't be afraid. I'm here to announce a great and joyful event that is meant for everybody, worldwide: A Savior has just been born in David's town,

GROUP:

a Savior who is Messiah and Master.

---

52. Scripture taken from *THE MESSAGE*. Copyright © 1993, 1994, 1995, 1996, 2000, 2001, 2002. Used by permission of NavPress Publishing Group.

VOICE 2:

This is what you're to look for: a baby wrapped in a blanket and lying in a manger."

VOICE 1:

At once the angel was joined by a huge angelic choir singing God's praises:

GROUP:

Glory to God in the heavenly heights,
Peace to all men and women on earth who please him.

VOICE 1:

As the angel choir withdrew into heaven, the shepherds talked it over.

VOICE 3:

"Let's get over to Bethlehem as fast as we can and see for ourselves what God has revealed to us."

VOICE 1:

[VOICE 3 and GROUP leave the room]
They left, running, and found Mary and Joseph, and the baby lying in the manger.

VOICE 2:

Seeing was believing.

VOICE 1:

They told everyone they met what the angels had said about this child. All who heard the shepherds were impressed.
[percussionist and singer slowly end]

CHRISTMAS EVE

CANDLELIGHT SERVICE

(Advent candles #1, 2, 3, and 4 are pre-lit before the service begins; each member of the congregation is given a candle as they enter the worship space; house lights are dimmed, but not completely off)

CALL TO WORSHIP

Welcome. Today is the last day of the Advent season. All that we have waited for arrives on this night. Jesus will be born. Messiah will come. As the world rests in silence, the King of kings will make his way into our world. And so we say, welcome, babe in a manger. Welcome, Light of the world. Welcome, blessed Redeemer. Welcome to our world.

HARK! THE HERALD ANGELS SING

Words by Charles Wesley, 1739; Music by Felix Mendelssohn, MENDELSSOHN, 1840
Public Domain

OPENING PRAYER

Emmanuel, God with us, we gather in this place to worship and adore you. During this season of Advent, we have awaited your birth. Now it is upon us. We can hear the faint cries of a baby in a manger, but not just any baby: the Creator of the universe held in the arms of the created; the Giver of all life dependent upon a mother's breast for nourishment; the One who spoke all things into existence not able to utter a single word.

Jesus Messiah has come. And yet today, we still wait; we wait for your coming again. Not as a baby, but as the King of kings and Lord of lords. We celebrate your birth in Bethlehem. And for those who know you as Lord and Savior, we celebrate your birth in us. This evening we pray the words of the old carol:

O holy Child of Bethlehem, descend to us we pray;
Cast out our sin and enter in, be born in us today.
We hear the Christmas angels, the great glad tidings tell;
O come to us, abide with us, our Lord Emmanuel.

Amen.

SCRIPTURE PRESENTATION

Isaiah 9:1–6

CAST:

5 Voices
[Voice 1 holding lit candle; Voices 2, 3, 4, and 5 holding unlit candles]

VOICE 1:

But there will be no gloom for her who was in anguish. In the former time he brought into contempt the land of Zebulun and the land of Naphtali, but in the latter time he has made glorious the way of the sea, the land beyond the Jordan, Galilee of the nations. The people who walked in darkness have seen a great light;

VOICE 2:

[light candle from Voice 1 candle before speaking]
those who dwelt in a land of deep darkness, on them has light shone.

VOICE 3:

[light candle from Voice 2 candle before speaking]
You have multiplied the nation;

VOICE 4:

[light candle from Voice 3 candle before speaking]
you have increased its joy;

VOICE 5:

[light candle from Voice 4 candle before speaking]

they rejoice before you as with joy at the harvest, as they are glad when they divide the spoil.

VOICE 1:

For the yoke of his burden, and the staff for his shoulder, the rod of his oppressor, you have broken as on the day of Midian. For every boot of the tramping warrior in battle tumult and every garment rolled in blood will be burned as fuel for the fire.
[Voice 1 lights the Christ Candle]

VOICES 1, 2, 3, 4, & 5:

For to us a child is born, to us a son is given; and the government shall be upon his shoulder, and his name shall be called Wonderful Counselor, Mighty God, Everlasting Father, Prince of Peace.

O COME, O COME EMMANUEL

12th century; Ancient Antiphons (Latin), versified in 18th century; John Mason Neale, trans., 1851
Public Domain

SING WE THE SONG OF EMMANUEL

Words and Music by Keith Getty, Matt Boswell, Matt Papa, and Stuart Townend
© 2015 Getty Music Hymns and Songs, Getty Music Publishing, Love Your Enemies Publishing, Messenger Hymns, Townend Songs

PRAYER OF ILLUMINATION

Loving God, on this Christmas Eve, we gather in your presence, with hearts filled with wonder and awe, eager to encounter the true meaning of this joyous occasion. As we prepare to celebrate the birth of your Son, we seek the illumination of your divine light, a light that shines brightly amidst the darkness of the world. In the glow of candlelight and the warmth of fellowship, may your Spirit guide our thoughts and reflections, opening our minds to the profound mysteries of your love.

As we hear the timeless story of Christ's humble birth, illuminate our understanding with the significance of this event. Let the miracle of his coming touch our souls deeply. As we reflect on the gift of your Son, our Savior, may the sermon draw us closer to your heart, igniting a renewed passion to live faithfully for you.

We offer this prayer with heartfelt gratitude and reverence, in the name of Jesus Christ, our Savior and Emmanuel, Amen.

SERMON

SILENT NIGHT

Words by Joseph Mohr; Music by Franz Gruber, 1818
Public Domain
[During the singing of "Silent Night," the pastor or worship leader lights a personal candle from the Christ candle. The congregation candles are lit from the pastor or worship leader's candle. It is significant to point out the light of Christ is spreading throughout the body of Christ.]

JOY TO THE WORLD

Words by Isaac Watts, 1719; Music by George F. Handel, ANTIOCH, 1742; adapted by Lowell Mason
Public Domain
[As the music for "Joy to The World" begins, the congregation is asked to stand (if not already standing) and lift their candles as they shine for Jesus. At the conclusion of the song, the congregation is asked to extinguish the candles, but to continue to shine their light for Christ as they depart from the worship space and go out into the world.]

BENEDICTION

May you be filled with the wonder of Mary, the obedience of Joseph, the joy of the angels, the eagerness of the shepherds, the determination of the magi, and the peace of the Christ child. May Almighty God, Father, Son, and Holy Spirit, bless you now and forever. Amen.

CHRISTMAS EVE
SCRIPTURE PRESENTATION

REJOICE, EMMANUEL!

Isaiah 9:2, 6–7 and Luke 2:10–14

CAST:

2 Voices
Congregation

[Music begins to "O Come, O Come Emmanuel"; plays quietly as underscore beneath reading]

VOICE 1:

The people who walked in darkness have seen a great light; Those who dwelt in the land of the shadow of death, upon them a light has shined.

VOICE 2:

For unto us a Child is born, unto us a Son is given; And the government will be upon his shoulder.

VOICE 1:

And his name will be called

CONGREGATION:

Wonderful Counselor, Mighty God, Everlasting Father, Prince of Peace.

VOICE 1:

Of the increase of his government and peace there will be no end,

VOICE 2:

upon the throne of David and over his kingdom,

VOICE 1:

to order it and establish it with judgment and justice from that time forward, even forever.

VOICE 2:

The zeal of the Lord of hosts will perform this.

ALL SING:

Rejoice! Rejoice! Emmanuel
Shall come to thee, O Israel

VOICE 1:

Then the angel said . . . "Do not be afraid, for behold, I bring you good tidings of great joy which will be to all people. For there is born to you this day in the city of David, a Savior, who is Christ the Lord. And this will be the sign to you: You will find a Babe wrapped in swaddling cloths, lying in a manger."

VOICE 2:

And suddenly there was with the angel a multitude of the heavenly host praising God and saying:

CONGREGATION:

"Glory to God in the highest, and on earth peace, goodwill toward men!"

ALL SING:

Rejoice! Rejoice! Emmanuel
Shall come to thee, O Israel.

O COME, O COME EMMANUEL

12th century; Ancient Antiphons (Latin), versified in 18th century; John Mason Neale, trans., 1851
Public Domain

CHAPTER 7

CHRISTMAS

The season of Christmas is a festive and joyous season, providing a time to celebrate Jesus, the Light of the world, who came to dispel darkness. The Christmas season begins on Christmas Day, December 25, and lasts until January 5, the day before Epiphany. Unfortunately, this season of the church year has been widely misunderstood and the commercialization of Christmas has created a distorted view of the season. Today, Christmas is popularly believed to end, not begin, on December 25, taking away the impact and importance of not only Advent, but also the feast of Epiphany following Christmas. The truth is, the Christmas season commences on December 25 and extends for twelve days—"on the first day of Christmas my true love gave to me..."[53] This is not merely a catchy song but an acknowledgment of the historical significance of the Christmas season, providing evidence that Christmas was genuinely celebrated for twelve days, not just one.[54]

The faith of the early church revolved around proclaiming the resurrection of Christ. It was so central to the life of the church that Paul wrote:

> Now if Christ is proclaimed as raised from the dead, how can some of you say there is no resurrection of the dead? If there is no resurrection of the dead, then Christ has not been raised; and

---

53. "The Twelve Days of Christmas" © 1909 by Novello and Company Limited.

54. The origin for the twelve days of Christmas lies in the early church. The early Christians of the East celebrated the birth of Jesus on January 6. In the West, Christians began to celebrate Christmas on December 25. Eventually these two dates came to bookend the Christmas season with the celebration of the birth of Jesus on December 25 representing the beginning of the season and the celebration of the manifestation of Christ to the world through the visit of the Magi on January 6 (Epiphany) representing the end of the Christmas season.

if Christ has not been raised, then our proclamation has been in vain, and your faith has been in vain. But in fact Christ has been raised from the dead, the first fruits of those who have died. (1 Cor 15:12–14, 20 NRSV)

Even though the proclamation of Christ's resurrection is the central focus of the Christian faith, many churches today give the birth of Christ equal or greater emphasis. Churches may be filled with people on Easter Sunday morning, but Christmas is given a whole month of musicals and celebrations. While we may provide excellent worship on Easter Sunday, it is common to invest more time, money, and effort in preparing for the Christmas musical, cantata, or pageant.

The importance of Christ's resurrection for the early Christians resulted in the celebration of his birth not becoming as a regular festivity until the fourth century. However, Thomas Talley presents the notion that the liturgical year in Rome in 336 was marked by the nativity of Christ on December 25, which would imply that the nativity had great meaning and importance to those in the early centuries. Earliest documents show that the observance of the nativity on December 25 was an integral turning point of the liturgical year, so much so that the calendar at that time was formed to run from December 25 to December 25.[55] And yet, the origin of Christmas is difficult to determine with scholars presenting two distinct viewpoints.

The first and more widely accepted viewpoint, known as the "History of Religions Theory," observes that the celebration of Christ's nativity on December 25 was an intentional alternative to an early pagan festival. In 274, the Roman emperor Aurelian established the date as a commemoration of Emesa, the Syrian god of the sun. By establishing the annual celebration of Christ's nativity to coincide with the pagan festival of the sun, the church could draw upon the sun/light imagery and witness to the pagans by telling them of the true Sun/Light. Adolf Adam has noted, "Christians could now make the triumphant claim to their pagan fellow citizens that they, the Christians, were celebrating the feast of the true Sun which alone can give light and salvation to the world."[56]

A second viewpoint was derived from a symbolic number system originally proposed by French church historian Louis Duchesne in his comprehensive work entitled *Christian Worship: Its Origin and Evolution*. Duchesne held that the date of December 25 for the celebration of Christ's nativity was determined by a series of computations (later termed the Calculation or Computation Theory). Witnesses of the early church, particularly Tertullian

---

55. Talley, *The Origins of the Liturgical Year*, 85.
56. Adam, *The Liturgical Year*, 123.

and Hippolytus, recognized March 25 as the date of Christ's death on the cross. Duchesne suggested, though without supporting evidence, that as an aspect of the paschal date itself, March 25 would also be the date in which Jesus was conceived. A perfect nine months later would make December 25 the birth date of Jesus. The use of the symbolic number system would not allow for imperfections (fractions). For as Duchesne put it, "fractions are imperfections which do not fall in with the demands of a symbolical system of numbers"; therefore, the date of Jesus' death would be taken as being that of his conception as well. To that hypothetical suggestion Duchesne added, "This explanation would be the more readily received if we could find it fully stated in some author. Unfortunately, we know of no text containing it, and we are therefore compelled to put it forward as an hypothesis, but it is an hypothesis which falls in with what we may call the recognized methods in such matters."[57] To this day the prevailing perspective on the origin of Christmas celebration on December 25 is its connection to the Christianization of the pagan festival of the sun. It is impossible, however, to know for certain.

The focus of a season of Christmas beginning on December 25 rather than ending on that day would be a challenge in our churches. Today, the commercialization of Christmas commences as early as September, with merchants displaying Christmas decorations and holiday promotions. This manipulation leads our congregations to feel like it's already Christmas before it actually is. Yet the church is supposed to stand against the prevailing culture. By following the Christian year, the church could eliminate some of the hectic busyness that we all feel and use the four Sundays before Christmas (Advent) as a time of preparation and the twelve days of Christmas as a time of celebration. Christmas parties and pageants could be planned to occur from December 25–January 5. Christmas carols could continue to be sung over the two Sundays following Christmas, long after radio stations and stores have forgotten about them. Maybe then we would hear less comments like, "isn't it sad that we're so busy at Christmas to realize what it's really all about?"

The primary meaning of Christmas is that we not only celebrate Jesus born in Bethlehem, but Christ crucified, risen, and returning—and Christ born *in us*. This perspective invites Christmas to be an important time in our spiritual lives. The fact that God became man—the Word became flesh—provides us an opportunity to be united with God. Because Jesus was united to God, we, through our union with Jesus in faith are united with God. Our spiritual lives are formed, and we experience unity with the triune

---

57. Duchesne, *Christian Worship*, 263.

God. Observing the Christmas season then, I maintain, has great spiritual value in strengthening spiritual formation.

INCORPORATING CHRISTMAS:

Consider leaving the Christmas decorations up for the two Sundays after December 25. Teach the congregation about the twelve days of Christmas (December 25–January 5) and use the two Sundays that fall within those twelve days as a celebration of Christ's birth. Just as a family with a recent newborn baby doesn't stop celebrating the child the day after they are born, we should not stop celebrating Jesus' birth on December 26. Let the congregation know of the plan to continue to celebrate over these two weeks. That way they are gaining an appreciation for the Christian year.

Continue to sing Christmas songs on the two Sundays after December 25. Long after the radio stations and stores have forgotten about Christmas, the church can still celebrate the birth of the Savior of the world.

Have light-themed worship services echoing the origins of the Christmas celebration, which were "light" focused. The Light of the world, Jesus, has come.

CHRISTMAS
OVERVIEW

TIME
December 25–January 5; a twelve-day season.

THEMES
From the beginning of the Christmas celebration in the early fourth century, the theme of the Christmas season has always been the arrival of the Light—the Light that has come to dispel darkness. What we are called to remember is that Christmas is a celebration of redemption. The prayers, Scripture readings, and songs for Christmas point us to the source of our redemption, namely, that in Christ's death and resurrection, we find salvation and that gives us the ultimate meaning for the incarnation.

SPIRITUAL CHALLENGE
Adopt an incarnational spirituality, allowing Christ to be born within you in a new way.

SCRIPTURE
- Old Testament: Isa 9:2–7; Isa 52:7–10; Isa 62:6–12; Isa 63:7–9
- Psalm: Ps 96; Ps 97; Ps 98; Ps 148
- New Testament: Gal 4:4–7; Phil 2:5–11; Titus 2:11–14; Titus 3:4–7; Heb 1:1–4 (5–12); Heb 2:10–18; Rev 21:1–6a
- Gospel: Matt 2:13–23; Matt 25:31–46; Luke 2:1–14, (15–20); John 1:1–14

SYMBOLS
- Manger

- Star
- Light

COLORS[58]

- White
- Gold

---

[58]. While the secular colors of Christmas are red and green, the liturgical colors of Christmas are white and gold, symbolizing light and kingship.

CHRISTMAS
SONG LIST

Many of us are acquainted with the standard traditional Christmas carols. I highly recommend including these carols in your Christmas worship services, as people have a strong desire to sing these songs. Even younger individuals and those who don't attend church regularly will be drawn to these beloved "favorites" during this season. Below, you'll find a list of these classics along with newer songs written to celebrate the birth of Jesus.

CONTEMPORARY

Christmas Offering Paul Baloche, 2003

Come Adore the Humble King Matt Boswell and Matt Papa, 2018

Come Behold the Wondrous Mystery Matt Boswell, Matt Papa, and Michael Bleecker, 2012

Creation Sings the Father's Song Keith Getty, Kristyn Getty, and Stuart Townend, 2008

Crown Him (Christmas) Chris Tomlin, Colby Taylor, Daniel Carson, DK Kim, and Matt Redman, 2021

Emmanuel (God with Us) Chris Tomlin, 2021

Emmanuel (Hallowed Manger Ground) Chris Tomlin and Ed Cash, 2009

Glory In the Highest Chris Tomlin, Daniel Carson, Ed Cash, Jesse Reeves, and Matt Redman, 2006

Glory In the Highest Travis Cottrell, Ben Cantelon, and Jeff Pardo, 2018

He Shall Reign Forevermore Chris Tomlin and Matt Maher, 2015

Hope Has A Name Kristian Stanfill, Sean Curran, and Jacob Sooter, 2020

How Suddenly a Baby Cries Fionán De Barra, Keith Getty, and Kristyn Getty, 2011

It Came to Pass (Worthy, Worthy) Jacob Scooter, Mia Fieldes, and Tyler Miller, 2013

Jesus, Joy of the Highest Heaven Keith Getty and Kristyn Getty, 2011

Joy Has Dawned Keith Getty and Stuart Townend, 2004

My Soul Magnifies the Lord Chris Tomlin and Daniel Carson, 2009

O Come All You Unfaithful Bob Kauflin and Lisa Clow, 2020

Sing We the Song of Emmanuel Keith Getty, Matt Boswell, Matt Papa, and Stuart Townend, 2015

This Is What Christmas Means to Me Tommy Walker, 2007

We Adore You Paul Baloche and Tim Janis, 2005

TRADITIONAL

Angels From the Realms of Glory James Montgomery, 1816

Angels We Have Heard on High James Chadwick, 1855

Away In a Manger Anonymous, 1885

Break Forth, O Beauteous Heavenly Light Johann von Rist, 1641

The First Noel Anonymous, 1833

Go Tell It on the Mountain John W. Work, adapt., 1907

God Rest Ye Merry, Gentlemen Unknown, 18th century

Good Christian Men Rejoice John Mason Neale, pp., 1400

Hark! The Herald Angels Sing Charles Wesley, 1739

How Great Our Joy Hugo Jungst, arr., 1890

Joyful, Joyful We Adore Thee Linda Lee Johnson, 1985

I Heard the Bells on Christmas Day Henry W. Longfellow, 1864

In the Bleak Midwinter Christina Rossetti, 1872

Infant Holy, Infant Lowly Piotrowi Skardze, 13th century; Edith M. G. Reed, pp., 1921

It Came Upon the Midnight Clear Edmund H. Sears, 1849

Lo, How a Rose 'Ere Blooming Unknown, 15th century

O Come All Ye Faithful John Francis Wade, 1743; Frederick Oakeley, transl., 1841

O Holy Night Placide Cappeau, 1843; John S. Dwight, transl., 1855

O Little Town of Bethlehem Phillips Brooks, 1868

Silent Night Joseph Mohr, 1818

What Child Is This? W. Chatterton Dix, 1865

While Shepherds Watched Their Flocks Nahum Tate, 1700

PRESENTATIONAL

A Strange Way to Save the World Dave Clark, Don Koch, and Mark Harris, 1993

Behold Dallas Jenkins, Phil Wickham, and Steven Furtick, 2022

Born Is the King (It's Christmas) Matt Crocker and Scott Ligertwood, 2011

God Made Low Bob Kauflin and Jason Hansen, 2014

Here With Us Ben Glover, Jason Ingram, and Joy Williams, 2005

Hope Was Born This Night Ben McDonald and David Frey, 2010

How Many Kings Jason Germain and Marc Martel, 2006

Light of the World Lauren Daigle, Paul Duncan, and Paul Mabury, 2014

Light of the World (Sing Hallelujah) Andrew Bergthold, Ed Cash, Franni Cash, Martin Cash, and Scott Cash, 2020

Noel Chris Tomlin, Ed Cash, and Matt Redman, 2015

O Come All You Unfaithful Bob Kauflin and Lisa Clow, 2020

Peace On Earth (Follow the Star) Don Chapman and Adam Fisher, 2011

So Much Joy Walt Harrah, 2009

Welcome to Our World Chris Rice, 1995

What A Glorious Night Ben McDonald, Casey Brown, David Frey, and Jonathan Smith, 2013

GLOBAL

Aya Yesu Yaar Sade Pas (Christ Our Friend Comes to Us) Talib Nasrani (Pakistan)

Don Oíche Úd I MBeithil (That Night in Bethlehem) Aodh Mac Aingil Mac Cathmhaoil (Ireland)

Ere Zij God (Glory to God) Frank Albert Schultz, 1987 (Netherlands)

Ghar Ghar Manglachar (Every Home Is Rejoicing) Punjabi folk song (Pakistan)

Gloria (Glory) Pablo Sosa, 1990 (Argentina)

He Came Down Traditional (Cameroon)

Masiha Aa Gaya (The Messiah Has Come) Aqeel Azeem, 2021 (Pakistan)

Mitt Hjerte Altivit Vanker (My Heart Will Always Wander) Hans Adolph Brorson, 1732 (Norway)

Різдвяна *(Christmas Song)* Andriy Hryfel, 2020 (Ukraine)

Щедрик *(Bountiful Evening; aka Carol of the Bells)* Mykola Leontovych, 1914 (Ukraine)

Sizalelwe Indodana (Unto Us A Son Is Born) Traditional (South Africa)

Stille Nacht (Silent Night) Franz Gruber, 1818 (Germany)

The Huran Carol Jean de Brébeuf, 1643 (Canada)

Talj Talj (Snow Snow) Assi Rhabani and Mansour Rhabani, 1977 (Lebanon)

Yesus Arti Natalku (Jesus, The Meaning of Christmas) Budianto Lim, Cindy Pelenkahu, Lidya Siah, and Mario W. Tananda, 2020 (Indonesia)

CHRISTMAS DAY
WORSHIP SERVICE

PRELUDE

[No matter how contemporary your church, people love traditional music at Christmas. Put together a brass quintet or string quartet to play traditional or classical prelude music.]

CALL TO WORSHIP

Wonder of wonders. Joy of all joys. Arise and shine, for the Light of the world has come. O come, let us adore him, Christ the Lord.

VIDEO: "ALL YE FAITHFUL" (IGNITER MEDIA)

O COME, ALL YE FAITHFUL

Words by John Francis Wade, 1743; translated by Frederick Oakeley, 1841
Public Domain
[If using the video above, omit verse 1; Optional—begin with verse 4, "Yea, Lord, we greet thee, born this happy morning . . . "]

SCRIPTURE READING

Luke 2:7–14

LEADER:

And she gave birth to her firstborn son and wrapped him in swaddling cloths and laid him in a manger, because there was no place for them in the inn.

CONGREGATION:

And in the same region there were shepherds out in the field, keeping watch over their flock by night.

LEADER:

And an angel of the Lord appeared to them, and the glory of the Lord shone around them, and they were filled with great fear. And the angel said to them,

CONGREGATION:

"Fear not, for behold, I bring you good news of great joy that will be for all the people. For unto you is born this day in the city of David a Savior, who is Christ the Lord. And this will be a sign for you: you will find a baby wrapped in swaddling cloths and lying in a manger."

LEADER:

And suddenly there was with the angel a multitude of the heavenly host praising God and saying,

CONGREGATION:

"Glory to God in the highest, and on earth peace among those with whom he is pleased!"

CAROL MEDLEY

[Arrange a medley of traditional Christmas carols to be sung. Or, if you are brave enough, ask the congregation to call out their favorites and sing those. You can sing these a cappella or have an instrumentalist ready with a hymnal.]

PRAYER

Divine and loving Creator, on this blessed Christmas Day, we gather in unity to celebrate the wondrous gift of your Son, Jesus Christ. Our hearts are filled with joy and gratitude as we embrace the true meaning of this season. Amid the festivities and joyous gatherings, we take a moment to reflect on the profound significance of Christ's birth. As we behold the beauty of the Christmas story, we are reminded of the boundless love and sacrifice that brought salvation to the world.

We offer our prayers of thanksgiving for the gift of your Son, whose presence in our lives brings peace, joy, and everlasting hope. Help us to share this light with those who are lost in darkness, offering them the warmth of your love and the promise of redemption. May the light of Christ shine brightly within us, transforming us to be instruments of your peace and agents of your love in a broken world.

In the name of Jesus, our Savior and Redeemer. Amen.

SERMON

[If observing the Lord's Supper, continue. If not, proceed to the next congregational song.]

THE LORD'S SUPPER INSTRUCTIONS AND INVITATION

[Instrumental music played or congregational singing.]

THE MYSTERY OF FAITH

And so, in remembrance of these your mighty acts in Jesus Christ, we offer ourselves in praise and thanksgiving as a holy and living sacrifice, in union with Christ's offering for us, as we proclaim the mystery of faith:

CONGREGATION:

Christ has died; Christ is risen; Christ will come again.

GO, TELL IT ON THE MOUNTAIN

African American Spiritual; John W. Work
Public Domain

BENEDICTION

May you be filled with the wonder of Mary, the obedience of Joseph, the joy of the angels, the eagerness of the shepherds, the determination of the magi, and the peace of the Christ child. May Almighty God, Father, Son, and Holy Spirit, bless you now and forever. Amen.

CHRISTMAS DAY
SCRIPTURE PRESENTATION

A HYMN ON THE NATIVITY OF MY SAVIOUR
with John 3:16-17 and 2 Corinthians 8:9

CAST:
Narrator
1 Voice
Harpist (plays musical underscore during the reading of the poem and short interludes between the stanzas)

NARRATOR:
The following poem, "A Hymn on the Nativity of My Saviour" was written by the sixteenth century English playwright and poet Benjamin Jonson. Jonson is generally regarded as the second most important English dramatist, after William Shakespeare. Starting as an announcement of Christ's birth, it ends with a question directed at each of us: what will we do with this information? Will we overlook it, or will we do something about it?

[Harp begins playing]

VOICE 1:
I sing the birth was born tonight,
The Author both of life and light;
The angels so did sound it,
And like the ravished shepherds said,
Who saw the light, and were afraid,
Yet searched, and true they found it.

[Musical interlude]

The Son of God, the eternal King,
That did us all salvation bring,
And freed the soul from danger;
He whom the whole world could not take,
The Word, which heaven and earth did make,
Was now laid in a manger.

[Musical interlude]

The Father's wisdom willed it so,
The Son's obedience knew no "No,"
Both wills were in one stature;
And as that wisdom had decreed,
The Word was now made Flesh indeed,
And took on Him our nature.

[Musical interlude]

What comfort by Him do we win?
Who made Himself the price of sin,
To make us heirs of glory?
To see this Babe, all innocence,
A Martyr born in our defense,
Can man forget this story?

[Musical outro; no musical underscore for Scripture reading]

NARRATOR:

[wait for music to end]
For God so loved the world that he gave his only begotten Son, that whoever believes in him should not perish but have everlasting life. For God did not send his Son into the world to condemn the world, but in order that the world might be saved through him. For you know the grace of our Lord Jesus Christ, that though he was rich, yet for your sake he became poor, so that you by his poverty might become rich.

Chapter 8

EPIPHANY AND AFTER EPIPHANY

The celebration of Christ's birth commences on December 25, signifying the incarnation of Christ to humanity, and culminates with the arrival of the Magi on January 6, known as the Feast of Epiphany. Scholars, utilizing the "History of Religions" approach, have postulated that Epiphany's origins, like that of Christmas, stem from the intentional Christianization of a pagan festival. Alternatively, some posit that January 6 was chosen through a series of calculations, rooted in the possibility of April 6 being the date of Christ's crucifixion.

Nevertheless, the general topic of Epiphany and the season that follows is Jesus' manifestation of himself as God. Epiphany means "manifestation" or "appearance" and is primarily observed in many churches to commemorate the arrival of the Magi. In Eastern churches however, Epiphany has come to be celebrated as the baptism of Jesus and his first miracle at Cana. The water theme comes from the intention to contradict the pagan festival that occurred on January 6—the "birthday" of the pagan god Aion (god of time and eternity), at which time the people would draw water from the Nile and store it away. The next day, the pagans would claim that overnight, the water from the Nile had been turned to wine. Christians sought to provide an alternative to this ceremony by commemorating Jesus' baptism and the miraculous turning of water into wine at the marriage feast in Cana. This day also became an important day for baptisms for the church. Laurence Stookey claims that the major theme of Epiphany is identification:

> *The coming of the Magi and the Baptism of Jesus help us to identify who it is that is born in Bethlehem and thus enable us to get past "the cute baby" approach that so vitiates the deep meaning*

of the incarnation and prevents us from appreciating the great exchange of divinity and humanity.[59]

Stookey continues the theme of identification:

Where the story of the wedding at Cana is used at this season, it bears yet one more mark of identification: Jesus is the One whose ministry is to be characterized by wonders. But these wonders were not, like those of the magicians of the day, intended merely to astound or amuse the observer. These wonders were to be seen as signs—reliable indicators that God was authentically at work in Jesus, so that the glory of God would be revealed and received by faith (see John 2:11).[60]

On the Feast of Epiphany (January 6), which falls under *Extraordinary Time*, and during the season after Epiphany (from January 6 to the beginning of Lent), observed as *Ordinary Time*, the church has traditionally celebrated the revelation of Jesus Christ to the world. During this time of the year, Bible readings and sermons deal with Jesus' identity. The purpose of the Christian year is to relive the major events in Jesus' life in real time. So, during this season after Epiphany, we remember Christ's life from his birth, as he grows and begins his public ministry.

Various events have been considered as significant occasions of revealing and making known our Lord:

THE MAGI

Now after Jesus was born in Bethlehem of Judea in the days of Herod the king, behold, wise men from the east came to Jerusalem, saying, "Where is he who has been born king of the Jews? For we saw his star when it rose and have come to worship him." When Herod the king heard this, he was troubled, and all Jerusalem with him; and assembling all the chief priests and scribes of the people, he inquired of them where the Christ was to be born. They told him, "In Bethlehem of Judea, for so it is written by the prophet:

'And you, O Bethlehem, in the land of Judah, are by no means least among the rulers of Judah; for from you shall come a ruler who will shepherd my people Israel.'"

Then Herod summoned the wise men secretly and ascertained from them what time the star had appeared. And he sent them

---

59. Stookey, *Calendar*, 112.
60. Stookey, *Calendar*, 114.

EPIPHANY AND AFTER EPIPHANY 99

to Bethlehem, saying, "Go and search diligently for the child, and when you have found him, bring me word, that I too may come and worship him." After listening to the king, they went on their way. And behold, the star that they had seen when it rose went before them until it came to rest over the place where the child was. When they saw the star, they rejoiced exceedingly with great joy. And going into the house, they saw the child with Mary his mother, and they fell down and worshiped him. Then, opening their treasures, they offered him gifts, gold and frankincense and myrrh. And being warned in a dream not to return to Herod, they departed to their own country by another way.

Matthew 2:1–12

The Magi were esteemed members of the religious hierarchy in ancient Persia and Media (the region corresponding to modern Iran), known for their expertise in astrology, divination, and dream interpretation. This made them be referred to as "wise men." In Babylonia, they likely interacted with exiled Jewish priests, who shared with them the Old Testament prophecies about the coming of Christ, including the mysterious "messianic star" passage in Numbers 24:17. This explains why the astral phenomenon described in Matthew 2:1–12 captivated the wise men in the gospel narrative.

Many legends about the wise men have arisen over the centuries. In the western Christian churches, these include the traditions that there were three Magi who visited Jesus, that their names were Gaspar, Melchior, and Balthazar, and that they were kings.

As the Magi informed King Herod of their mission to find Jesus, the new King, they were making Jesus known publicly.

THE PRESENTATION OF THE LORD

And when the time came for their purification according to the Law of Moses, they brought him up to Jerusalem to present him to the Lord (as it is written in the Law of the Lord, "Every male who first opens the womb shall be called holy to the Lord") and to offer a sacrifice according to what is said in the Law of the Lord, "a pair of turtledoves, or two young pigeons." Now there was a man in Jerusalem, whose name was Simeon, and this man was righteous and devout, waiting for the consolation of Israel, and the Holy Spirit was upon him. And it had been revealed to him by the Holy Spirit that he would not see death before he had seen the Lord's Christ. And he came in the Spirit into the temple, and when the parents brought in the child Jesus, to do for him according to

> the custom of the Law, he took him up in his arms and blessed God and said,
>
> "Lord, now you are letting your servant depart in peace, according to your word; for my eyes have seen your salvation that you have prepared in the presence of all peoples, a light for revelation to the Gentiles, and for glory to your people Israel."
>
> And his father and his mother marveled at what was said about him. And Simeon blessed them and said to Mary his mother, "Behold, this child is appointed for the fall and rising of many in Israel, and for a sign that is opposed (and a sword will pierce through your own soul also), so that thoughts from many hearts may be revealed."
>
> And there was a prophetess, Anna, the daughter of Phanuel, of the tribe of Asher. She was advanced in years, having lived with her husband seven years from when she was a virgin, and then as a widow until she was eighty-four. She did not depart from the temple, worshiping with fasting and prayer night and day. And coming up at that very hour she began to give thanks to God and to speak of him to all who were waiting for the redemption of Jerusalem.
>
> Luke 2:22-38

To fulfill the requirements of Leviticus 12:2-8, Mary had to present Jesus at the temple and offer a sacrifice. If Jesus was born on December 25, then this would have occurred on February 2. Therefore, February 2 is known in the historic church as "The Presentation" or "The Presentation of Our Lord Jesus Christ in the Temple."

According to Luke 2:22-24, Mary and Joseph followed the regulations in the Law of Moses after the birth of Jesus. On the eighth day, Jesus was circumcised. Thirty-three days later, Mary and Joseph took Jesus to the temple for the priest to make atonement on their behalf. Leviticus 12:2-8 informs us that Mary and Joseph were to bring a year-old lamb for a burnt offering, and a pigeon or a turtledove for a sin offering. However, if they couldn't afford a lamb, they had the option to offer two turtledoves or two pigeons—one for a burnt offering and the other for a sin offering. When we look at Luke 2:22-24, we discover that Mary and Joseph were poor, since they only brought two birds to the temple. Or did they? Luke infers that Mary and Joseph only brought two turtledoves or two pigeons, and not a lamb. Yet, they indeed brought a lamb—Jesus, the Lamb who would later be sacrificed for the sins of the world.

In the temple, a priest named Simeon publicly declared who Jesus was. He had received a divine promise that he wouldn't die before seeing the Messiah. When Mary and Joseph brought Jesus to the temple, Simeon joyfully embraced him, lifted him up, and proclaimed with great conviction, "Lord, now you are letting your servant depart in peace, according to your word; for my eyes have seen your salvation that you have prepared in the presence of all peoples, a light for revelation to the Gentiles, and for glory to your people Israel." Luke 2:29-32 Following Simeon's declaration, the prophetess Anna also spoke about Jesus to all those present in the temple.

THE BAPTISM OF JESUS

> As the people were in expectation, and all were questioning in their hearts concerning John, whether he might be the Christ, John answered them all, saying, "I baptize you with water, but he who is mightier than I is coming, the strap of whose sandals I am not worthy to untie. He will baptize you with the Holy Spirit and fire. His winnowing fork is in his hand, to clear his threshing floor and to gather the wheat into his barn, but the chaff he will burn with unquenchable fire" . . . Now when all the people were baptized, and when Jesus also had been baptized and was praying, the heavens were opened, and the Holy Spirit descended on him in bodily form, like a dove; and a voice came from heaven, "You are my beloved Son; with you I am well pleased."
>
> Luke 3:15-17, 21-22

Prior to commencing his ministry, Jesus' cousin, John the Baptizer, had been proclaiming to the people across Jerusalem and Judea to get ready for the arrival of the Messiah. He urged them to repent, turn away from their sins, and receive baptism as a symbol of their readiness. John served as a guide, pointing the way to Jesus. While baptizing people in the Jordan river, Jesus approached John to be baptized. Although John hesitated, Jesus insisted, stating that it was necessary to fulfill righteousness. Consequently, John baptized Jesus.

Immediately after Jesus' baptism, while he was praying, the skies (heavens) opened, and the Holy Spirit, in the form of a dove, descended and alighted upon him. Simultaneously, a resonant voice from heaven proclaimed, "You are my beloved Son; with you I am well pleased" (Luke 3:22). This passage also beautifully illustrates the Trinity: God the Father speaking from heaven, God the Son being baptized, and God the Holy Spirit descending upon Jesus.

THE MIRACLE AT CANA

> On the third day there was a wedding at Cana in Galilee, and the mother of Jesus was there. Jesus also was invited to the wedding with his disciples. When the wine ran out, the mother of Jesus said to him, "They have no wine." And Jesus said to her, "Woman, what does this have to do with me? My hour has not yet come." His mother said to the servants, "Do whatever he tells you." Now there were six stone water jars there for the Jewish rites of purification, each holding twenty or thirty gallons. Jesus said to the servants, "Fill the jars with water." And they filled them up to the brim. And he said to them, "Now draw some out and take it to the master of the feast." So, they took it. When the master of the feast tasted the water now become wine and did not know where it came from (though the servants who had drawn the water knew), the master of the feast called the bridegroom and said to him, "Everyone serves the good wine first, and when people have drunk freely, then the poor wine. But you have kept the good wine until now." This, the first of his signs, Jesus did at Cana in Galilee, and manifested his glory. And his disciples believed in him.
>
> John 2:1–11

What captivates me the most about this biblical story is how it portrays the humanity of Jesus. He proves to be just like us—enjoying time with friends, cherishing special occasions, and honoring his parents even when it's inconvenient. Bobby Gross expands upon this when he writes, "If nothing else [this miracle] reveals Christ's humanity—he revels with friends at a wedding—and underscores the earthy goodness of creation—wine to gladden the heart! . . . This extravagant, gracious gesture foreshadows a greater glory—a messianic abundance—yet to be revealed . . . Jesus reveals his glory—his authority and power and love—in the place of worship, yes, but also inside a home, out in a front yard, down by the riverside and in the midst of a wedding. It's in these everyday contexts that he invites belief. . . ."[61]

There's one aspect of this story that leaves me perplexed—the last sentence (John 2:11): "And his disciples believed in him." I find myself questioning which disciples the Scripture refers to. Were they the ones who witnessed the miracle and instantly chose to follow Jesus? Or were they the ones who had already left their jobs, livelihoods, and families to become his followers? Did this moment mark their newfound belief? They are called disciples, indicating they were already following Jesus, yet their belief seems

---

61. Gross, *Living the Christian Year*, 102–3.

to solidify at this particular moment. Perhaps this moment, like our own spiritual growth, is another step in a series of events that strengthened their faith in Jesus as the Son of God. Regardless, this manifestation served as another opportunity for people to witness who Jesus truly was—the Son of the Most High—which led them to believe.

THE TRANSFIGURATION

> *And after six days Jesus took with him Peter and James and John and led them up a high mountain by themselves. And he was transfigured before them, and his clothes became radiant, intensely white, as no one on earth could bleach them. And there appeared to them Elijah with Moses, and they were talking with Jesus. And Peter said to Jesus, "Rabbi, it is good that we are here. Let us make three tents, one for you and one for Moses and one for Elijah." For he did not know what to say, for they were terrified. And a cloud overshadowed them, and a voice came out of the cloud, "This is my beloved Son; listen to him." And suddenly, looking around, they no longer saw anyone with them but Jesus only. And as they were coming down the mountain, he charged them to tell no one what they had seen, until the Son of Man had risen from the dead.*

Mark 9:2–9 (see also Matthew 17:1–9 and Luke 9:28–36)

The Transfiguration acknowledges Jesus' radical change of appearance while in the presence of Peter, James, and John, on a mountain. Matthew records that Jesus "was transfigured before them, and his face shone like the sun, and his clothes became white as light" (Matt 17:2). At this moment Moses and Elijah appeared, and they were talking with Jesus. Peter, misunderstanding the meaning of this manifestation, offered to make three tents for Jesus, Moses, and Elijah. A bright cloud overshadowed them and a voice from the cloud stated, "This is my beloved Son, with whom I am well pleased; listen to him" (Matt 17:5b). The disciples fell on their faces in awe, but Jesus encouraged them to rise and to not be afraid. When they did, they saw only Jesus standing there. This event is alluded to in 2 Peter 1:16–18, which records that "we were eyewitnesses of his majesty" and "we were with him on the holy mountain." The Transfiguration showcased Christ's glory before the crucifixion, foreshadowing his resurrection and ascension. It likely offered strength and solace to his disciples during the challenging times that followed.

The celebration of the Transfiguration originated in the Eastern church during the late fourth century, marking August 6 as the date when the first church on Mount Tabor was dedicated, traditionally considered the Mount of Transfiguration. Some also associate the Transfiguration with Mount Hermon or the Mount of Olives. In the Western church, celebrating the Transfiguration was not widespread until the ninth century. However, Pope Callistus III declared it a universal feast in 1457, and it is now observed on the last Sunday after Epiphany. The Transfiguration is listed among the holy days of the church year as a Feast of our Lord. As an Epiphany story, the Transfiguration stands out as one of the most extraordinary and dramatic displays of Jesus' divinity within the holy days of the church year.

Theological struggles were vast regarding Epiphany. Varying theologians believed January 6 to be: the date of Jesus' birth according to Epiphanius and Ephrem Syrus; the date of Jesus' baptism as reported by Clement of Alexandria; and the date of his manifestation according to the church in the West, particularly noting its observance in Gaul by the emperor Julian in 361.

In the West, Epiphany became the day to celebrate the manifestation of Jesus through three great events: the visit of the Magi, the baptism of Jesus, and the marriage feast of Cana. Epiphany brings us to the end of the Christmas season and points to the beginning of Christ's manifestation to the world. Epiphany reminds us of the mandate that we are to be a witness to Christ in our everyday lives. The mission of the church and of every member of Christ's body is a mandate that cannot be denied. We are Christ's body, the church, and the church is sent on a mission by God—a mission that involves us all.

Just as the word itself means a manifestation of Jesus as the Christ, we find a spiritual emphasis for our own lives during Epiphany. As we gather for worship, the glory of God is to be "seen in the face of Christ Jesus (2 Cor 4:6), so that, being by that beholding changed from glory into glory (3:18), the righteous by faith may at last shine like the sun (Matt 13:43)."[62] Because God's glory has been manifested in Jesus Christ, we, as his disciples, have been called to manifest Christ's glory, not only through our words and actions, but through our lives as we reach out to be the epiphany to those with whom we come in contact.

---

62. Wainwright, "Beginning with Easter," 15.

INCORPORATING EPIPHANY:

Plan for your church to have baptisms either on Epiphany Sunday or during the short season after Epiphany. Offer a short devotional on Jesus' baptism before baptizing those in the congregation.

Select representatives from three distinct ethnic backgrounds to portray the Magi during the worship service. These individuals will don attire resembling the Magi and present gifts to symbolize the offerings brought to Jesus. Additionally, consider having the Magi distribute gifts to the children of the congregation, illustrating the idea of Jesus bestowing blessings upon those who are his children.

EPIPHANY AND AFTER EPIPHANY

OVERVIEW

TIME

The Feast of Epiphany is January 6, the day after the season of Christmas; The season after Epiphany is January 7 until the day before Ash Wednesday (the beginning of Lent).

THEMES

Christians have traditionally celebrated the making known of Jesus Christ to the world on the Feast of Epiphany, January 6. It celebrates the "Feast of the Baptism of Our Lord" in the Eastern church, and the Magi following the star in the Western church. The Western church celebrates Jesus' baptism the Sunday after Epiphany. The Last Sunday after Epiphany, before Lent begins, is Transfiguration Sunday.

SPIRITUAL CHALLENGE

Renew your dedication to let Jesus be manifest in and through your life.

SCRIPTURE

- Old Testament: Exod 24:12–18; Deut 30:15–20; Isa 9:1–4; Isa 42:1–9; Isa 49:1–7; Isa 58:1–9a; Isa 60:1–6; Micah 6:1–8; Mal 3:1–4
- Psalm: Ps 2; Ps 15; Ps 27:1, 4–9; Ps 29; Ps 40:1–11; Ps 72:1–7, 10–14; Ps 84; Ps112:1–9; Ps119:1–8
- New Testament: Acts 10:34–43; 1 Cor 1:1–9; 1 Cor 1:10–18; 1 Cor 1:18–31; 1 Cor 2:1–12; 1 Cor 3:1–9; Eph 3:1–12; Heb 2:14–18; 2 Pet 1:16–21
- Gospel: Matt 2:1–12; Matt 3:13–17; Matt 4:12–23; Matt 5:1–12; Matt 5:13–20; Matt 5:21–37; Matt 17:1–9; Luke 2:22–40; John 1:5; John 1:9; John 1:29–42

SYMBOLS
- Water
- Light

COLORS
- White
- Green

EPIPHANY AND AFTER EPIPHANY

SONG LIST

CONTEMPORARY

All Glory Be to Christ Dustin Kensrue, 2012

Christ Our Glory David Zimmer and Nathan Stiff, 2019

Christ Our Hope in Life and Death Keith Getty, Matt Boswell, Jordan Kauflin, Matthew Merker, and Matt Papa, 2020

Christmas Offering Paul Baloche, 2003

Come Behold the Wondrous Mystery Matt Boswell, Matt Papa, and Michael Bleecker, 2012

Come to the Water Kristian Stanfill and Brett Younker, 2012

Everyday Joel Houston, 1999

Great Are You Lord David Leonard, Jason Ingram, and Leslie Jordan, 2012

Holy and Anointed One John Barnett, 1988

Honor and Praise Twila Paris, 1996

Jesus, Only Jesus Chris Tomlin, Christy Nockles, Kristian Stanfill, Matt Redman, Nathan Nockles, and Tony Wood, 2013

Joy Has Dawned Keith Getty and Stuart Townend, 2004

Let It Rise Holland Davis, 1997

Living Waters Ed Cash and Kristyn Getty, 2016

Marvelous Light Charlie Hall, 2005

May the Words of My Mouth Rob Hill and Tim Hughes, 2000

O Church Arise (Arise Shine) Chris Tomlin, Keith Getty, Kristyn Getty, and Stuart Townend, 2016

Our God Chris Tomlin, Jesse Reeves, Jonas Myrin, and Matt Redman, 2010

Our God Will Go Before Us Matt Boswell, Keith Getty, and Matt Papa, 2023

Shine Jesus Shine Graham Kendrick, 1987

That's Why We Praise Him Tommy Walker, 1999

Turn Your Eyes Helen Lemmel, George Romanacce, Kevin Winebarger, Nathan Stiff, and Nic Trout, 2019

Who You Say I Am Ben Fielding and Reuben Morgan, 2017

TRADITIONAL

Abide with Me Henry F. Lyte, 1847

All the Way My Savior Leads Me Fanny Crosby, 1875

As With Gladness Men of Old W. Chatterton Dix, 1859

Be Thou My Vision Mary E. Byrne, transl., 8th century; Eleanor H. Hull, versifier

Brightest and Best of the Stars of the Morning Reginald Heber, 1811

Christ, Whose Glory Fills the Skies Charles Wesley, 1740

I Heard the Voice of Jesus Say Horatius Bonar, 1846

I Saw the Light Hank Williams, Sr., 1948

Immortal, Invisible, God Only Wise Walter C. Smith, 1867

O Love That Will Not Let Me Go George Matheson, 1882

Praise to the Lord, the Almighty Joachim Neander, 1680

We Three Kings John H. Hopkins, 1857

PRESENTATIONAL

Here I Am, Lord Daniel L. Schutte, 1981

How Suddenly A Baby Cries Keith Getty, Kristyn Getty, and Fionan de Barra, 2011

O Love George Matheson; Arr. by Elaine Hagenberg

We Are Chuck Butler, Ed Cash, Hillary McBride, and James Tealy, 2011

You Say Bebo Norman, Jason Ingram, Lauren Daigle, Mike Donehey, and Paul Mabury, 2016

GLOBAL

Carol of the Epiphany John Bell, 1992 (Scotland)

Dans Nos Obscurités (Within the Darkest Night) Communauté de Taizé, 1991 (France)

De Tierra Lejana Venimos (From a Distant Home) Traditional Puerto Rican carol (Puerto Rico)

Galikin (Come Here) Traditional (Philippines)

MaNn Mandir May Tera Deep Jale (The Temple of My Heart) Eric Sarwar, 2018 (Pakistan)

Way Maker Osinachi Kalu Okoro Egbu, 2016 (Nigeria)

Yesu, Yesu (Jesus, Jesus) Eric Sarwar, 2009 (Pakistan)

EPIPHANY AND AFTER EPIPHANY
WORSHIP SERVICE

CALL TO WORSHIP

As we gather this morning, let us consider Jesus, God's Son, remembering his life here on earth. Let's read this portion of Psalm 72 (1–4, 12–14), responsively:

LEADER:

Give the king your justice, O God,

CONGREGATION:

and your righteousness to the royal son!

LEADER:

May he judge your people with righteousness,

CONGREGATION:

and your poor with justice!

LEADER:

Let the mountains bear prosperity for the people,

CONGREGATION:

and the hills, in righteousness!

LEADER:

May he defend the cause of the poor of the people, give deliverance to the children of the needy,

CONGREGATION:

and crush the oppressor!

LEADER:

For he delivers the needy when he calls,

CONGREGATION:

the poor and him who has no helper.

LEADER:

He has pity on the weak and the needy,

CONGREGATION:

and saves the lives of the needy.

LEADER:

From oppression and violence he redeems their life,

CONGREGATION:

and precious is their blood in his sight.

LIVING WATERS

Words and Music by Ed Cash and Kristyn Getty
© 2016 Getty Music Publishing and Alletrop Music

OPENING PRAYER

Jesus, you invited all who are weary and heavy-laden to come to you, and that you would give them rest. You said that your yoke is easy, and that your burden is light. You said that whoever drinks of the water you give them will never thirst again, that in fact the water you give us becomes a spring of water welling up to eternal life. You promised us the Holy Spirit, to teach us and to guide us; you promised to never leave us, and that you would come again. And because you are trustworthy, we have someone to place our hope in. God of hope, fill us with all joy and peace this morning as we worship you, so that we can overflow with hope by the power of your Holy Spirit. Amen.

Jesus was in his hometown of Nazareth in the synagogue that he had been attending for 30 years. He stood up and stunned all the worshippers by taking the Isaiah scroll and opened it up to a passage that predicted his ministry. He began to read:
"The Spirit of the Lord is upon me, because he has anointed me to proclaim good news to the poor. He has sent me to proclaim liberty to the captives and recovering of sight to the blind, to set at liberty those who are oppressed, to proclaim the year of the Lord's favor."
And he rolled up the scroll and gave it back to the attendant and sat down. And the eyes of all in the synagogue were fixed on him. And he began to say to them, "Today this Scripture has been fulfilled in your hearing."
Luke 4:18–21

OUR GOD

Words and Music by Chris Tomlin, Jesse Reeves, Jonas Myrin, and Matt Redman
© 2010 Atlas Mountain Songs, sixsteps Music, Thankyou Music, Vamos Publishing, worshiptogether.com songs

Jesus made the following promise, a call that was open to all to respond:
Come to me, all who labor and are heavy laden, and I will give you rest. Take my yoke upon you, and learn from me, for I am gentle and lowly in heart, and you will find rest for your souls.
Matthew 11:28–29

We are invited to run to Jesus. He can turn anything in our lives from the most difficult situation, into something that's glorious . . . if we listen and respond to his call.

I HEARD THE VOICE OF JESUS SAY

Words by Horatius Bonar, 1846; Music: Traditional English melody, KINGSFOLD
Public Domain

OFFERING PRAYER

Gracious and loving God, we come before you with hearts full of reverence and adoration. We thank you for revealing the glorious truth of your Son, Jesus Christ, to the world. As the wise men followed the guiding star to find the newborn King, we too seek your guidance and wisdom to illuminate our paths and lead us closer to you. We offer our worship and praise, acknowledging you as the source of all wisdom and light in our lives.

During this season of revelation and enlightenment, we ask for your guidance in discerning your will for our lives. May the light of your truth shine brightly within us, dispelling any darkness and uncertainty. Just as the Magi presented their gifts of gold, frankincense, and myrrh, we offer our gifts and offerings with gratitude and humility. May these offerings be a symbol of our commitment to honor and serve you in all aspects of our lives.

In the name of Jesus Christ, our Savior and Lord, we pray. Amen.

OFFERTORY
ALL THE WAY MY SAVIOR LEADS ME

Words by Fanny Crosby, 1875; Music by Robert Lowry, ALL THE WAY, 1875
Public Domain

PRAYER OF ILLUMINATION

Gracious God, we come before you with hearts filled with awe, seeking the illumination of your divine wisdom. In this moment before the sermon, we pause, to open our spirits to the revelation of your truth. May your light shine brightly upon the scriptures proclaimed.

As the Magi followed the star to find the Christ child, guide us on our own journey of faith, that we may encounter the profound significance of this season. As we reflect on the manifestation of your glory, open our minds to comprehend the fullness of your plan, and empower us to shine your light brightly in the world. In the wonder of this Epiphany moment, may your truth be unveiled in our lives, leading us to walk more closely with you each day.

We offer this prayer with gratitude and anticipation, trusting in your faithfulness and unfailing love, in the name of Jesus Christ, our Savior and Lord, Amen.

SERMON

[If observing the Lord's Supper, continue. If not, proceed to the next congregational song.]

THE LORD'S SUPPER INSTRUCTIONS AND INVITATION

[Instrumental music played or congregational singing.]

THE MYSTERY OF FAITH

And so, in remembrance of these your mighty acts in Jesus Christ, we offer ourselves in praise and thanksgiving as a holy and living sacrifice, in union with Christ's offering for us, as we proclaim the mystery of faith:

CONGREGATION:

Christ has died; Christ is risen; Christ will come again.

CHRIST OUR HOPE IN LIFE AND DEATH

Words and Music by Keith Getty, Matt Boswell, Jordan Kauflin, Matthew Merker, and Matt Papa
© 2020 Getty Music Publishing, Messenger Hymns, Jordan Kauflin Music, Matthew Merker Music, Getty Music Hymns and Songs, Love Your Enemies Publishing

BENEDICTION

Go now as a light to the nations, honoring the Lord and proclaiming the risen Christ. And may God strengthen you and bless you with peace; may Jesus bring forth justice for you and among you; and may the Holy Spirit shine upon you and affirm you as God's beloved ones. We go in peace to love and serve the Lord, in the name of Jesus Christ. Amen.

EPIPHANY AND AFTER EPIPHANY
SCRIPTURE PRESENTATION

ABIDE WITH ME

Psalm 27

CAST:

2 Voices
Congregation sings hymn verses

HYMN VERSE 1:

Abide with me: fast falls the eventide; the darkness deepens; Lord, with me abide.
When other helpers fail and comforts flee, Help of the helpless, O abide with me.

VOICE 1:

The Lord is our light and our salvation; whom shall we fear?

VOICE 2:

The Lord is the stronghold of our lives; of whom shall we be afraid?

VOICE 1:

Though enemies come, our hearts are steadfast.

VOICE 2:

Though wars break out, we are confidant.

HYMN VERSE 2:

I fear no foe with thee at hand to bless, ills have no weight, and tears no bitterness.
Where is death's sting? Where, grave, thy victory? I triumph still, if thou abide with me.

VOICE 1:

One thing we ask, one thing we seek, that we may live in your presence for all our days, for all our days!

VOICE 2:

Lord, to gaze upon your beauty, to seek you in your temple,

VOICES 1 & 2:

hide us in your shelter

VOICE 1:

and set us high upon your rock.

HYMN VERSE 3:

I need thy presence every passing hour. What but thy grace can foil the tempter's power?
Who like thyself my guide and strength can be? Through cloud and sunshine, O abide with me.

VOICE 2:

I believe that I shall look upon the goodness of the Lord in the land of the living!

VOICE 1:

Wait for the Lord;

VOICE 2:

be strong and let your heart take courage;

VOICES 1 & 2:

we will wait for the Lord!

HYMN VERSE 4:

Hold thou thy cross before my closing eyes. Shine through the gloom and point me to the skies.
Heaven's morning breaks and earth's vain shadows flee; in life, in death, O Lord, abide with me.

ABIDE WITH ME

Words by Henry Francis Lyte, 1847; Music by William H. Monk, 1861
Public Domain

SEASONS OF LIFE

CHAPTER 9

LENT

THE WORD LENT IS derived from the Anglo-Saxon word meaning "spring."[63] The season of Lent lasts for forty days concluding on Easter Sunday. Lent begins on Ash Wednesday, which is forty-six days before Easter. Since Sundays are considered "resurrection days," in which observers celebrate and do not fast, Sundays are not counted as part of the forty days of fasting, praying, and almsgiving.

Have you ever heard the term "spring cleaning"? Each year in the spring we look around our homes and say, "I should really get rid of a bunch of this stuff. It's time for some spring cleaning!" Well, maybe not those words exactly. But we all go through the cycle of cleaning out the clutter in our homes, bedrooms, or dorm rooms. This is what Lent is about. It is a "spring cleaning" for our souls. We search within to find all the stuff that really doesn't need to be there, or shouldn't be there, and we empty them from our lives, inviting Christ to dwell in their place.

Robert Boyd Munger wrote a little book called *My Heart, Christ's Home*. In it he likens inviting Christ into our lives to inviting him into our homes. Once Christ has entered the door (our hearts) we must then give him a tour of the house. That means allowing him access to certain parts of our lives that might not be very attractive. Munger begins his book with these words:

63. The English word Lent is a shortened form of the Old English word *lencten*, meaning "spring" or the "season of spring." According to the Oxford English Dictionary, the shorter form seems to be a derivative of 'lango-long' and may possibly refer to the lengthening of the days as characterized by the season of spring. In Latin it is called *quadragesima*, which means the "40 days" (or more literally the "40th day" before Easter). This term identifies the season with the 40-day period of preparation before the celebration of Jesus's resurrection from the dead.

> *I will never forget the evening I invited [Jesus Christ] into my heart. What an entrance he made! It was not a spectacular, emotional thing, but very real, occurring at the very center of my soul. He came into the darkness of my heart and turned on the light. He built a fire in the cold hearth and banished the chill. He started music where there had been stillness and harmony where there had been discord. He filled the emptiness with his loving fellowship. I have never regretted opening the door to Christ, and I never will.*
>
> *In the joy of this new relationship I said to Jesus Christ, "Lord I want this heart of mine to be yours. I want you to settle down here and be fully at home. I want you to use it as your own. Let me show you around."* [64]

Munger goes on to write about showing Jesus every part of our lives, even the most intimate, and how difficult it is to turn those over to Christ. This embodies the essence of Lent—a period to introspect and, more importantly, to let God examine our hearts, removing anything that fails to glorify him (Ps 139:23–24).

The Apostle Paul gives us an example of emptying ourselves to be filled with the things of Jesus.

> *If then you have been raised with Christ, seek the things that are above, where Christ is, seated at the right hand of God. Set your minds on things that are above, not on things that are on earth. For you have died, and your life is hidden with Christ in God. When Christ who is your life appears, then you also will appear with him in glory.*
>
> *Put to death therefore what is earthly in you: sexual immorality, impurity, passion, evil desire, and covetousness, which is idolatry. On account of these the wrath of God is coming. In these you too once walked, when you were living in them. But now you must put them all away: anger, wrath, malice, slander, and obscene talk from your mouth. Do not lie to one another, seeing that you have put off the old self with its practices and have put on the new self, which is being renewed in knowledge after the image of its creator. Here there is not Greek and Jew, circumcised and uncircumcised, barbarian, Scythian, slave, free; but Christ is all, and in all.*
>
> *Put on then, as God's chosen ones, holy and beloved, compassionate hearts, kindness, humility, meekness, and patience, bearing with one another and, if one has a complaint against another,*

---

64. Munger, *My Heart, Christ's Home*, 10–11

forgiving each other; as the Lord has forgiven you, so you also must forgive. And above all these put on love, which binds everything together in perfect harmony. And let the peace of Christ rule in your hearts, to which indeed you were called in one body. And be thankful. Let the word of Christ dwell in you richly, teaching and admonishing one another in all wisdom, singing psalms and hymns and spiritual songs, with thankfulness in your hearts to God. And whatever you do, in word or deed, do everything in the name of the Lord Jesus, giving thanks to God the Father through him. (Col 3:1-17)

Lent is a season for both personal and corporate spiritual renewal. During this season, the Christ follower is to look within and ask, "Am I living my life as though it were worthy of someone to die?" The history of Lent unveils traditions rich with meaning including times of intense study of God's Word, meditation, prayer, and self-examination.

The origin of Lent remains intricate. It was commonly believed that Lent evolved as the ultimate preparation for catechumens (converts in training) who, after extensive preparation, were set apart for baptism during the Easter Vigil. However, recent evidence reveals an earlier form of Lent in Egypt, consisting of a post-Epiphany fast lasting forty days, linked to Christ's forty-day fast in the wilderness. The Council of Nicaea, A.D. 325, first referred to Lent as "forty days" and made it immediately precede Easter. Theologian Thomas Talley suggests that Lent, as a time for public exercises of penitents, may have been implied as early as the second decade of the fifth century (Innocent I, Epistle 25, caput 7, PL 20.559).

The season of Lent begins on Ash Wednesday, which is intended to be a bold confrontation with death. The imposition of ashes serves as a poignant reminder that, just as ashes can enrich the soil and aid in the growth of new plants, we need to let go of our old selves and let Christ bring forth new life within us. Although the beginning of the observance of Ash Wednesday is difficult to date with certainty, historical documents show it probably began around 600 A.D.

The Scriptures do not prescribe the keeping of Ash Wednesday. But there are signs in Scripture that are used on Ash Wednesday. The first is the sign of the cross. The origin of the sign of the cross goes back to the early church and expresses the self-denial that is associated with Jesus. In the early church the sign of the cross accompanied sacred actions, such as baptism. Baptism, like the cross, is the way of death. What is brought to death is the old life, the old way, the influence of the powers of evil. So, the sign of the cross, used in the Ash Wednesday service symbolizes a willingness to put to death a life lived after the flesh and a willingness to follow Jesus, even to death.

The second sign of Ash Wednesday is ashes. You have probably seen ashes placed on foreheads (configured into the sign of the cross). Maybe you have even participated in an Ash Wednesday service yourself. In Scripture, ashes are a sign of repentance. When Daniel discovered the impending desolation of Jerusalem, he "turned to the Lord God, seeking him by prayer and pleas for mercy with fasting and sackcloth and ashes." (Dan 9:3; see also 2 Sam 13:19; Job 42:6; Esth 4:1). The ashes used in the imposition traditionally come from the burning of the palm branches from the year before. The symbolism here is powerful as the palms used to praise Jesus are now ash used to remind us of his death and our mortality. Ashes are applied to the forehead of Christians in the sign of the cross as a symbol of humility and repentance. Throughout the Middle Ages ashes were sprinkled on the head. The ashes are a reminder that we are "dust, and to dust you shall return" (Gen 3:19). Thus, they are a reminder of our mortality cursed as it is by sin. Moreover, the ashes remind us of our limits, of what we are, and how greatly we need God's mercy in Christ. We don't wear ashes to proclaim our holiness but to acknowledge that we sin and are in need of repentance and renewal.

Additional Lenten symbols include barren stones symbolizing overcoming temptation, desolation, and sadness; fish symbolizing the obligation to fast; praying hands symbolizing strengthening one's relationship with God through prayer; money bag/coin pouch symbolizing the penitential practice of almsgiving; and pretzels. Pretzels? Yes, pretzels. Pretzels actually had their origin in early Christian Lenten practice. Since fat, eggs, and milk were not used during Lent as part of the fast, a special bread was made with dough consisting of only flour, salt, and water. These thin breads were shaped in the form of arms crossed in prayer and were called *bracellae* (Latin meaning "little arms"). Germans took this Latin word and called it "bretzel." These pretzels were a common Lenten food throughout the Middle Ages in Europe and became a year-round snack, in its original shape, only in the nineteenth century.[65]

Ultimately, Lent is a time to die to self and to the power that sin has over our lives. The desire during this season is that God would create in us clean, broken, and contrite hearts. Webber states,

> *While it is God who creates that new heart in us through grace, we are called on to receive God's grace in repentance, a turning from our sin, and in faith, a turning toward God. We are assisted in this journey of turning through fasting, prayer, and*

---

65. Dues, *Catholic Customs and Traditions*, 76–77.

almsgiving—external disciplines that order and organize the internal experience of our continuing conversion.[66]

Thomas Talley would agree, suggesting that a shift occurred in the emphasis of Lent from "preparation for baptism to a general public penitential observance predicated upon what were once exercises for penitents seeking formal reconciliation with the church."[67] Instead of Lent being a time strictly for those desiring baptism, it became a time for the whole church to reflect upon how they are living their lives, with a desire to become more like Christ. This time of penitence moves us toward *Pascha* as "the time of *metanoia*, the time of conversion, the time of repentance, the time that identifies our human lives and all our human history as the process of conversion moving now and always to meet the coming of the Lord at the consummation of the age."[68]

An authentic journey through Lent leads to repentance—to turn away from sin and to turn to God. Our lives are shaped internally through external disciplines as we spiritually prepare to experience the power of the resurrection in our own lives. Lent provides an opportunity to be spiritually formed through the external disciplines of fasting, prayer, and almsgiving.

The tradition of giving up something during Lent, like chocolate, soda, or social media, has its roots in the historical practice of fasting. Fasting was observed by Moses, Elijah, Daniel, and many others in the Bible. Jesus himself fasted for forty days, which is why Lent also lasts for forty days, as it symbolizes his focus on his mission and journey to the cross.

Fasting helps us prioritize what truly matters, and the hunger pangs we experience during our fast serve as a reminder of the sacrifice required by our faith. It aids in developing discipline and character. As we have witnessed, fasting is not solely about giving something up but also about embracing something, or more accurately, someone else. We relinquish something to adopt a greater likeness to Christ and deepen our relationship with God.

Regardless of how one feels about the season of Lent, followers of Christ should strive to be more like Jesus in every word and deed. The season of Lent provides the church the opportunity to ask God to cleanse us of what should not be within, and to make us more like Jesus.

---

66. Webber, *Ancient-Future Time*, 120–21.
67. Talley, *The Origins of the Liturgical Year*, 224.
68. Talley, *The Origins of the Liturgical Year*, 225.

INCORPORATING LENT:

Offer an Ash Wednesday service for your congregation. One creative Ash Wednesday service idea is to plan for the service to be held in various homes in small group settings.

Two aspects of worship that are sorely lacking in many of today's Protestant worship services are stillness and confession. Take advantage of this season to incorporate these elements within your worship services. Somewhere near the beginning of the service, invite the congregation to spend time in silence, confessing sin before God. Conclude the time of silence with a corporate prayer of confession recited aloud. An example of one such prayer is:

> Father in heaven, we have sinned against You and others; and we need to be forgiven. We have tried to heal ourselves. Instead of trusting in the death of Jesus Christ, we have tried to work off our guilt. We have tried so hard to pile up good deeds that outweigh our sins. When this doesn't work, we quickly turn to denial and distraction. Instead of trusting in the resurrection of Jesus Christ, we have tried to change through our own efforts. We have tried to change our hearts through sheer will power. This has left some of us arrogant. This has left most of us anxious and depressed. Forgive us for trying to heal ourselves. Forgive us for neglecting your grace. Forgive us and heal us, for Jesus' sake. Amen.

"Give up" and "take on" something during the season of Lent. There are two primary forms of spiritual discipline: abstaining habits such as fasting and silence; and engaging habits such as prayer, meditation, journaling, and service. Select a spiritual discipline from each category to practice during Lent. Encourage the members of your congregation to do the same.

Pretzel Making and Sharing. A wonderful group activity idea is to bake pretzels together, perfect for Sunday school or youth groups, while incorporating a teaching about the significance of Lent, prayer, and fasting. You can make the pretzels during the worship service and invite the congregation or other Sunday school classes to join in eating them. Alternatively, you can distribute the baked pretzels in brown bags to the children as a takeaway. Another option is to create small pretzel baggies accompanied by a card or sheet of paper with an overview of Lent. Ensure the pretzels are in the correct shape. Use these baggies as a prayer challenge—"whenever you come across the pretzel over the next forty days, take a moment to pray for yourself and others." You can also include a Lenten prayer or poem on the card to enhance the spiritual experience.

ASH WEDNESDAY
OVERVIEW

TIME

The first day of Lent, forty-six days prior to Easter. The precise date varies according to the date of Easter, which can range from March 22 to April 25.

THEMES

In ancient times, people wore sackcloth and ashes as a symbol of grief and regret. The Bible contains various references to ashes, symbolizing death, sorrow, and remorse. Centuries ago, a tradition emerged where ashes were used as an object lesson at the beginning of Lent, representing death and the subsequent renewal, rebirth, and transformation. Ashes remind us of the earth from which we came and to which we shall return (Genesis 3:19). They also symbolize new life, analogous to how ashes enrich the soil, fostering the growth of new plants.

SPIRITUAL CHALLENGE

Confront your own mortality and confess your sin before God within the community of faith.

SCRIPTURE

- Old Testament: Gen 3:19; Esth 4:1; Isa 61:3; Job 42:1–6; Dan 9:3; Joel 2:1–2, 12–17
- Psalm: Ps 51:1–17
- New Testament: 2 Cor 5:20b–6:10
- Gospel: Matt 6:1–6, 16–21; Luke 10:13

SYMBOLS

- Ashes
- Cross

COLORS

- Black
- Purple/Violet
- Gray

ASH WEDNESDAY

SONG LIST

CONTEMPORARY

At the Foot of the Cross Kathryn Scott, 2003

Beautiful Things Michael Gungor and Lisa Gungor, 2009

Brokenness Aside David Leonard and Leslie Jordan, 2011

Christ Our Hope in Life and Death Keith Getty, Matt Boswell, Jordan Kauflin, Matthew Merker, and Matt Papa, 2020

Create In Me A Clean Heart Keith Green, 1984

Desert Song Brooke Ligertwood, 2008

Healer Michael Guglielmucci, 2007

Lead Me to the Cross Brooke Ligertwood, 2006

Lord Have Mercy Eoghan Heaslip, 2002

O Come to the Altar Chris Brown, Mack Brock, Steven Furtick, and Wade Joye, 2015

Refiner's Fire Brian Doerksen, 1990

Search Me, Know Me Kathryn Scott and Mildred Rainey, 2003

We Confess Glenn Packiam and Ian Morgan Cron, 2011

Wonderful Merciful Savior Dawn Rodgers and Eric Wyse, 1989

TRADITIONAL

Have Thine Own Way, Lord Adelaide A. Pollard, 1906

I Need Thee Every Hour Annie S. Hawks, 1872

Just As I Am Charlotte Elliot, 1834

Nearer My God to Thee Sarah F. Adams, 1841

Turn Your Eyes Upon Jesus Helen Lemmel, 1922

PRESENTATIONAL

Dust We Are and Shall Return John Arndt, David Gungor, and Kate Gungor, 2012

Even Unto Death Audrey Assad and Matt Maher, 2016

From the Dust Paul Zach and Kate Bluett, 2021

God Be Merciful to Me (Psalm 51) Keith Getty, Kristyn Getty, and Cindy Morgan, 2018

Healer Of My Soul John Michael Talbot, 1983

It Is Not Death to Die Bob Kauflin, George Washington Bethune, and Henri Abraham Cesar Malan, 2008

Kyrie Eleison Chris Tomlin, Jason Ingram, Matt Maher, and Matt Redman, 2016

GLOBAL

God Is Forgiveness Communauté de Taizé, 2007 (France)

Kyrie Guarany (Kyrie Eleison) Traditional; arr. John Bell, 1991 (Paraguay)

ASH WEDNESDAY
WORSHIP SERVICE

WORDS OF WELCOME

Welcome. Listen to these words of Jesus from Matthew 22:37–40:
"You shall love the Lord your God with all your heart and with all your soul and with all your mind. This is the great and first commandment. And a second is like it: You shall love your neighbor as yourself. On these two commandments depend all the Law and the Prophets."

OPENING PRAYER

Let us pray: Almighty God, who, through the redemption of your Son Jesus Christ, provided a way of redemption for all who repent and turn from sin: Create in us a clean heart and renew a steadfast and willing spirit, that we, acknowledging our sinfulness, may live an upright and holy life by the power of your Holy Spirit; through Jesus Christ our Lord, who, with you and the Holy Spirit, lives and reigns, Amen.

Today is the first day of the season of Lent. We can trace the word Lent back to the Old English word *lencten* (related to the modern English word "lengthen") that simply refers to the season of spring—a time for renewal. Just as flowers find new life in the spring, we too can find renewed life during this season. During Lent we begin our journey toward Easter by looking within ourselves to see how we as individuals and a society fall short of God's vision for us. To the Hebrew people, "sin" meant "missing the mark" or falling short of who we are meant to be. It means separating ourselves from the love of God and others. Today we confess the many ways that we, too, "miss the mark." We seek God's forgiveness and new life.

As we begin this service, pause for a few moments to present yourself before the Lord, sharing your current state of mind and concerns. Offer a heartfelt confession of your yearning to encounter God during this time.

[Optional: for this next portion of the service, you can proceed or utilize the Scripture presentation immediately following this worship service example.]

In church, we confess our sins directly to God and seek forgiveness in our services of worship. We admit our mistakes and learn to love others as Christ has loved us. In ancient times, people wore sack cloth and ashes as a symbol of grief and regret of the sin they had committed. There are many references in the Bible to ashes as a symbol of death, sorrow, and remorse.

When Mordecai learned about all that had been done, he tore his clothes, put on burlap and ashes, and went out into the city, crying with a loud and bitter wail.
Esther 4:1

To all who mourn in Israel, he will give a crown of beauty for ashes, a joyous blessing instead of mourning, festive praise instead of despair. In their righteousness, they will be like great oaks that the Lord has planted for his own glory.
Isaiah 61:3

Then Job replied to the LORD: "I know that you can do anything, and no one can stop you. You asked, 'Who is this that questions my wisdom with such ignorance?' It is I—and I was talking about things I knew nothing about, things far too wonderful for me. You said, 'Listen and I will speak! I have some questions for you, and you must answer them.' I had only heard about you before, but now I have seen you with my own eyes. I take back everything I said, and I sit in dust and ashes to show my repentance."
Job 42:1–6

So I turned to the LORD God and pleaded with him in prayer and fasting. I also wore rough burlap and sprinkled myself with ashes.
Daniel 9:3

Jesus says in Luke 10:13, "What sorrow awaits you, Korazin and Bethsaida! For if the miracles I did in you had been done in wicked Tyre and Sidon, their people would have repented of their sins long ago, clothing themselves in burlap and throwing ashes on their heads to show their remorse."

[If using the Ash Wednesday Scripture presentation, resume order of service at this point.]

A tradition started centuries ago, that at the beginning of Lent, ashes would be used as an object lesson to symbolize death and renewal out of death. It was called Ash Wednesday.
In our time together today, we will use the symbol of ashes [hold up a bowl of the ash mixture and place it down again].

These ashes remind us of the earth from which we came and to which we shall return. It reminds us of new life, just as ashes serve to fertilize the earth and help new plants to grow. Throughout the history of the church, versions of Lent can be found not only in the Catholic church but also in many Protestant traditions as well. Simply put, Lent is a time of reflection and recommitment, as we ready ourselves for Easter and all that it means in our lives.

CALL TO WORSHIP

Now let us worship together in prayer, in meditation, in confession, in the search for forgiveness and new life. Join with me in this prayer:

Almighty and Ever-living God, who, through your Son, Jesus Christ, provided a way of redemption for all who repent and turn from sin: Create in us a clean heart and renew a steadfast and willing spirit, that we, acknowledging our sinfulness, may live an upright and holy life by the power of your Holy Spirit; through Jesus Christ our Lord, who, with you and the Holy Spirit, lives and reigns, one God, world without end. Amen.

Please join with me in our responsive call to worship:

LEADER:

We stand in need of God's grace and mercy. Let us turn to the Lord.

CONGREGATION:

May God look upon us with compassion and grant us forgiveness.

LEADER:

We stand in need of God's healing power. Let us turn to the Lord.

CONGREGATION:

May God's Spirit and redemptive power make us whole and restore us in body, mind, and spirit.

LEADER:

We stand in need of God's word of hope. Let us turn to the Lord.

CONGREGATION:

May God's voice be heard anew proclaiming hope to all who in trust come to our God.

LEADER:

We stand in faith before the all-righteous and all-loving God. Let us offer worship and praise.

CONGREGATION:

May the worship we bring be to the glory and honor of God.

TURN YOUR EYES UPON JESUS

Words and Music by Helen H. Lemmel, 1922
Public Domain

THE FIRST READING

The prophet Joel points to the fact that we need to repent of our ways and turn to God. Whatever has happened in the past, God is merciful and willing to forgive.

Now, a reading from the prophet Joel. This is the Word of God:

A day of darkness and gloom, a day of clouds and thick darkness! Like blackness there is spread upon the mountains a great and powerful people; their like has never been before, nor will be again after them through the years of all generations.

Fire devours before them, and behind them a flame burns. The land is like the garden of Eden before them, but behind them a desolate wilderness, and nothing escapes them.

Their appearance is like the appearance of horses, and like war horses they run. As with the rumbling of chariots, they leap on the tops of the mountains, like the crackling of a flame of fire devouring the stubble, like a powerful army drawn up for battle.

Before them peoples are in anguish; all faces grow pale. Like warriors they charge; like soldiers they scale the wall. They march each on his way; they do not swerve from their paths. They do not jostle one another; each marches in his path; they burst through the weapons and are not halted. They leap upon the city, they run upon the walls, they climb up into the houses, they enter through the windows like a thief.

The earth quakes before them; the heavens tremble. The sun and the moon are darkened, and the stars withdraw their shining. The Lord utters his voice before his army, for his camp is exceedingly great; he who executes his word is powerful. For the day of the Lord is great and very awesome; who can endure it?

"Yet even now," declares the Lord, "return to me with all your heart, with fasting, with weeping, and with mourning."

Joel 2:2–12

PRAYER

Join with me as we pray this prayer together:

CONGREGATION:

Loving God, how great and wonderful you are. You want us to journey with you, to be your hands and feet and heart and mind, to bring your healing love to a hurting world. Be with us now as we look deeply within ourselves, as we seek your presence and your guidance, as we begin our Lenten journey this day. Amen.

THE SECOND READING

Listen to the words of the Apostle Paul as he discusses the importance of being reconciled with God.

Therefore, we are ambassadors for Christ, God making his appeal through us. We implore you on behalf of Christ, be reconciled to God. For our sake he made him to be sin who knew no sin, so that in him we might become the righteousness of God.

Working together with him, then, we appeal to you not to receive the grace of God in vain. For he says,

"In a favorable time I listened to you, and in a day of salvation I have helped you."

Behold, now is the favorable time; behold, now is the day of salvation. We put no obstacle in anyone's way, so that no fault may be found with our ministry, but as servants of God we commend ourselves in every way: by great endurance, in afflictions, hardships, calamities, beatings, imprisonments, riots, labors, sleepless nights, hunger; by purity, knowledge, patience, kindness, the Holy Spirit, genuine love; by truthful speech, and the power of God; with the weapons of righteousness for the right hand and for the left; through honor and dishonor, through slander and praise. We are treated as impostors, and yet are true; as unknown, and yet well known; as dying, and behold, we live; as punished, and yet not killed; as sorrowful, yet always rejoicing; as poor, yet making many rich; as having nothing, yet possessing everything.
2 Corinthians 5:20–6:10

THE GOSPEL READING

And these words from Jesus on the importance of prayer and fasting, two pillars of the season of Lent.

Beware of practicing your righteousness before other people in order to be seen by them, for then you will have no reward from your Father who is in heaven. Thus, when you give to the needy, sound no trumpet before you, as the hypocrites do in the synagogues and in the streets, that they may be praised by others. Truly, I say to you, they have received their reward. But when you give to the needy, do not let your left hand know what your right hand is doing, so that your giving may be in secret. And your Father who sees in secret will reward you.

And when you pray, you must not be like the hypocrites. For they love to stand and pray in the synagogues and at the street corners, that they may be seen by others. Truly, I say to you, they have received their reward. But when you pray, go into your room and shut the door and pray to your Father who is in secret. And your Father who sees in secret will reward you.

And when you fast, do not look gloomy like the hypocrites, for they disfigure their faces that their fasting may be seen by others. Truly, I say to you, they have received their reward. But when you fast, anoint your head and wash your face, that your fasting may not be seen by others but by your Father who is in secret. And your Father who sees in secret will reward you.
Do not lay up for yourselves treasures on earth, where moth and rust destroy and where thieves break in and steal, but lay up for yourselves treasures in

heaven, where neither moth nor rust destroys and where thieves do not break in and steal. For where your treasure is, there your heart will be also.
Matthew 6:1–6, 16–21

Dear Brothers and Sisters in Christ: Since the beginning of the church, Christians have always observed the days of our Lord's passion and resurrection with great devotion. It became one of the great traditions of the church to prepare for these events through serious examination of our spiritual lives through prayer, repentance, and fasting. New believers were prepared for baptism during Lent. Those who were separated from the church through serious sin were reconciled and restored to fellowship. The body of Christ was challenged to seek pardon and absolution for those areas where sin had found a place, to find reconciliation with God and with each other and to renew their faith.

I invite you, therefore, in Christ, to observe this season of renewal, by engaging in self-examination, repentance, prayer, fasting, and sacrificial giving; to further your discipline of reading and meditating on the Word of God, and to make a right beginning to walk in newness of life. Therefore, I invite you to kneel before the Lord, our Creator and Redeemer.

CONFESSION OF SIN

If we confess our sins, he is faithful and just to forgive us our sins and to cleanse us from all unrighteousness.
[Using 1 John 1:9 as the text, invite the congregation to pray and ask God to reveal areas of sin and weakness in our lives.]

WE CONFESS

Words and Music by Glenn Packiam and Ian Morgan Cron
© 2013 Integrity Worship Music

PRAYER OF THANKSGIVING

Let's join together in this prayer as we prepare to receive the ashes:

CONGREGATION:

Almighty God, we thank you for your promise to forgive us our sin. You created us out of the dust of the earth. Grant that these ashes may be to us a reminder of our mortality, humility, and repentance, that we may remember that it is only by your gracious gift that we are given everlasting life, through Jesus Christ our Lord (adapted from the Book of Common Prayer).

ASHES AND ANOINTING[69]

[While the imposition of ashes dates back to the eleventh century, more recent liturgies make this optional, referencing Jesus' words in Matthew 6:16–18 concerning penitence. The leader may want to explain before the people come forward that the ashes are a symbol of sorrow and repentance for sin. They are a sign of intention to die to the old ways and live a new life for Christ. The Leader may say something like . . .]

There are many ways to show we are truly sorry and seek to live in God's way. Our words, our actions, and our way of being will tell the tale. To show our repentance and our commitment to new life, we now invite you to receive the symbol of ashes. This symbol will be in the shape of a cross, and you can choose to have it placed on your forehead or on the back of your hand. If you choose to have it placed on your hand, just simply hold out your hand when you come forward. The ashes, a symbol of how sorry we are, have been mixed with oil, a symbol of God's healing.

[Should the imposition of ashes be done, the following words can be used when people come forward:]
Remember that you are dust and to dust you shall return. Repent and believe the gospel of our Lord Jesus Christ.

[Instruments begin playing "At the Foot of the Cross" while congregation comes forward to receive ashes. Once everyone has received the ashes, sing "At the Foot of the Cross" as a time for reflection and self-examination.]

AT THE FOOT OF THE CROSS

Words and Music by Kathryn Scott
© 2003 Integrity Worship Music

---

69. Although this is a powerfully symbolic worship element, it is optional. If you choose not to include the imposition of ashes, you can substitute distributing cards to the congregation. Prepare cards (place ashes in a small jewelry bag and attach the bag to a card) that explains the purpose behind using ashes as part of our spiritual development. These cards become a reminder throughout the Season of Lent to invite God to examine our lives, cleanse us, and prepare us for the celebration of Easter.

PRAYER

Let's pray together:

CONGREGATION:

Loving and merciful God, we have made our honest confessions before you and before one another. We thank you for your forgiveness and for your healing. We pray for your continued forgiveness and healing in a hurting world. May nothing separate us from you as we follow Jesus during this Lenten journey. Amen.

BENEDICTION

Jesus said, *"Come to me all you who labor and are heavily burdened, and I will give you rest. Take my yoke upon you, and learn from me; for I am gentle and lowly in heart, and you will find rest for your souls."*
Matthew 11:28–29

Let us go from this place, knowing that we are not alone on our journey. God is with us! Let us go, seeking new life in Christ, and with the peace of Christ in our hearts. Amen.

ASH WEDNESDAY
SCRIPTURE PRESENTATION

HIS GLORY AND GRACE

Matthew 22:37-40; Esther 4:1; Isaiah 61:3; Job 42:1-6; Daniel 9:3; Luke 10:13

CAST:

Narrator
4 Voices

NARRATOR:

Listen to these words spoken by Jesus:
"You shall love the Lord your God with all your heart and with all your soul and with all your mind. This is the great and first commandment. And a second is like it: You shall love your neighbor as yourself. On these two commandments depend all the Law and the Prophets."

In ancient times, when people broke the commandments of God, failing to obey what he had taught and commanded, they wore sackcloth and ashes as a symbol of grief and regret. There are many references in the Bible to ashes as a symbol of death, sorrow, and remorse.

VOICE 1:

Esther chapter 4, verse 1
When Mordecai learned all that had been done, Mordecai tore his clothes and put on sackcloth and ashes, and went out into the midst of the city, and he cried out with a loud and bitter cry.

VOICE 2:

Isaiah chapter 61, verse 3
To grant to those who mourn in Zion—to give them a beautiful headdress instead of ashes, the oil of gladness instead of mourning, the garment of praise instead of a faint spirit; that they may be called oaks of righteousness, the planting of the Lord, that he may be glorified.

VOICE 3:

Job chapter 42, verses 1–6
Then Job answered the Lord and said: "I know that you can do all things, and that no purpose of yours can be thwarted. 'Who is this that hides counsel without knowledge?' Therefore I have uttered what I did not understand, things too wonderful for me, which I did not know. 'Hear, and I will speak; I will question you, and you make it known to me.' I had heard of you by the hearing of the ear, but now my eye sees you; therefore I despise myself, and repent in dust and ashes."

VOICE 4:

Daniel chapter 9, verse 3
Then I turned my face to the Lord God, seeking him by prayer and pleas for mercy with fasting and sackcloth and ashes.

NARRATOR:

In Luke 10:13, Jesus says, "Woe to you, Chorazin! Woe to you, Bethsaida! For if the mighty works done in you had been done in Tyre and Sidon, they would have repented long ago, sitting in sackcloth and ashes."

And yet there is the promise that God is full of grace, offering us new mercies each morning. There is joy in the presence of the Lord when we stay focused on him and live within his purposes for this world and our lives.

Let's sing the chorus of the hymn "Turn Your Eyes Upon Jesus."

CONGREGATION:

Turn your eyes upon Jesus,
Look full in his wonderful face,
And the things of earth will grow strangely dim,
In the light of his glory and grace.

TURN YOUR EYES UPON JESUS

Words and Music by Helen Lemmel, 1922
Public Domain

LENT
OVERVIEW

TIME
Ash Wednesday–Easter Vigil (Saturday, the day before Easter).

THEMES
During the season of Lent, indicating the season of spring or renewal, we prepare ourselves for Easter, examining our spiritual lives through prayer, repentance, and fasting. We confess our sins to God and seek forgiveness.

SPIRITUAL CHALLENGE
Repent through self-examination and experience renewal by identifying with the journey of Jesus. Engage in a time of prayer and fasting.

SCRIPTURE
- Old Testament: Gen 2:15–17, 3:1–7; Gen 12:1–4a; Exod 17:1–7; 1 Sam 16:1–13; Isa 7:10–14; Isa 50:4–9a; Ezek 37:1–14; Joel 2:1–2, 12–17
- Psalm: Ps 23; Ps 31:9–16; Ps 32; Ps 45; Ps 51:1–17; Ps 95; Ps 118:1–2, 19–29; Ps 121; Ps 130
- New Testament: Rom 4:1–5, 13–17; Rom 5:1–11; Rom 5:12–19; Rom 8:6–11; 2 Cor 5:20b–6:10; Eph 5:8–14; Phil 2:5–11; Heb 10:4–10
- Gospel: Matt 4:1–11; Matt 6:1–6, 16–21; Matt 26:14–27:66; Luke 1:26–38; John 3:1–17; John 4:5–42; John 9:1–41; John 11:1–45

SYMBOLS
- Ashes
- Cross

- Barren stones
- Fish
- Praying hands
- Money bag/coin pouch
- Pretzel

COLORS
- Black
- Purple/Violet
- Grey
- Red

LENT

SONG LIST

CONTEMPORARY

Beneath the Cross Keith Getty and Kristyn Getty, 2005

Beautiful Things Lisa Gungor and Michael Gungor, 2009

Blessed Be Your Name Beth Redman and Matt Redman, 2002

Christ Our Hope in Life and Death Keith Getty, Matt Boswell, Jordan Kauflin, Matthew Merker, and Matt Papa, 2020

Christ the Sure and Steady Anchor Matt Boswell, 2014

Create In Me A Clean Heart Keith Green, 1984

Desert Song Brooke Ligertwood, 2008

Don't Ever Let Me Go Corey Voss, Jennie Lee Riddle, and Melanie Tierce, 2016

He Will Hold Me Fast Ada Ruth Habershon and Matthew Merker, 2013

Healer Michael Guglielmucci, 2007

His Mercy Is More Matt Boswell and Matt Papa, 2016

Lead Me to the Cross Brooke Ligertwood, 2006

Lord From Sorrows Deep I Call Matt Boswell and Matt Papa, 2018

Lord Have Mercy Eoghan Heaslip, 2002

Lord, I Need You Christy Nockles, Daniel Carson, Jesse Reeves, Kristian Stanfill, and Matt Maher, 2011

Our God Chris Tomlin, Jesse Reeves, Jonas Myrin, and Matt Redman, 2010

The Power of the Cross Keith Getty and Stuart Townend, 2005

Refiner's Fire Brian Doerksen, 1990

Search Me, Know Me Kathryn Scott and Mildred Rainey, 2003

The Goodness of Jesus Fiona Aghajanian, Harrison Druery, Jaywan Maxwell, Jonny Robinson, Michael Farren, and Rich Thompson, 2018

The Wonderful Cross Isaac Watts, J.D. Walt, Chris Tomlin, Lowell Mason, and Jesse Reeves, 2000

What the Lord Has Done In Me Reuben Morgan, 1998

We Confess Glenn Packiam and Ian Morgan Cron, 2011

TRADITIONAL

Are You Washed in the Blood Elisha A. Hoffman, 1878

Have Thine Own Way, Lord Adelaide A. Pollard, 1906

I Need Thee Every Hour Annie S. Hawks, 1872

It Is Well With My Soul Horatio Spafford, 1873

Just As I Am Charlotte Elliot, 1834

Lord, Who Throughout These Forty Days Caludia F. Hernaman, 1873

Man of Sorrows Philip P. Bliss, 1875

Near to the Heart of God Cleland B. McAfee, 1903

Nearer My God to Thee Sarah F. Adams, 1841

Out of the Depths I Cry to Thee Martin Luther, 1524; Catherine Winkworth, transl., 1855

Rock of Ages Augustus Toplady, 1776

Take Time to Be Holy William D. Longstaff, 1882

There Is A Fountain William Cowper, 1772

Turn Your Eyes Upon Jesus Helen Lemmel, 1922

PRESENTATIONAL

40 Days Ben Glover and Mark Schultz, 2006

40 Days Matt Maher, 2003

Clean Natalie Grant, 2015

Even Unto Death Audrey Assad and Matt Maher, 2016

God Be Merciful to Me (Psalm 51) Keith Getty, Kristyn Getty, and Cindy Morgan, 2018

I Repent Dave Noel, Phil Nash, and Steve Green, 1998

Kyrie Eleison Chris Tomlin, Jason Ingram, Matt Maher, and Matt Redman, 2016

Left It In the Water Andrew Bergthold, Ed Cash, Franni Cash, Jeremy Gifford, Martin Cash, Scott Cash, 2022

Remember Surrender Sara Groves, 2002

The River Colby Wedgeworth, Jordan Feliz, and Joshua Silverberg, 2015

You Alone Can Rescue Jonas Myrin and Matt Redman, 2008

You Have Searched Me (Psalm 139) Keith Getty, Kristyn Getty, and Matt Papa, 2018

GLOBAL

Great God and Lord of the Earth John Bell, 2002 (Scotland)

Le Chal Meri Aatma Ko Tu (Lead My Soul, O God) Punjabi folk song (Pakistan)

Somlandela (We Will Follow) Traditional (South Africa)

Somos Pueblo Que Camina (We Are People On A Journey) Manuel Dávila (Nicaragua)

Tenemos Esperanza (We Have Hope) Federico J. Pagura, 1979 (Argentina)

LENT

WORSHIP SERVICE

BLESSED BE YOUR NAME

Words and Music by Beth Redman and Matt Redman
© 2002 Thankyou Music

We welcome you to this time of worship in the name of our glorious Lord Jesus Christ, who draws us, through his Body, the church, into friendship with God and with one another. This morning is the first Sunday of a new season in the church year. Historically this season has been called Lent. That word simply means the lengthening of days, such as during the season of spring. Spring is a time of renewal and rebirth, and during this season in the church year, we are reminded that because of Christ's death and resurrection, we are offered new life. As we begin our time of worship, let us still our minds and claim the divine promise: "Be still, and know that I am God! [pause briefly] I am exalted among the nations, I am exalted in the earth" (Psalm 46:10).

A TIME TO BE STILL

[Give the congregation the opportunity to settle their minds. Place Psalm 46:10 on the screen or in the bulletin to draw their attention to being still before the Lord; who is and will be exalted in the earth.]

The Apostle James exhorts us to,
Draw near to God, and he will draw near to you. Cleanse your hands, you sinners, and purify your hearts, you double-minded. Humble yourselves before the Lord, and he will exalt you.
James 4:8, 10

CALL TO CONFESSION

Earlier in his letter, James promises, "Blessed is anyone who endures temptation" (1:12). Yet we know that too often we give in to temptation and do what is wrong. Let us confess our sins together before God.

UNISON PRAYER OF CONFESSION

O God, we too often want to be a friend of the world and still be your friend. Yet, Jesus taught us: no one can serve two masters. Lord, forgive us for dividing our allegiance between you and another. Give us strength and courage to get our priorities straight: help us to seek your kingdom first. Help us to live faithfully and joyfully in the world, and to be friends with the people you call us to serve. Help us also to remember that our best relationship is the one we have with you, we pray in the name of Jesus Christ our Lord. Amen.

ASSURANCE OF FORGIVENESS

"But the wisdom from above is first pure, then peaceable, gentle, open to reason, full of mercy and good fruits, impartial and sincere" (James 3:17). In Jesus Christ, we are forgiven, and we are given a new way to live. Let us accept God's grace, and live new lives of faith, obedience, and joy.

LORD, I NEED YOU

Words and Music by Christy Nockles, Daniel Carson, Jesse Reeves, Kristian Stanfill, and Matt Maher
© 2011 sixsteps Music, Sweater Weather Music, Thankyou Music, Valley Of Songs Music, worshiptogether.com songs

BEAUTIFUL THINGS

Words and Music by Lisa Gungor and Michael Gungor
© 2009 worshiptogether.com songs

SCRIPTURE READING

Matthew 4:1–11

LEADER:

Then Jesus was led up by the Spirit into the wilderness to be tempted by the devil. And after fasting forty days and forty nights, he was hungry. And the tempter came and said to him, "If you are the Son of God, command these stones to become loaves of bread." But he answered,

CONGREGATION:

"It is written, 'Man shall not live by bread alone, but by every word that comes from the mouth of God.'"

LEADER:

Then the devil took him to the holy city and set him on the pinnacle of the temple and said to him, "If you are the Son of God, throw yourself down, for it is written, 'He will command his angels concerning you,' And 'On their hands they will bear you up, lest you strike your foot against a stone.'" Jesus said to him,

CONGREGATION:

"Again it is written, 'You shall not put the Lord your God to the test.'"

LEADER:

Again, the devil took him to a very high mountain and showed him all the kingdoms of the world and their glory. And he said to him, "All these I will give you, if you will fall down and worship me." Then Jesus said to him,

CONGREGATION:

"Be gone, Satan! For it is written, 'You shall worship the Lord your God and him only shall you serve.'"

LEADER:

Then the devil left him, and behold, angels came and were ministering to him.

HE WILL HOLD ME FAST

Words and Music by Ada Ruth Habershon and Matthew Merker
© 2013 Getty Music Publishing and Matthew Merker Music

OFFERING PRAYER

Heavenly Father, as we gather during this solemn and sacred Lenten season, we come before you with hearts humbled and contrite. We thank you for the opportunity to draw nearer to you during this season of reflection and repentance. In this time of Lent, we remember the great sacrifice of your Son, Jesus Christ, who willingly gave his life on the cross for our redemption. We offer our worship and praise, acknowledging your unfathomable love and mercy that knows no bounds.

As we embark on this journey of self-examination and renewal, we seek your forgiveness for our shortcomings and sins. Help us to turn away from all that separates us from you and to embrace a life of righteousness and compassion.

We offer our gifts and offerings with a spirit of surrender and dedication. May they be used to further your kingdom, to serve the marginalized and oppressed, and to bring comfort to those in need. During this Lenten season, may your Holy Spirit guide us in deeper understanding and reflection on the significance of Christ's sacrifice. May our hearts be transformed, and our lives be a testimony to the transformative power of your grace.

In the name of Jesus, who endured the cross for our sake, we pray. Amen.

OFFERTORY

O THE DEEP, DEEP LOVE OF JESUS

Words by Samuel T. Francis, 1875; Music by Thomas J. Williams, EBENEZER, 1897
Public Domain

PRAYER OF ILLUMINATION

Loving God, you teach us that if we are lacking in wisdom, we should turn to you and ask for what we need, because you give to all generously and ungrudgingly. We know that we have so much to learn; open wide your word to us and give us wisdom to understand the things you want to teach us. We pray in Jesus' name. Amen.

SERMON

[If observing the Lord's Supper, continue. If not, proceed to the next congregational song.]

THE LORD'S SUPPER INSTRUCTIONS AND INVITATION

[Instrumental music played or congregational singing.]

THE MYSTERY OF FAITH

And so, in remembrance of these your mighty acts in Jesus Christ, we offer ourselves in praise and thanksgiving as a holy and living sacrifice, in union with Christ's offering for us, as we proclaim the mystery of faith:

CONGREGATION:

Christ has died; Christ is risen; Christ will come again.

CHRIST THE SURE AND STEADY ANCHOR

Words and Music by Matt Boswell
© 2014 Doxology & Theology, Love Your Enemies Publishing

BENEDICTION

In the book of James, we are reminded not to confidently plan our future, saying, "Today or tomorrow we will travel to a certain city, stay there for a year, conduct business, and make profits." We are advised against this because we cannot predict what the future holds. Instead, we are encouraged to acknowledge, "If it is the Lord's will, we will live and do this or that." Our lives are under the care of God. Move forward with the confidence that he will accompany you, provide guidance, and illuminate your path each day. Amen.

LENT

SCRIPTURE PRESENTATION

HOW LONG, O LORD?

Psalm 13

CAST:

3 Voices

Optional: Voice 2 could be a language different from Voice 1 & 3; this reminds us that lament is a global practice.

VOICE 1:

How long, O Lord?

VOICE 2:

How long?

VOICE 3:

How long, O Lord?

VOICE 1:

Will you forget me forever?
How long?
[pause]

VOICE 2:

How long?
[pause]

VOICE 3:

How long?
[pause]

VOICE 1:

How long will you hide your face from me?
How long?
[pause]

VOICE 2:

How long?
[pause]

VOICE 3:

How long?
[pause]

VOICE 1:

How long must I take counsel in my soul and have sorrow in my heart all the day?
How long?
[pause]

VOICE 2:

How long?
[pause]

VOICE 3:

How long?
[pause]

VOICE 1:

How long shall my enemy be exalted over me? Consider and answer me, O Lord my God; light up my eyes, lest I sleep the sleep of death,

VOICE 2:

lest my enemy say, "I have prevailed over him,"

VOICE 3:

lest my foes rejoice because I am shaken.

VOICES 1, 2, 3:

But I have trusted in your steadfast love; my heart shall rejoice in your salvation.

VOICE 1:

I will sing to the Lord,

VOICE 2:

I will sing to the Lord,

VOICE 3:

I will sing to the Lord,

VOICE 1:

because he has dealt bountifully with me.

VOICE 2:

With me.

VOICE 3:

With me.

VOICES 1, 2, 3:

He has dealt bountifully . . . [pause] . . . with you.

CHAPTER 10

HOLY WEEK AND THE GREAT TRIDUUM

Holy Week[70] is the last full week of Lent and begins with Palm/Passion Sunday, the Sunday before Easter Sunday. According to Egeria, in fourth-century Jerusalem, what we now call Holy Week was known as "The Great Week." This week encapsulates the climactic events of the arrest, conviction, crucifixion, death, burial, and resurrection of Jesus Christ, making this the most extraordinary week in the Christian year calendar. A week in which the redemption of the world happened and in which the recreation of the world began.

PALM/PASSION SUNDAY

The first day of Holy Week is known as both Palm Sunday and Passion Sunday. It is the Sunday immediately preceding Easter Sunday, when the church remembers and celebrates the day Jesus rode into Jerusalem on a donkey, fulfilling the prophetic words of Zechariah (Zech 9:9). A group of people in Jerusalem laid their cloaks down in front of Jesus. Others grabbed palm branches and began waving them (a Jewish national symbol conveying the notion of victory over one's enemies) as they hailed Jesus as king. Most in the crowd that day shouted praises toward Jesus, "Hosanna to the Son of David! Blessed is he who comes in the name of the Lord! Hosanna in the highest!" (Matt 21:9; echoing the words of the psalmist; Ps 118:25–26).

This is a celebration! Shouts of praise, symbols of victory, and a kingly entrance. But we can't stop at the waving of palm branches and not read further. Luke shares with us the event immediately after Jesus' entrance to Jerusalem. The people are shouting praises, the Pharisees are upset, Jesus

---

70. For more on Holy Week, see my book *The Week that Changed the World*.

tells them that he won't silence the crowd because if he does, the rocks will begin to shout praises, and then he looks over the city of Jerusalem and weeps. This is a deep, grieving cry. You see, Jesus knows the path that is set before him. The path that he has begun with this entrance. He knows that by the end of the week, the shouts of praise will turn to cries for his death. He sees the sin in the people's hearts and their refusal to let him cleanse them. He knows that their shouts of "hosanna," meaning "Lord, save us" are just words. They don't really mean it. At least not in the sense that really matters—spiritually. In fact, their cries of "hosanna" are directing Jesus to the moment and place where he can fulfill their request—the cross. And so, Jesus weeps. And each step Jesus takes from this point forward takes him one step closer to the cross.

THE GREAT TRIDUUM

The conclusion of Holy Week includes three special days known as "The Great Triduum." This term may be unfamiliar to many Christians. Triduum is a Latin word that means "three days." So, the Great Triduum is the Great Three Days of Maundy Thursday, Good Friday, and the Easter Vigil or Paschal Vigil (Easter Saturday), tracing the last three days of Jesus' life before his resurrection. The intriguing part of the Great Triduum is that these three days are seen as one single event. The service that begins on Maundy Thursday with foot washing and the Lord's Supper is completed only by the announcement of the resurrection and its celebration at the Easter Vigil on Saturday evening or early Sunday morning—Easter Sunday.

The word *triduum* was first used by Augustine to express the essential unity of this single, three-day service. This unified service occurs in three separate time periods with Good Friday bridging the beginning and end. The important aspect for today is not that the term *triduum* be reintroduced to our congregations, but that the idea of a unified observance across the three days be evident to those in attendance of the triduum to help worshipers grasp the truth that dying he destroyed our death and rising he restored our life.

Maundy Thursday

Maundy Thursday (*maundy* meaning "mandate" or "command") remembers the time Jesus spent with his disciples in the upper room. It was there Jesus gave the ultimate example of being a servant as he washed the disciples' feet: "Jesus, knowing that the Father had given all things into his hands, and that he had come from God, got up from the table, took off his outer robe, and tied a towel around himself. Then he poured water into a basin and began to wash the disciples' feet and to wipe them with the towel that was tied around him" (John 13:3–5 NRSV). Jesus gave a new command when he said, "This is my commandment, that you love one another as I have loved you" (John 15:12 NRSV). Now, this command wasn't new to the disciples in the sense that they had never heard these words before. This is a command found in the Old Testament Law (Lev 19:18), which would have been familiar to them. They would have known these words well. Yet it was new to them because Jesus was showing them how to love one another—through acts of service.

Jesus also gave new meaning to the Passover when he took the bread and called it his body and took the cup of wine and called it his blood (Matt 26:26–29; Mark 14:22–25; Luke 22:14–20), instituting what we now know as the Lord's Supper, or communion. Maundy Thursday worship naturally features the Lord's Supper with its rich theological elements, including its attention to communal love and its clear eschatological orientation (its focus on hopeful anticipation of the coming kingdom).

The Maundy Thursday service generally begins in celebration with light and joy as the congregation gives thanks for Christ and his example of servanthood. The service ends in shadows and darkness as the congregation begins to prepare to reflect upon Christ's sacrifice on the cross.

Good Friday

Good Friday reflects upon the death of Jesus on the cross and is the bridge between Maundy Thursday and the Easter Vigil of the triduum. This is a day filled with horrendous events and yet it is called good. Frequently, we hear it is called good because of what Jesus accomplished for us on the cross. Although the events on the cross bring us something truly good, the actual meaning of the day's name originates from the Middle English root of "good" as "holy" or "righteous." This day is a holy day—the Friday of Holy Week.

The cross of Christ holds immense significance. It goes beyond being a symbol for Good Friday and stands as the most recognizable emblem of Christianity. Yet, its importance surpasses mere decoration on church buildings or necklaces. The cross primarily serves as an instrument of redemption. In Adam's transgression, the wood of a tree brought sin and death; however, in Christ's obedience, the wood of the cross brings forgiveness and life. Jesus Christ is the once for all sacrifice (Heb 7:27; 10:10), the Passover Lamb (1 Cor 5:6–8), slain to take away the sins of the world (John 1:29; Eph 1:5–7; Heb 9:12–14). Our sins were eliminated by the sacrifice of our Savior, covered by the blood of the Lamb. And yes, that is good.

While texts from Matthew, Mark, and Luke are used for the celebration of Palm/Passion Sunday, the gospel of John (18:1–19:42) is the primary Scripture used for Good Friday.

Easter Vigil

The triduum concludes with the Easter Vigil, which traditionally began late on Easter Saturday and ended in the early morning of Easter Sunday. The Easter Vigil begins in darkness as it continues from Good Friday with Christ remaining in the tomb. Traditionally, there are four parts to the Easter Vigil or Great Paschal Vigil; these include the Service of Light, the Service of Readings, the Service of Baptism, and the Easter Eucharist. The congregation sings songs of the resurrection and reads the story of God from creation, the fall, the Exodus (Exod 14:10–15:1), and the incarnation of God in Jesus Christ. At the end of the service, the lights are illuminated (or it is daybreak) and the music grows in intensity with energy and praise as the transition is made into Easter.

There are many theological speculations concerning what Jesus did on this day; mainly because Scripture does not tell us. Now, you may be asking, what do you mean, "what Jesus did on this day"? Wasn't he dead? Well yes . . . and no.

If you are a Christian, you must become accustomed to paradox. Throughout Scripture, we are told not to fear and to fear the Lord. We are told to be bold and to be humble. And then there's Jesus . . . another paradox. Jesus was 100 percent man and 100 percent Divine. So, on this Saturday following his crucifixion and the day before his resurrection, the 100 percent God-man was dead, but the 100 percent God-Divine was very much still alive. And I do not believe that Jesus, the Divine, just sat in the tomb twiddling his thumbs, waiting for Sunday.

Here is what we do know about this day:

- Jesus, the man, is dead and his body lay in the grave.
- His disciples are hiding behind locked doors and closed windows in fear for their lives. This day is the Sabbath, a day of worship. And not just any Sabbath, but the Sabbath of Passover, a "special Sabbath." The disciples should be worshiping in the temple rejoicing in the deliverance of the people of God. And yet the disciples are hiding away, full of fear and grief, instead of participating in celebratory worship.
- The women, identified as Mary Magdalene, Mary the mother of James, and Salome in Mark 16:1, but most likely others as well, are waiting for Sunday so they can take spices and ointments to prepare Jesus' body. John tells us that Nicodemus brought to the tomb with Jesus' body, a

mixture of myrrh and aloes, as well as linen cloths and spices, as was the Jewish burial custom. So why does Mark tell us the women went to the tomb on Sunday morning with spices to anoint Jesus? Did the women not know that Nicodemus already prepared Jesus' body? Did they feel more was required? Or did they simply want to participate in the custom as well? Scripture does not tell us.
- According to Matthew (27:62–66), guards are placed at the tomb to deter Jesus' disciples from stealing his body and claiming he rose from the dead.

One temptation on this day is to jump right to Easter and the Resurrection—to celebrate our risen Savior. But this day before Easter Sunday is critically important to our spiritual growth. It is a day of waiting. As Christians, we need to better learn how to wait. Although it may seem like God is silent, he is actively at work behind the scenes. Don't you think Jesus could have raised from the dead on Saturday . . . or within a couple hours after his crucifixion? Yes, of course he could have. But he waited . . . and he made his disciples wait . . . and sometimes, he makes us wait. Oftentimes, the waiting period is a time to see if we truly trust in God and his sovereignty.

This day is also a day of mourning, a time to grieve the loss of a loved one and to stand vigil at their graveside. We must permit ourselves to grieve the death of Jesus, but we do so with hope and anticipation for what lies ahead. It is vital not to overlook the significance of this day.

Christian spirituality, and our salvation history, is ultimately based on these three events—Maundy Thursday, Good Friday, and the Easter Vigil—as Jesus Christ was crucified, dead, buried, and eventually rose again so we could have new life. Throughout these three days, we experience the highs and lows in our faith, ending with the ultimate high—the new life of the resurrection. These are the events that establish our spirituality. It is important for the church today to remember these events, not simply as historical events, but as events that spiritually form our lives as we live in the death and resurrection of Jesus Christ as a foundation for our own dying to self and rising to new life in the Spirit.

INCORPORATING HOLY WEEK AND THE GREAT TRIDUUM:

Encourage your congregation to utilize a devotional book/resource during Holy Week. If you are able, create a devotional resource using people from within your own congregation to write the daily devotionals. Otherwise, I would recommend *The Week That Changed the World: Daily Reflections for Holy Week* (Westbow Press, 2021).

Palm/Passion Sunday

Plan a worship service that begins in celebration, utilizing palms and triumphal entry themes, and transitions to a passion theme focusing on the suffering of Jesus as he deliberately takes steps toward the cross.

Maundy Thursday

Plan a Maundy Thursday service and incorporate the three main aspects of the day within the service: 1) communion; 2) foot-washing; 3) a focus on the command to love one another.

Good Friday

Plan a Good Friday service that concludes by encouraging the congregation to exit in silence.

Easter Vigil

Rather than a worship service, plan an event utilizing stations (see Easter Saturday/Vigil Reflective Worship Experience).

PALM/PASSION SUNDAY

OVERVIEW

TIME
The Sunday immediately preceding Easter Sunday; the first day of Holy Week.

THEMES
Two commonly used themes on this day are the palm theme, which centers on Christ's triumphant entry into Jerusalem while riding on a donkey's colt amid people shouting, "Hosanna! Blessed is he who comes in the name of the Lord" (John 12:13); involving the waving of palm branches and laying down of cloaks. The passion theme, on the other hand, emphasizes Jesus' entry into Jerusalem, signifying the commencement of the last week of his life, leading to his suffering and death.

SPIRITUAL CHALLENGE
Be like the donkey, presenting Jesus to people; like the palms, praising Jesus; like the people, seeking salvation; and like Jesus, with eyes fixed on the cross.

SCRIPTURE
- Old Testament: Isa 7:10–14; Isa 50:4–9a
- Psalm: Ps 31:9–16; Ps 45; Ps 118:1–2, 19–29
- New Testament: Phil 2:5–11; Heb 10:4–10
- Gospel: Matt 21:1–11; Matt 26:14—27:66; Mark 11:1–10; Mark 14:1—15:47; Luke 1:26–38; Luke 19:28–44; Luke 22:14—23:56; John 12:12–19

SYMBOLS
- Palms
- Cross

COLORS
- Purple/Violet
- Red

PALM/PASSION SUNDAY

SONG LIST

CONTEMPORARY

All Hail to the King Jack Hayford, 1984

Ancient of Days Gary Sadler and Jamie Harvill, 1992

Ancient of Days Jonny Robinson, Rich Thompson, Michael Farren, and Jesse Reeves, 2018

Christ Be Magnified Cody Carnes, Cory Asbury, and Ethan Hulse, 2019

Glorious Chris Tomlin and Jesse Reeves, 2006

Great In Power Russel Fragar, 1998

He Has Made Me Glad Leona Von Brethorst, 1976

Holy, Holy, Holy Lord Peter Scholtes, 1966

Hosanna Brooke Ligertwood, 2006

Hosanna Carl Tuttle, 1985

Hosanna (Praise Is Rising) Paul Baloche and Brenton Brown, 2005

Jesus Messiah Daniel Carson, Ed Cash, Jesse Reeves, and Chris Tomlin, 2008

Mighty To Save Ben Fielding and Reuben Morgan, 2006

Only A God Like You Tommy Walker, 2000

Saved My Soul James Ferguson, Dustin R. Smith, and Rich Thompson, 2016

Shout For Joy Jason Ingram, Lincoln Brewster, and Paul Baloche, 2010

That's Why We Praise Him Tommy Walker, 1999

To the King Angela Cottrell and Travis Cottrell, 2009

Victory Chant Joseph Vogels, 1985

We Will Glorify Twila Paris, 1982

What the Lord Has Done in Me Reuben Morgan, 1998

TRADITIONAL

All Glory, Laud and Honor Theodulf, Bishop of Orleans, 9th century; John Mason Neale, transl., 1854

All Hail the Power of Jesus' Name Edward Perronet, 1780

Hosanna, Loud Hosanna Jennette Threlfall, 1873

My Song Is Love Unknown Samuel Crossman, 1664

O Worship the King Robert Grant, 1833

Prepare the Royal Highway Frans Mikael Franzen, 17th century

Rejoice, O Zion's Daughter Herman G. Stuempfle, 1997

Ride On, Ride On In Majesty! Henry H. Milman, 1827

Victory In Jesus Eugene Bartlet, 1939

PRESENTATIONAL

Ain't No Rock LaMarquis Jefferson, 1987

Blessed Is He Joel Lindsey and Sue C. Smith, 1998

Glorious Ed Cash, Franni Cash, Martin Cash, Scott Cash, and Andrew Bergthold, 2021

Hosanna Deborah D. Smith and Michael W. Smith, 1983

Hosanna Song Jon Guerra, Kate Bluett, and Paul Zach, 2021

In the Name of the Lord Sandi Patty, Phil McHugh, and Gloria Gaither, 1986

Prepare Ye the Way Michael W. Smith, 2008

Psalm 24 (The King of Glory) Keith Getty, Kristyn Getty, Ed Cash, and Chris Tomlin, 2016

Sing Hosanna Joshua Blakesley, 2007

GLOBAL

Gbemi Jesu (Lift Me, Jesus) Unknown (Nigeria)

Mantos y Palmas (Cloaks and Palms) Rubén Ruíz Avila, 1972 (Mexico)

Rab Khudawand Badshah Hai (Psalm 24) Traditional Punjabi Psalm (Pakistan)

Sanna Sannanina (Holy, Most Holy Lord) South African folk song (Tanzania)

Seyun Diyo Betiyo (O Daughter of Zion) Traditional (Pakistan)

PALM/PASSION SUNDAY
WORSHIP SERVICE

CALL TO WORSHIP

[A percussion and horn ensemble can play a triumphant processional to call the people to worship. Incorporate the ensemble on the first congregational song.]

SCRIPTURE READING

Psalm 24:7–10

LEADER:

Lift up your heads, you gates; be lifted up, you ancient doors,

CONGREGATION:

that the King of glory may come in.

LEADER:

Who is this King of glory?

CONGREGATION:

The Lord strong and mighty, the Lord mighty in battle.

LEADER:

Lift up your heads, you gates; lift them up, you ancient doors,

CONGREGATION:

that the King of glory may come in.

LEADER:

Who is he, this King of glory?

CONGREGATION:

The Lord Almighty—he is the King of glory.

TO THE KING

Words and Music by Angela Cottrell and Travis Cottrell
© 2009 First Hand Revelation Music, Indelible Creative Songs

Today is Palm Sunday, the day that marks the beginning of the greatest week in human history, culminating in the death and resurrection of our Lord and Savior, Jesus Christ. He willingly sacrificed himself for our sins, enabling us to be reconciled with a holy God and restoring our relationship with him.

Rejoice greatly, O daughter of Zion! Shout aloud, O daughter of Jerusalem! Behold, your king is coming to you; righteous and having salvation is he, humble and mounted on a donkey, on a colt, the foal of a donkey.
Zechariah 9:9

This is the day that the Lord has made; let us rejoice and be glad in it. Save us, we pray, O Lord! O Lord, we pray, give us success! Blessed is he who comes in the name of the Lord! We bless you from the house of the Lord. The Lord is God, and he has made his light to shine upon us. Bind the festal sacrifice with cords, up to the horns of the altar! You are my God, and I will give thanks to you; you are my God; I will extol you. Oh give thanks to the Lord, for he is good; for his steadfast love endures forever!
Psalm 118:24–29

And so today, we join with those who praised Jesus on that road to Jerusalem, declaring "Hosanna," meaning "Lord, save us." Let us pray,

OPENING PRAYER

Lord, save us from our own selfish desires. Save us from our sinful ways. Save us from turning our eyes away from you, Jesus. And we already know, you have promised to do just that—for all those who believe in you—you have saved us by your sacrifice on the cross.

SAVED MY SOUL

Words and Music by James Ferguson, Dustin R. Smith, and Rich Thompson
© 2016 CityALight Music, Integrity's Praise! Music

VICTORY CHANT

Words and Music by Joseph Vogels
© 1985 Universal Music—Brentwood Benson Publishing

OFFERING PRAYER

Loving and gracious God, on this Palm Sunday, we come before you with hearts full of praise and thanksgiving. We rejoice in the triumphal entry of your Son, Jesus Christ, into Jerusalem, and we celebrate the beginning of Holy Week. We offer our worship and adoration, acknowledging Jesus as our King and Savior. We thank you for the gift of his life, his teachings, and his sacrificial love that brings salvation to all who believe in him.

During this Holy Week, we are reminded of the price of redemption paid on the cross. We offer our gratitude for the selflessness and obedience of Jesus, who humbly accepted his fate for the sake of humanity.

As we present our gifts and offerings, we do so with hearts that are open and willing to follow Jesus' example of love and service. May these gifts be used to further your kingdom and to support those who are in need.

In the spirit of this season, may we also reflect on our own lives and the ways we can emulate Christ's humility, compassion, and forgiveness. Help us to walk the path of discipleship with faithfulness and dedication.

In the name of Jesus, who came to save us and reconcile us to you, we pray. Amen.

OFFERTORY

ANCIENT OF DAYS

Words and Music by Jonny Robinson, Rich Thompson, Michael Farren, and Jesse Reeves
© 2018 CityALight Music, Farren Love And War Publishing, Integrity's Alleluia! Music, BEC Worship, WriterWrong Music

PRAYER OF ILLUMINATION

Heavenly Father, on this blessed Palm Sunday, we gather in your presence, with hearts filled with gratitude and reverence, seeking the illumination of your divine truth. As we commemorate the triumphant entry of your Son into Jerusalem, we humbly approach your throne of grace, longing to understand the significance of this pivotal moment.

In the waving of palm branches and shouts of "Hosanna," may we grasp the profound meaning of this event, and may it remind us of the depth of your sacrificial love. As we journey through this Holy Week, illuminate our hearts with the path of humility and service, teach us to follow in the footsteps of our Savior, Jesus Christ.

As we prepare to celebrate Christ's resurrection, may this sermon ignite a fire in our souls, renewing our commitment to live faithfully for you.

We offer this prayer with thanksgiving and anticipation, trusting in your infinite wisdom and guidance, in the name of Jesus Christ, our Lord and Redeemer, Amen.

SERMON

[If observing the Lord's Supper, continue. If not, proceed to the next congregational song.]

THE LORD'S SUPPER INSTRUCTIONS AND INVITATION

[Instrumental music played or congregational singing.]

THE MYSTERY OF FAITH

And so, in remembrance of these your mighty acts in Jesus Christ, we offer ourselves in praise and thanksgiving as a holy and living sacrifice, in union with Christ's offering for us, as we proclaim the mystery of faith:

CONGREGATION:

Christ has died; Christ is risen; Christ will come again.

VICTORY IN JESUS

Words and Music by Eugene M. Bartlett, 1939

Arrangement by Travis Cottrell © 2009 First Hand Revelation Music

BENEDICTION

Brothers and sisters, as we enter this holy week, let us keep our eyes on Jesus. As we walk in step with Jesus and the Holy Spirit this week, he will show us where we need to go. Go in peace.

PALM/PASSION SUNDAY
SCRIPTURE PRESENTATION

HOSANNA TO THE SON OF DAVID

Mark 11:1–11; with Zechariah 9:9 and Philippians 4:4

CAST:

3 Voices
Congregation

VOICE 1:

"Rejoice greatly, O daughter of Zion! Shout aloud, O daughter of Jerusalem!

CONGREGATION:

Rejoice in the Lord always; again I will say, rejoice.

VOICE 2:

Behold, your king is coming to you; righteous and having salvation is he, humble and mounted on a donkey, on a colt, the foal of a donkey."

VOICE 3:

Now when they drew near to Jerusalem, to Bethphage and Bethany, at the Mount of Olives, Jesus sent two of his disciples and said to them,

VOICE 1:

"Go into the village in front of you, and immediately as you enter it you will find a colt tied, on which no one has ever sat. Untie it and bring it. If anyone says to you, 'Why are you doing this?' say, 'The Lord has need of it and will send it back here immediately.'"

VOICE 3:

And they went away and found a colt tied at a door outside in the street, and they untied it. And some of those standing there said to them,

VOICE 2:

"What are you doing, untying the colt?"

VOICE 3:

And they told them what Jesus had said, and they let them go. And they brought the colt to Jesus and threw their cloaks on it, and he sat on it. And many spread their cloaks on the road, and others spread leafy branches that they had cut from the fields. And those who went before and those who followed were shouting,

CONGREGATION:

"Hosanna! Blessed is he who comes in the name of the Lord!
Blessed is the coming kingdom of our father David!
Hosanna in the highest!"

VOICE 3:

And he entered Jerusalem and went into the temple. And when he had looked around at everything, as it was already late, he went out to Bethany with the twelve.

MAUNDY THURSDAY

OVERVIEW

TIME
The Thursday before Easter Sunday.

THEMES
Marks three key events in Jesus' last week:
- Washing of the disciples' feet
- Institution of the Lord's Supper
- Command to love one another

SPIRITUAL CHALLENGE
Take time to contemplate Jesus' example of love and service, reaffirming your commitment to lead a life dedicated to serving others.

SCRIPTURE
- Old Testament: Exod 12:1-4, (5-10), 11-14
- Psalm: Ps 116:1-2, 12-19
- New Testament: 1 Cor 11:23-26
- Gospel: John 13:1-17, 31b-35

SYMBOLS
- Bread and Cup
- Basin and Towel

COLORS
- White
- Red

MAUNDY THURSDAY

SONG LIST

CONTEMPORARY

Behold the Lamb Keith Getty, Kristyn Getty, and Stuart Townend, 2007

In This Very Room Carol Harris and Ron Harris, 1979

Let Me Be a Servant Today Philip Bardowell, 2007

Meekness and Majesty Graham Kendrick, 1986

Remembrance Chris Davenport and Benjamin Hastings, 2018

There's Something About That Name Gloria Gaither and William Gaither, 1970

They'll Know We Are Christians Peter Scholtes, 1966

This Is My Body Jack Hayford, 1984

We Are the Body of Christ David Hampton and Scott Wesley Brown, 1997

Who You Say I Am Ben Fielding and Reuben Morgan, 2018

Wonderful Merciful Savior Dawn Rodger and Eric Wyse, 1989

Yet Not I But Through Christ In Me Michael Farren, Jonny Robinson, Rich Thompson, 2018

TRADITIONAL

Ah, Holy Jesus, How Hast Thou Offended Johann Heermann, 1630

For the Bread Which You Have Broken Louis F. Benson, 1924

Let Us Break Bread Together Unknown; African American Spiritual

'Tis Midnight and on Olive's Brow William Tappan, 1822

What Wondrous Love Is This Anonymous, 1811

PRESENTATIONAL

Alabaster Box Janice Lyn Sjostrand, 2004

Communion Brooke Ligertwood, Scott Ligertwood, Jason Ingram, 2022

Gethsemane Keith Getty and Stuart Townend, 2009

How Beautiful Twila Paris, 1990

I Am the Bread of Life John Michael Talbot, 1982

Pour My Love On You Dan Dean and Gary Sadler, 2001

Remember Laura Story, 2009

The Basin and the Towel Michael Card, 1994

The Last Supper Wes King and Cindy Morgan, 1998

The Servant King Graham Kendrick, 1983

The Song of the Supper John Bell, 1988

GLOBAL

Eat This Bread Communauté de Taizé, 1984; Robert J. Batastini, adapt. (France)

Jesu, Jesu, Fill Us With Your Love Tom Colvin, 1969 (Ghana)

Stay With Me Communauté de Taizé, 1984 (France)

Ubi Caritas Communauté de Taizé, 1981 (France)

We Are Coming, Lord, to the Table Unknown (Sierra Leone)

MAUNDY THURSDAY
WORSHIP SERVICE

[There is beauty in the simplicity of this evening. All songs are sung a cappella, and the tables are sparsely decorated. A cross is placed at the center of the platform. The rest of the platform is decorated with water jugs and plants surrounding the cross—leaving room for the liturgical dance that occurs later in the service.]

WELCOME

[During the welcome, the congregation is asked to save a piece of bread and a portion of juice for communion later in the service.]

FELLOWSHIP AT MEAL

[The congregation is invited to enjoy fellowship and finger foods at their tables.]

SERMON (PART 1)—JESUS WASHES THE DISCIPLES' FEET

John 13:1–20

FOOT WASHING

[Multiple stations may be needed depending on the size of the congregation. For hygiene purposes, you will want to either change the water after each person or pour the water over the foot into the basin below. If you choose to place the foot in the water, it will require "runners" to empty the dirty water and refresh the basins with clean water. This takes extra time, but don't worry, congregants would rather have the clean water. Plus, this is a beautiful time of worship so taking time here is okay. No matter how you choose to execute the foot washing, be sure the water is warm. Cold water makes for an uncomfortable experience. Songs are sung a cappella during foot washing.]

SERMON (PART 2)—THE PASSOVER WITH THE DISCIPLES

Luke 22:7–13

LITURGICAL DANCE

HOW BEAUTIFUL

Words and Music by Twila Paris
© 1990 Ariose Music; Mountain Spring Music
[Live performance or pre-recorded track.]

THE LORD'S SUPPER INSTRUCTIONS AND INVITATION

Read Luke 22:14–20

PRAYER

Loving God, on this solemn and sacred Maundy Thursday, we gather in your presence with hearts of humility, to remember the last supper of your beloved Son.

As we approach the table of communion, we reflect on the depth of his selfless love, in the breaking of bread and sharing of the cup. In the act of washing his disciples' feet, Jesus demonstrated the essence of true service, teaching us to love and care for one another.

On this night of remembrance, we seek your illumination, to understand the significance of Christ's sacrifice, and the redemption that flows from his precious blood. May the spirit of Maundy Thursday dwell within us, compelling us to embrace unity and reconciliation, as we partake in this solemn feast of remembrance.

We offer this prayer with thanksgiving and devotion, in the name of Jesus Christ, our Savior and Redeemer, Amen.

SERMON (PART 3) — A NEW COMMAND

John 13:31–35

BENEDICTION

And when they had sung a hymn, they went out to the Mount of Olives.
Mark 14:26

PRAISE GOD FROM WHOM ALL BLESSINGS FLOW

Words by Thomas Ken, 1674; Music by Louis Bourgeois, OLD HUNDREDTH, 1551
Public Domain
[Sung a cappella; invite congregation to stand and hold hands]

DISMISSAL

Go in peace and thankfulness.

MAUNDY THURSDAY

SCRIPTURE PRESENTATION

WHO IS LIKE THE LORD OUR GOD?
Psalm 113

CAST:
3 Voices
Congregation

VOICE 1:
Psalm 113 begins with the words: "Praise the Lord!"
We will repeat this phrase throughout this Psalm. Every time I point to you, like this (hold hand outward toward the congregation, palm facing up), let's declare our praise to the Lord. Let's try it. [Hold hand out toward congregation and let them respond with "Praise the Lord!"]

VOICE 2:
Praise, O servants of the Lord, praise the name of the Lord!

CONGREGATION:
Praise the Lord!

VOICE 1:
Blessed be the name of the Lord from this time forth and forevermore!

CONGREGATION:
Praise the Lord!

VOICE 3:

From the rising of the sun to its setting, the name of the Lord is to be praised!

CONGREGATION:

Praise the Lord!

VOICE 2:

The Lord is high above all nations, and his glory above the heavens!

CONGREGATION:

Praise the Lord!

VOICE 1:

Who is like the Lord our God, who is seated on high, who looks far down on the heavens and the earth?

VOICE 3:

He raises the poor from the dust and lifts the needy from the ash heap, to make them sit with princes, with the princes of his people.

VOICE 2:

He gives the barren woman a home, making her the joyous mother of children.

VOICES 1, 2, & 3:

Praise the Lord!

CONGREGATION:

Praise the Lord!

GOOD FRIDAY

OVERVIEW

TIME

The Friday before Easter Sunday.

THEMES

The death of Jesus on the cross.

SCRIPTURE

- Old Testament: Isa 52:13—53:12
- Psalm: Ps 22
- New Testament: Heb 10:16–25
- Gospel: John 18:1—19:42

SPIRITUAL CHALLENGE

Engage in reflection and repentance as you remember Jesus' sacrifice.

SYMBOLS

- Cross

COLORS

- Black
- Red
- Or no color

GOOD FRIDAY
SONG LIST

CONTEMPORARY

Agnus Dei Michael W. Smith, 1990

At the Cross Darlene Zschech and Reuben Morgan, 2006

Be Lifted Up Paul Oakley, 2001

Come Behold the Wondrous Mystery Matt Boswell, Matt Papa, and Michael Bleecker, 2012

Forever (The Nails in Your Hands) Richard Camino, 1995

How Deep the Father's Love for Us Stuart Townend, 1995

How Vast the Love Joel Sczebel, Lacy Hudson, and Marc Willerton, 2019

I Cling to the Cross Matt Redman and Paul Baloche, 2007

I See the Cross Brian Doerksen, 2000

In Christ Alone Keith Getty and Stuart Townend, 2001

Is He Worthy? Andrew Peterson and Ben Shive, 2018

It Was Finished Upon That Cross Jonny Robinson, Nigel Hendroff, and Rich Thompson, 2021

King of Kings Brooke Ligertwood, Jason Ingram, and Scott Ligertwood, 2019

Lamb of God Twila Paris, 1985

Lead Me to The Cross Brooke Ligertwood, 2006

Lord Have Mercy Eoghan Heaslip, 2002

Mighty Is the Power of the Cross Chris Tomlin, Jesse Reeves, and Shawn Craig, 2004

No Other Fount David Moffitt, Tommee Profitt, and Travis Cottrell, 2018

The Power of the Cross Keith Getty and Stuart Townend, 2005

You Are My All in All Dennis Jernigan, 1991

TRADITIONAL

Alas! and Did My Savior Bleed? Isaac Watts, 1707

And Can It Be? Charles Wesley, 1738

At the Cross Isaac Watts and Ralph Hudson, 1883

Beneath the Cross of Jesus Elizabeth C. Clephane, 1868

Blessed Redeemer Avis Christiansen, 1920

Go to Dark Gethsemane James Montgomery, 1825

I Will Sing of My Redeemer Philip P. Bliss, 1876

In the Cross of Christ I Glory John Bowring, 1825

Jesus Paid It All Elvina M. Hall, 1865

Lead Me to Calvary Jennie Evelyn Hussey, 1921

Man of Sorrows, What a Name Philip P. Bliss, 1875

Near the Cross Fanny Crosby, 1869

Nothing But the Blood Robert Lowry, 1876

O Sacred Head, Now Wounded Bernard of Clairvaux, 12th century; James W. Alexander, transl., 1829

Tell Me the Story of Jesus Fanny Crosby, 1880

The Old Rugged Cross George Bennard, 1913

There Is a Fountain William Cowper, 1772

We Sing the Praise of Him Who Died Thomas Kelly, 1815

Were You There? Anonymous, 1899

What Wondrous Love Is This? Anonymous, 1811

When I Survey the Wondrous Cross Isaac Watts, 1707

Why Should He Love Me So? Robert Harkness, 1925

PRESENTATIONAL

Behold the Lamb Dottie Rambo, 1979

I Believe in a Hill Called Mount Calvary Dale Oldham, Gloria Gaither, and William Gaither, 1968

In Christ Alone Shawn Craig and Don Koch, 1990

Via Dolorosa Billy Sprague and Niles Borop, 1984

GLOBAL

Hatha Pairan Wich Kell (Nails in His Feet and Hands) Punjabi folk song (Pakistan)

Jesus, Remember Me Communauté de Taizé and Jacques Berthier, 1981 (France)

Kalvary De Saharay (By the Cross of Calvary) Punjabi folk song (Pakistan)

Kandaalo Aalariyukilla (You Will Not Recognize the Man) Anil Adoor, 2021 (India)

Karna SalibMu (Because of Your Cross) Maria Shandi, 2014 (Indonesia)

Thuma (Lamb) Adrian Dewan, 2019 (Nepal)

GOOD FRIDAY

WORSHIP SERVICE

COME, BEHOLD THE WONDROUS MYSTERY

Words and Music by Matt Boswell, Matt Papa, and Michael Bleecker
© 2013 Getty Music Songs, McKinney Music Inc., Love Your Enemies Publishing, Bleecker Publishing
[For Good Friday, it is appropriate to omit verse 4.]

OPENING PRAYER

O God of infinite love and power, we gather on this Good Friday to reflect on the passion of the Christ. We are utterly humbled in the presence of such love and mercy. Open our hearts this day to the goodness of Good Friday and fill us with your love and powerful Spirit of Holiness. Remove from us all sin. Offer us anew this Life in Christ that makes all things new. Amen.

THE SON OF MAN MUST BE LIFTED UP

John 12:27–36

READER 1:

Now is my soul troubled. And what shall I say? "Father, save me from this hour"? But for this purpose I have come to this hour. Father, glorify your name. Then a voice came from heaven: "I have glorified it, and I will glorify it again." The crowd that stood there and heard it said that it had thundered. Others said, "An angel has spoken to him." Jesus answered, "This voice has come for your sake, not mine. Now is the judgment of this world; now will the ruler of this world be cast out. And I, when I am lifted up from the earth, will draw all people to myself." He said this to show by what kind of death he was going to die. So the crowd answered him, "We have heard from the Law that the Christ remains forever. How can you say that the Son of Man must be lifted up? Who is this Son of Man?" So Jesus said to them, "The light is among you for a little while longer. Walk while you have the light, lest darkness overtake you. The one who walks in the darkness does not know where he is going. While you have the light, believe in the light, that you may become sons of light."

INSTRUMENTAL MUSIC FOR CONTEMPLATION

[I suggest using instruments such as a cello or oboe to match the ambience of the evening.]

BETRAYAL AND ARREST OF JESUS

John 18:1

READER 1:

. . . Jesus . . . went out with his disciples across the brook Kidron, where there was a garden, which he and his disciples entered.

GO TO DARK GETHSEMANE (VERSE 1)

Words by James Montgomery, 1825; Music by Richard Redhead, RED-HEAD NO. 76, 1853
Public Domain

Go to dark Gethsemane, you who feel the tempter's pow'r;
Your Redeemer's conflict see; Watch with him one bitter hour;
Turn not from his griefs away; Learn of Jesus Christ to pray.

JUDAS, WHO BETRAYED HIM

John 18:2–11

READER 2:

Now Judas, who betrayed him, also knew the place, for Jesus often met there with his disciples. So Judas, having procured a band of soldiers and some officers from the chief priests and the Pharisees, went there with lanterns and torches and weapons. Then Jesus, knowing all that would happen to him, came forward and said to them, "Whom do you seek?" They answered him, "Jesus of Nazareth." Jesus said to them, "I am he." Judas, who betrayed him, was standing with them. When Jesus said to them, "I am he," they drew back and fell to the ground. So he asked them again, "Whom do you seek?" And they said, "Jesus of Nazareth." Jesus answered, "I told you that I am he. So, if you *seek me, let these men go." This was to fulfill the word that he had spoken: "Of those whom you gave me I have lost not one." Then Simon Peter, having a sword, drew it and struck the high priest's servant and cut off his right ear. (The servant's name was Malchus.) So Jesus said to Peter, "Put your sword into its sheath; shall I not drink the cup that the Father has given me?"*

JESUS FACES ANNAS AND CAIAPHAS

John 18:12–14

READER 1:

So the band of soldiers and their captain and the officers of the Jews arrested Jesus and bound him. First they led him to Annas, for he was the father-in-law of Caiaphas, who was high priest that year. It was Caiaphas who had advised the Jews that it would be expedient that one man should die for the people.

PETER DENIES JESUS

John 18:15–18

READER 2:

Simon Peter followed Jesus, and so did another disciple. Since that disciple was known to the high priest, he entered with Jesus into the courtyard of the high priest, but Peter stood outside at the door. So the other disciple, who was known to the high priest, went out and spoke to the servant girl who kept watch at the door, and brought Peter in. The servant girl at the door said to Peter, "You also are not one of this man's disciples, are you?" He said, "I am not." Now the servants and officers had made a charcoal fire, because it was cold, and they were standing and warming themselves. Peter also was with them, standing and warming himself.

GO TO DARK GETHSEMANE (VERSE 2)

Follow to the judgment hall; View the Lord of life arraigned;
O the worm-wood and the gall! O the pangs his soul sustained!
Shun not suff'ring, shame, or loss; Learn of him to bear the cross.

THE HIGH PRIEST QUESTIONS JESUS

John 18:19–24

READER 1:

The high priest then questioned Jesus about his disciples and his teaching. Jesus answered him, "I have spoken openly to the world. I have always taught in synagogues and in the temple, where all Jews come together. I have said nothing in secret. Why do you ask me? Ask those who have heard me what I said to them; they know what I said." When he had said these things, one of the officers standing by struck Jesus with his hand, saying, "Is that how you answer the high priest?" Jesus answered him, "If what I said is wrong, bear witness about the wrong; but if what I said is right, why do you strike me?" Annas then sent him bound to Caiaphas the high priest.

PETER DENIES JESUS AGAIN

John 18:25–27

READER 2:

Now Simon Peter was standing and warming himself. So they said to him, "You also are not one of his disciples, are you?" He denied it and said, "I am not." One of the servants of the high priest, a relative of the man whose ear Peter had cut off, asked, "Did I not see you in the garden with him?" Peter again denied it, and at once a rooster crowed.

JESUS BEFORE PILATE

John 18:28–32

READER 1:

Then they led Jesus from the house of Caiaphas to the governor's headquarters. It was early morning. They themselves did not enter the governor's headquarters, so that they would not be defiled, but could eat the Passover. So Pilate went outside to them and said, "What accusation do you bring against this man?" They answered him, "If this man were not doing evil, we would not have delivered him over to you." Pilate said to them, "Take him yourselves and judge him by your own law." The Jews said to him, "It is not lawful for us to put anyone to death." This was to fulfill the word that Jesus had spoken to show by what kind of death he was going to die.

MY KINGDOM IS NOT OF THIS WORLD

John 18:33–40

READER 2:

So Pilate entered his headquarters again and called Jesus and said to him, "Are you the King of the Jews?" Jesus answered, "Do you say this of your own accord, or did others say it to you about me?" Pilate answered, "Am I a Jew? Your own nation and the chief priests have delivered you over to me. What have you done?" Jesus answered, "My kingdom is not of this world. If my kingdom were of this world, my servants would have been fighting, that I might not be delivered over to the Jews. But my kingdom is not from the world." Then Pilate said to him, "So you are a king?" Jesus answered, "You say that I am a king. For this purpose I was born and for this purpose I have come into the world—to bear witness to the truth. Everyone who is of the truth listens to my voice." Pilate said to him, "What is truth?"

After he had said this, he went back outside to the Jews and told them, "I find no guilt in him. But you have a custom that I should release one man for you at the Passover. So do you want me to release to you the King of the Jews?" They cried out again, "Not this man, but Barabbas!" Now Barabbas was a robber.

JESUS DELIVERED TO BE CRUCIFIED

John 19:1–11

READER 1:

Then Pilate took Jesus and flogged him. And the soldiers twisted together a crown of thorns and put it on his head and arrayed him in a purple robe. They came up to him, saying, "Hail, King of the Jews!" and struck him with their hands. Pilate went out again and said to them, "See, I am bringing him out to you that you may know that I find no guilt in him." So Jesus came out, wearing the crown of thorns and the purple robe. Pilate said to them, "Behold the man!" When the chief priests and the officers saw him, they cried out, "Crucify him, crucify him!" Pilate said to them, "Take him yourselves and crucify him, for I find no guilt in him." The Jews answered him, "We have a law, and according to that law he ought to die because he has made himself the Son of God." When Pilate heard this statement, he was even more afraid. He entered his headquarters again and said to Jesus, "Where are you from?" But Jesus gave him no answer. So Pilate said to him, "You will not speak to me? Do you not know that I have authority to release you and authority to crucify you?" Jesus answered him, "You would have no authority over me at all unless it had been given you from above. Therefore he who delivered me over to you has the greater sin."

JESUS DELIVERED TO BE CRUCIFIED

John 19:12–16

READER 2:

From then on Pilate sought to release him, but the Jews cried out, "If you release this man, you are not Caesar's friend. Everyone who makes himself a king opposes Caesar." So when Pilate heard these words, he brought Jesus out and sat down on the judgment seat at a place called The Stone Pavement, and in Aramaic Gabbatha. Now it was the day of Preparation of the Passover. It was about the sixth hour. He said to the Jews, "Behold your King!" They cried out, "Away with him, away with him, crucify him!" Pilate said to them, "Shall I crucify your King?" The chief priests answered, "We have no king but Caesar." So he delivered him over to them to be crucified.

GO TO DARK GETHSEMANE (VERSE 3)

Calv'ry's mournful mountain climb there adoring at his feet,
Mark the miracle of time, God's own sacrifice complete:
"It is finished!" Hear the cry; Learn of Jesus Christ to die.

THE CRUCIFIXION

John 19:16b–22

READER 1:

So they took Jesus, and he went out, bearing his own cross, to the place called The Place of a Skull, which in Aramaic is called Golgotha. There they crucified him, and with him two others, one on either side, and Jesus between them. Pilate also wrote an inscription and put it on the cross. It read, "Jesus of Nazareth, the King of the Jews." Many of the Jews read this inscription, for the place where Jesus was crucified was near the city, and it was written in Aramaic, in Latin, and in Greek. So the chief priests of the Jews said to Pilate, "Do not write, 'The King of the Jews,' but rather, 'This man said, I am King of the Jews.'" Pilate answered, "What I have written I have written."

JESUS IS CRUCIFIED

John 19:23–27

READER 2:

When the soldiers had crucified Jesus, they took his garments and divided them into four parts, one part for each soldier; also his tunic. But the tunic was seamless, woven in one piece from top to bottom, so they said to one another, "Let us not tear it, but cast lots for it to see whose it shall be." This was to fulfill the Scripture which says,
"They divided my garments among them, and for my clothing they cast lots."
So the soldiers did these things, but standing by the cross of Jesus were his mother and his mother's sister, Mary the wife of Clopas, and Mary Magdalene. When Jesus saw his mother and the disciple whom he loved standing nearby, he said to his mother, "Woman, behold, your son!" Then he said to the disciple, "Behold, your mother!" And from that hour the disciple took her to his own home.

THE DEATH OF JESUS

John 19:28–30

READER 1:

After this, Jesus, knowing that all was now finished, said (to fulfill the Scripture), "I thirst." A jar full of sour wine stood there, so they put a sponge full of the sour wine on a hyssop branch and held it to his mouth. When Jesus had received the sour wine, he said, "It is finished," and he bowed his head and gave up his spirit.

NO OTHER FOUNT

Words and Music by David Moffitt, Tommee Profitt, and Travis Cottrell
© 2018 Timechangemusic, Universal Music—Brentwood Benson Publishing, Capitol CMG Genesis

NOTHING BUT THE BLOOD

Words and Music by Robert Lowry, 1876
Public Domain

JESUS' SIDE IS PIERCED

John 19:31–37

READER 2:

Since it was the day of Preparation, and so that the bodies would not remain on the cross on the Sabbath (for that Sabbath was a high day), the Jews asked Pilate that their legs might be broken and that they might be taken away. So the soldiers came and broke the legs of the first, and of the other who had been crucified with him. But when they came to Jesus and saw that he was already dead, they did not break his legs. But one of the soldiers pierced his side with a spear, and at once there came out blood and water. He who saw it has borne witness—his testimony is true, and he knows that he is telling the truth—that you also may believe. For these things took place that the Scripture might be fulfilled: "Not one of his bones will be broken." And again another Scripture says, "They will look on him whom they have pierced."

JESUS IS BURIED

John 19:38–42

READER 1:

After these things Joseph of Arimathea, who was a disciple of Jesus, but secretly for fear of the Jews, asked Pilate that he might take away the body of Jesus, and Pilate gave him permission. So he came and took away his body. Nicodemus also, who earlier had come to Jesus by night, came bringing a mixture of myrrh and aloes, about seventy-five pounds in weight. So they took the body of Jesus and bound it in linen cloths with the spices, as is the burial custom of the Jews. Now in the place where he was crucified there was a garden, and in the garden a new tomb in which no one had yet been laid. So because of the Jewish day of Preparation, since the tomb was close at hand, they laid Jesus there.

IT WAS FINISHED UPON THAT CROSS

Words and Music by Jonny Robinson, Rich Thompson, and Nigel Hendroff
© 2021 SHOUT! Music Publishing Australia, CityAlight Music

BENEDICTION

We wait by the tomb, with feelings of grief and loss. We wait with broken hearts knowing that Jesus took upon himself the grief of us all. We hear his words echo in our minds, "It is finished." And this brings us hope. Yet, just as the disciples had to wait, we must wait. We go . . . and we wait. And as we wait, we worship you God our Father, for the gift of your Son.

GOOD FRIDAY

SCRIPTURE PRESENTATION

THE CRUCIFIXION—AS TOLD BY THE GOSPELS

with portions of Psalm 22 & Isaiah 53

CAST:

3 Voices

VOICE 1:

Now from noon there was darkness over all the earth until 3:00PM. And about that time Jesus cried out with a loud voice, saying, "Eli, Eli, lema sabachthani?" that is, "My God, my God, why have you forsaken me?"

VOICE 2:

My God, my God, why have you forsaken me? Why are you so far from saving me, from the words of my groaning? O my God, I cry by day, but you do not answer, and by night, but I find no rest.

VOICE 1:

And those who passed by derided him, wagging their heads and saying, "You who would destroy the temple and rebuild it in three days, save yourself! If you are the Son of God, come down from the cross."

VOICE 2:

But I am a worm and not a man, scorned by mankind and despised by the people. All who see me mock me; they make mouths at me; they wag their heads;

VOICE 3:

He was despised and rejected by men, a man of sorrows and acquainted with grief; and as one from whom men hide their faces he was despised, and we esteemed him not.

VOICE 1:

and they twisted together a crown of thorns, they put it on his head and put a reed in his right hand. And kneeling before him, they mocked him, saying, "Hail, King of the Jews!"

VOICE 2:

All who see me mock me; they make mouths at me; they wag their heads;

VOICE 1:

"He trusts in God; let God deliver him now, if he desires him. For he said, 'I am the Son of God.'"

VOICE 2:

"He trusts in the Lord; let him deliver him; let him rescue him, for he delights in him!"

VOICE 1:

And the soldiers led him away inside the palace (that is, the governor's headquarters) and they called together the whole battalion. And they clothed him in a purple cloak, and twisting together a crown of thorns, they put it on him. And they began to salute him, "Hail, King of the Jews!" And they were striking his head with a reed and spitting on him and kneeling down in homage to him. And when they had mocked him, they stripped him of the purple cloak and put his own clothes on him. And they led him out to crucify him.

VOICE 2:

Many bulls encompass me; strong bulls of Bashan surround me;
They open wide their mouths at me, like a ravening and roaring lion.

VOICE 1:

But one of the soldiers pierced his side with a spear, and at once there came out blood and water.

VOICE 2:

For dogs encompass me; a company of evildoers encircles me;
they have pierced my hands and feet—

VOICE 3:

But he was pierced for our transgressions; he was crushed for our iniquities; upon him was the chastisement that brought us peace, and with his wounds we are healed.

VOICE 1:

When the soldiers had crucified Jesus, they took his garments and divided them into four parts, one part for each soldier; also his tunic. But the tunic was seamless, woven in one piece from top to bottom, so they said to one another, "Let us not tear it, but cast lots for it to see whose it shall be." This was to fulfill the Scripture which says, "They divided my garments among them, and for my clothing they cast lots."

VOICE 2:

I can count all my bones—they stare and gloat over me;
they divide my garments among them, and for my clothing they cast lots.

VOICE 1:

And Jesus uttered a loud cry and breathed his last.

VOICE 2:

I am poured out like water, and all my bones are out of joint; my heart is like wax; it is melted within my breast; my strength is dried up like a potsherd, and my tongue sticks to my jaws; you lay me in the dust of death.

VOICE 3:

And they made his grave with the wicked and with a rich man in his death, although he had done no violence, and there was no deceit in his mouth.

EASTER SATURDAY/VIGIL
OVERVIEW

TIME

Easter Vigil (or Paschal Vigil) traditionally begins late on Easter Saturday and ends in the early morning of Easter Sunday.

THEMES

On this day in history Christ remained in the tomb.

SPIRITUAL CHALLENGE

Devote yourself to living according to the pattern of Jesus' death and resurrection, the very pattern of life into which we are baptized.

SCRIPTURE

- Old Testament: Job 14:1–14
- Psalm: Ps 31:1–4; 15–16
- New Testament: 1 Pet 4:1–8
- Gospel: Matt 27:57–66; Mark 15:42–47; Luke 23:50–56; John 19:38–42

SYMBOLS

- Tomb
- Darkness (beginning of service)
- Light (end of service)

COLORS

- Black
- Red

- Or no color

EASTER SATURDAY/VIGIL
SONG LIST

CONTEMPORARY
Awakening Chris Tomlin and Reuben Morgan, 2010

Christ Is Mine Forevermore Jonny Robinson and Rich Thompson, 2016

Christ Our Hope in Life and Death Keith Getty, Matt Boswell, Jordan Kauflin, Matthew Merker, and Matt Papa, 2020

My Savior, My God Aaron Shust and Dorothy Greenwell, 2005

O Praise the Name (Anástasis) Marty Sampson, Benjamin Hastings, and Dean Ussher, 2015

Our God Chris Tomlin, Jesse Reeves, Jonas Myrin, and Matt Redman, 2010

The Power of the Cross Keith Getty and Stuart Townend, 2005

Yet Not I But Through Christ in Me Michael Farren, Jonny Robinson, Rich Thompson, 2018

TRADITIONAL
Christ Jesus Lay in Death's Strong Bands Martin Luther, 1524

In the Cross of Christ, I Glory John Bowring, 1825

Lead Me to Calvary Jennie Evelyn Hussey, 1921

O Paradise Frederick Faber, 1862

Worthy the Lamb Gloria Gaither and William Gaither, 1974

PRESENTATIONAL
Higher Cindy Morgan, 1998

Take My Life Cindy Morgan, 1998

The Night Before Easter Donnie Sumner and Dwayne Friend, 1969

GLOBAL

Exsultet (Rejoice) Unknown, 5th century (Italy)

Hellelujah, Bolo Yesu Zinda Ho Gaya (Hallelujah, Jesus Is Alive) Punjabi folk song (Pakistan)

Wait for the Lord Communauté de Taizé, 1991 (France)

EASTER SATURDAY/VIGIL
REFLECTIVE WORSHIP EXPERIENCE

Rather than a worship service example, I would like to provide an "experiential worship time" which includes stations in a room (i.e., sanctuary, chapel, etc.) for the congregation to visit. The stations should focus on a variety of elements such as reconciliation, forgiveness, praise, prayer, etc. Those in attendance may visit the stations alone or in a group, spending time at each to reflect upon Christ's life, death, and resurrection. A booklet should be provided explaining each station and encouraging the visitor to reflect on a specific focus based on that station.

Offer this as an open house with no set program. Visitors may come when they like and stay for as long as they want (between the designated hours that your church determines; generally, a period of three hours is sufficient). Provide quiet background music throughout the evening. Live musicians are a great addition: solo cello . . . quiet piano . . . clarinet accompanied by piano, etc. Make every effort to not distract from the experience. Include times of silence where no music is being played in order to give the visitor time to reflect and meditate.

Here are suggestions for stations:

LISTENING AND MEDITATION

Isaiah 50:4: Provide space in the stations booklet for journaling or sketching what God might be revealing to them.

REPENTANCE AND FORGIVENESS

Matthew 27:1–5: Challenge the participant to make this evening a turning point in their life as they repent and accept the fact that Jesus willingly hung on a tree and died so that they wouldn't have to.

THE WEIGHT OF THE CROSS

Psalm 38:4: There should be a heavy beam at this station. Encourage the participant to lift the beam and feel its weight. As they bear this weight, they should name the burdens they are carrying. Prompt them to thank Jesus Christ for taking their place in bearing their burdens. As they set the beam back in place, encourage them to leave the burdens where they belong. We were never meant to carry these alone, so leave them at the cross. Trust them to the finished work of Christ.

PARTICIPATION (COMMUNION)

1 Corinthians 10:16-17; Luke 22:19; 1 Corinthians 11:23-26: When we observe communion, we show our participation in the body of Christ. His life becomes our life and we become members with each other. Encourage the participant to ask God to reveal any unresolved sin issues in their life before taking communion. Take the time and necessary steps to repent and ask forgiveness. When they are ready, either alone or preferably with others, they should tear off a piece of bread from the loaf, dip it into the bowl, and participate in communion.

SHINE MY LIGHT

Matthew 5:14-16: Encourage the participant to bring to light the abilities they've been too shy or embarrassed to let shine before now. Light a candle as they commit to shine bright in your hurting and lost world.

EXCHANGE ANXIETY FOR PEACE

Philippians 4:6-7: Create a prayer wall for prayer requests to be offered. Establish a prayer team to pray through the prayer requests within a few days of the event.

PALMS

John 12:12-13 and Matthew 27:22-23: How ironic that the very outstretched hands that waved palm branches in honoring Jesus as king would be the very hands turned to closed fists and guilty of crucifying him. Provide palm buds for the participant to fold into the shape of a cross. Instructions can be found on the internet.

TRANSPARENCY

John 4:23: Create a three-sided box approximately seven feet high by five feet wide. Spread white bed sheets around the frame. Place two flood lights on the open end shining into the box. Encourage the participant to step into the box, all the while praying for the courage to be fully honest before God and others. Ask them to think about what they need to be transparent about. Provide thick Sharpie markers and ask them to write it on the "wall" in the light of God's love.

EASTER SATURDAY/VIGIL

SCRIPTURE PRESENTATION

WHAT WONDROUS LOVE IS THIS

with portions of Psalm 22 & Isaiah 53

CAST:

2 Voices
Congregation sings hymn verses

VOICE 1:

My God, my God, why have you forsaken me?
Why are you so far from saving me, from the words of my groaning?
O my God, I cry by day, but you do not answer,
and by night, but I find no rest.

VOICE 2:

Yet you are holy, enthroned on the praises of Israel.
In you our fathers trusted; they trusted, and you delivered them.
To you they cried and were rescued;
in you they trusted and were not put to shame.

HYMN VERSE 1:

What wondrous love is this, O my soul, O my soul?
What wondrous love is this, O my soul?

VOICE 1:

But I am a worm and not a man,
scorned by mankind and despised by the people.

All who see me mock me; they make mouths at me; they wag their heads;
"He trusts in the Lord; let him deliver him;
let him rescue him, for he delights in him!"

HYMN VERSE 2:

When I was sinking down, sinking down, sinking down,
When I was sinking down, sinking down . . .

VOICE 2:

He was despised and rejected by men,
a man of sorrows and acquainted with grief;
and as one from whom men hide their faces
he was despised, and we esteemed him not.
Surely he has borne our griefs and carried our sorrows;
yet we esteemed him stricken, smitten by God, and afflicted.

VOICE 1:

But he was pierced for our transgressions;
he was crushed for our iniquities;
upon him was the chastisement that brought us peace,
and with his wounds we are healed.
All we like sheep have gone astray;
we have turned—every one—to his own way;
and the Lord has laid on him the iniquity of us all.
He was oppressed, and he was afflicted, yet he opened not his mouth;
like a lamb that is led to the slaughter,
and like a sheep that before its shearers is silent, so he opened not his mouth.

HYMN VERSE 3:

To God and to the Lamb, I will sing, I will sing.
To God and to the Lamb, I will sing.

VOICE 2:

Yet it was the will of the Lord to crush him;
he has put him to grief;
when his soul makes an offering for guilt,
he shall see his offspring; he shall prolong his days;
the will of the Lord shall prosper in his hand.
Out of the anguish of his soul he shall see and be satisfied;
by his knowledge shall the righteous one, my servant,

make many to be accounted righteous, and he shall bear their iniquities.

VOICES 1 & 2 together:
All the ends of the earth shall remember and turn to the Lord,
and all the families of the nations shall worship before you.

VOICE 1:
it shall be told of the Lord to the coming generation;

VOICE 2:
they shall come and proclaim his righteousness to a people yet unborn, that
...

VOICES 1 & 2 together:
he has done it.

HYMN VERSE 4:
And when from death I'm free, I'll sing on, I'll sing on!
And when from death I'm free, I'll sing on!

WHAT WONDROUS LOVE IS THIS

Words: American Folk Hymn (Anonymous); Music: William Walker's *Southern Harmony*, 1835
Public Domain

CHAPTER 11

EASTER

WHILE MANY ASSUME THAT Easter is just one day, the Christian year is designed to celebrate Easter for fifty days. During these days, the church celebrates Christ's resurrection, remembers the post-resurrection appearances of Christ, celebrates Christ's ascension into heaven, the coming of the Spirit at Pentecost, and begins to explore the implications of the resurrection for the future of God's kingdom.

The tone of Easter is drastically different than that of Lent. While Lent is characterized by austerity, Easter is a most joyous occasion. It is a season of the Alleluia, which serves as a hopeful sign of the time when we shall do nothing but praise God. James White quotes Augustine:

> *These days after the Lord's resurrection form a period, not of labor, but of peace and joy. That is why there is no fasting and we pray standing, which is a sign of resurrection. This practice is observed at the altar on all Sundays, and the Alleluia is sung, to indicate that our future occupation is to be no other than the praise of God.*[71]

The times of self-examination and reflection throughout the season of Lent are replaced by praise and celebration.

Although details on the origin of Easter are unclear, scholars widely agree that the celebration of the resurrection of the Lord became a standard annual observance very early in the life of the church. In fact, there are good reasons to believe that Christians would have observed the resurrection the very next year after the Crucifixion. In addition to the weekly Sunday

---

71. White, *Introduction to Christian Worship*, 61–62.

memorial of the death and resurrection of Christ ("Resurrection Day"),[72] there seems also to have been an annual commemoration of the *Pascha* (Passover). Although there is no clear mention of an annual commemoration in Scripture, the writings of the early church fathers regularly used the word *Pascha* to refer to the crucifixion/resurrection event and the new meaning for Christians: "For Christ, our paschal lamb, has been sacrificed" (1 Cor 5:7 NRSV). Those belonging to Christ are free of the "old leaven" and have become new "unleavened bread." Thus, the Apostle Paul appeals to us saying, "Let us, therefore, celebrate the festival, not with old leaven, the leaven of malice and evil, but with the unleavened bread of sincerity and truth" (1 Cor 5:8). This new meaning given to the Jewish feast suggests that during the days of the Jewish Passover the apostolic communities celebrated the memory of the Christian paschal mystery with heightened intensity.[73]

The season of Easter is also referred to as "the Great Fifty Days," comprised of eight Sundays. It is no mistake that this season consists of fifty days as it is based on the Jewish festival of fifty days that began the harvest season two days after the start of Passover and extended until what came to be called the Day of Pentecost (the Greek word for "fiftieth").

The eight Sundays of Easter traditionally include:
- Easter Sunday
  The greatest Sunday in the history of the church—*the* Resurrection Day! The event of Jesus' resurrection was so important for those who followed Christ's teaching, that the day of meeting was changed from Saturday to Sunday to commemorate his resurrection.
- The Second Sunday of Easter
  The Apostle Thomas was not at Jesus' appearance after his resurrection and questioned the resurrection. The focus of this day, however, is not on the doubt of Thomas, but the graciousness he received from Jesus and the graciousness that God continues to show to us (see John 20:24–29).
- The Third Sunday of Easter
  Post-resurrection Jesus eats with the disciples (see Luke 24:41–43), with those in Emmaus (see Luke 24:30) and on the shore of Tiberius

---

72. The Jewish Passover feast had been fixed on the 14th Nisan and could, therefore, fall on any day of the week. But since the triumphal conclusion of the Passion, the Resurrection, had immediately acquired pre-eminent position in the minds of Christian communities it was inevitable that they would change the Passover celebration to a Sunday. In the West, the change had already been completed by the second half of the second century. In the East, the process took much longer and led to what is called the *Paschal controversy* as serious divisions occurred between the conservative and progressive groups of the church.

73. Adam, *The Liturgical Year*, 58.

(see John 21:9–14). These stories reveal the presence of Christ that we celebrate in Eucharist.
- The Fourth Sunday of Easter
A reprise of ancient practice of focusing on God as the "Good Shepherd" as a metaphor for divine care (see John 10 and Psalm 23).
- The Fifth Sunday of Easter
This Sunday points to the fact that 1) there is a continuity between the Risen One and the God at the burning bush (see Exod 3:2–4) and 2) just as the Jews refused to speak the name "I AM" (see Exod 13:13–15), there is a holy grandeur to the resurrection.
- The Sixth Sunday of Easter
Preparations are being made for the Ascension, the day in which Jesus returned to heaven following his post-resurrection appearances (Acts 1:9).
- The Seventh Sunday of Easter
This Sunday focuses on the great high priestly prayer in which Jesus prays "that all may be one"—a call for unity (John 17:11); in many congregations, this day is instead observed as Ascension Day (see Acts 1:9). Since Ascension Day (forty days after Easter Sunday) falls on a Thursday, churches may choose to celebrate Ascension either on the Sixth Sunday of Easter or the Seventh Sunday of Easter.
- The Final Sunday of Easter
This is Pentecost Sunday and celebrates the coming of the Holy Spirit and the calling of the church by the Spirit of the Risen One (see Acts 2:1–47).

The Biblical precedent for a fifty-day Easter season is found when Jesus met with his disciples and taught about his kingdom over the course of forty days after his resurrection, preparing his disciples for the coming of the Holy Spirit ten days later (Acts 2:1–47). With this history of the post-resurrection account, Easter developed into the seven-week season celebrated today.

According to Robert Webber, Easter includes these two facets: God makes all things new, and we have been raised with Christ. He also claimed that,

> in the postmodern world of violence and uncertainty, there is a great need to recover the Christus Victor theme that God in Christ has defeated all the powers of evil, that he has conclusively abolished sin, death, and all that is evil in the world, and that because of his death and resurrection, he will return for his final victory

over all that is evil and set up his kingdom and reign over all the earth.[74]

Thomas Talley agrees, "Pascha itself is celebration of Christ's victorious passion and death, his resurrection and ascension, and the sending of the Spirit upon the church,"[75] which is known as Pentecost.

The Season of Easter is filled with significant events as Jesus continues his ministry post-resurrection, yet pre-glorification. Three important events within the season of Easter which we must take notice is, of course, Easter Sunday, Ascension of Jesus, and Pentecost.

The Ascension of Jesus, which occurs forty days after his resurrection, celebrated Jesus returning to his Father. A regular occurrence of celebrating the Ascension began near the end of the fourth century in several places, including Antioch, Nyssa, and northern Italy, and became almost universal early in the fifth century.

As we have observed, Pentecost, occurring fifty days after Jesus' resurrection, was a well-established feast known as the Feast of Weeks, celebrated by the Jewish community for centuries even before Jesus' time. During the year of Jesus' death and resurrection, thousands of Jews gathered in Jerusalem to participate in the Jewish harvest festival known as Pentecost.

On the tenth day after Jesus' ascension, about one hundred twenty of his followers were gathered together in a room, expecting to partake in the festivities. However, their plans took an unexpected turn when the Holy Spirit descended from heaven, giving birth to the church on earth. God the Father sent his Spirit to indwell his people, bringing forth the harvest known as the church.

Early Christian author Tertullian addresses Pentecost in his treatise on baptism, where he describes it as a "most joyous period" (*laetissimum spatium*),

> *because the Lord's resurrection was celebrated among the disciples and the grace of the Holy Spirit was inaugurated and the hope of the Lord's coming indicated, because it was then, when he had been take back into heaven, the angels told the apostles that he would come exactly as he had gone up into heaven—meaning, of course, during the Pentecost.*[76]

---

74. Webber, *Ancient-Future Worship*, 86.
75. Talley, *The Origins of the Liturgical Year*, 57.
76. Tertullian, *De baptismo*, 91.

It is evident that the whole fifty-day Easter season celebrated the resurrection and ascension of Jesus and the gift of the Holy Spirit at Pentecost, looking ahead to Christ's coming in glory.

The first evidence of a special feast to commemorate the gift of the Holy Spirit comes from the fourth century. The earliest testimony to the feast links the descent of the Spirit to the ascent of Christ, which is a connection that continues to be made to this day; although a separate observance of the Ascension on the fortieth day is attested to only later than the evidence for the feast of Pentecost on the fiftieth.

The Easter season revolves around our resurrection spirituality. Through worship, we immerse ourselves in the pattern of Christ's death and resurrection, embracing the new life offered to us through his resurrection. This resurrection spirituality not only influences the manner in which we worship but also impacts our daily lives and how we choose to live.

INCORPORATING EASTER:

This may not seem a difficult task as most churches celebrate Easter. My encouragement is to not limit the celebration of the risen Christ to only Easter Sunday, but to continue the celebration for the entire eight Sundays of the Easter season, culminating with a focus on Pentecost. You don't have to create fully produced Easter celebration services each of the eight Sundays, but an acknowledgement of Jesus' resurrection, such as, "As we continue celebrating our risen Lord and Savior, Jesus Christ . . ." would remind the congregation that the resurrection season continues.

Sing Easter songs after Easter Sunday. "Christ Arose" or "Jesus Is Alive" is just as appropriate on the Sundays after Easter Sunday.

Be sure to observe Ascension (forty days after Easter Sunday) and Pentecost (fifty days after Easter Sunday). The Ascension of Jesus is important for our spiritual faith formation as we remember Jesus returning to heaven, now seated at the right hand of the Father. For Pentecost, incorporate Scripture readings and songs in various languages within the church worship service. Consider decorating the worship space with flames or mission's themes. For example, red ribbon hanging from the ceiling is a great visual reminder of the flames of fire on the disciples' heads. These are important days in the life of the church. Let's not ignore them.

EASTER SUNDAY

OVERVIEW

TIME

A fifty-day season that commences on the evening before Easter Sunday and extends for seven Sundays until Pentecost. In the Protestant church, Easter Sunday is observed on the Sunday after the first full moon following the Spring equinox (March 21), as per the Gregorian calendar. Conversely, the Orthodox church celebrates Easter Sunday according to the Julian calendar, on the Sunday after the first full moon following Passover, which falls between April 4 and May 8.

THEMES

The greatest Sunday in the history of the church—*the* Resurrection Day! Christ is risen! He is risen indeed! At Easter we believe in these two facets: God makes all things new, and we have been raised with Christ. All year long, but particularly on Easter Sunday, we join Christ in his resurrection as those who have been raised to new life in Christ.

SPIRITUAL CHALLENGE

Embrace the death of Jesus, freeing you from sin, and rise to a life filled with the Spirit through resurrection spirituality.

SCRIPTURE

- Old Testament: Isa 25:6–9
- Psalm: Ps 114; Ps 118:1–2, 14–24
- New Testament: 1 Cor 5:6b–8; Col 3:1–4
- Gospel: Matt 28:1–7; Mark 16:1–8; Luke 24:1–12; John 20:1–18

SYMBOLS

- Empty tomb
- New life

COLORS

- White
- Gold

EASTER SUNDAY

SONG LIST

CONTEMPORARY

Alive Forever Amen David Moffitt, Sue C. Smith, and Travis Cottrell, 2003

All the Earth Will Sing Your Praises Paul Baloche, 2003

Because He Lives (Amen) Ed Cash, Gloria Gaither, Jason Ingram, Matt Maher, Daniel Carson, William Gaither, and Chris Tomlin, 2014

Christ Be Magnified Cody Carnes, Cory Asbury, and Ethan Hulse, 2019

Christ Is Risen Matt Maher and Mia Fieldes, 2009

Christ the Lord Is Risen Today (He Is Not Dead) Charles Wesley, Kurtis Parks, and Samuel Arnold, 2014

Christ Our Hope in Life and Death Keith Getty, Matt Boswell, Jordan Kauflin, Matthew Merker, and Matt Papa, 2020

Come Behold the Wondrous Mystery Matt Boswell, Matt Papa, and Michael Bleecker, 2012

Come People of the Risen King Keith Getty, Kristyn Getty, and Stuart Townend, 2007

Glorious Day Kristian Stanfill, Jason Ingram, Jonathan Smith, and Sean Curran, 2017

Great Things Jonas Myrin and Phil Wickham, 2018

Happy Day Tim Hughes and Ben Cantelon, 2006

He Is Lord Steve Vest, 1969

He Lives Anthony Skinner, Chris McClarney, and Jonathan Smith, 2019

In Christ Alone Keith Getty and Stuart Townend, 2001

In Jesus' Name Darlene Zschech and Israel Houghton, 2013

It Was Finished Upon That Cross Jonny Robinson, Nigel Hendroff, and Rich Thompson, 2021

Jesus Is Alive Ron Kenoly, 1987

Jesus Messiah Daniel Carson, Chris Tomlin, Ed Cash, and Jesse Reeves, 2008

The Lamb Has Overcome Travis Cottrell, David Moffitt, and Sue C. Smith, 2005

Man of Sorrows Brooke Ligertwood and Matt Crocker, 2012

Mighty to Save Ben Fielding and Reuben Morgan, 2006

My Redeemer Lives Reuben Morgan, 1998

My Savior Lives Jon Egan and Glenn Packiam, 2006

O Praise the Name (Anástasis) Marty Sampson, Benjamin Hastings, and Dean Ussher, 2015

Praise the King Corey Voss, Michael Bryce Jr., Michael Farren, and Dustin Smith, 2014

Resurrection Day Matt Maher, 2005

Turn Your Eyes George Romanacce, Kevin Winebarger, Nathan Stiff, and Nic Trout, 2019

What I See Jason Ingram, Pat Barrett, Chris Brown, Steven Furtick, 2022

TRADITIONAL

Because He Lives Gloria Gaither and William Gaither, 1971

Christ Arose Robert Lowry, 1874

Christ the Lord Is Risen Today Charles Wesley, 1739

Crown Him with Many Crowns Matthew Bridges, 1851

He Lives Alfred H. Ackley, 1933

I Know That My Redeemer Lives Samuel Medley, 1775

One Day J. Wilbur Chapman, 1910

Rejoice, the Lord Is King Charles Wesley, 1744

Worship Christ, the Risen King Jack Hayford, 1986

PRESENTATIONAL

Death Was Arrested Adam Kersh, Brandon Coker, Heath Balltzglier, Paul Taylor Smith, 2015

Easter Song Annie Herring, 1974

He's Alive Don Francisco, 1977

My Jesus Anne Wilson, Jeff Pardo, and Matthew West, 2021

Our Heart Still Burns D.A. Carson and Matt Boswell, 2013

Redeemer Nicole C. Mullen, 2000

Resurrection Hymn Keith Getty and Stuart Townend, 2003

GLOBAL

À Toi la Gloire, O Ressuscité (Thine Is the Glory) Edmond Budry, 1884 (France)

Cristo Vive (Christ Is Risen) Nicolas Martinez, 1962 (Argentina)

Hallelujah Dumisani Maraire (Zimbabwe)

Mfurahini, haleluya (Christ Has Arisen, Alleluia) Bernard Kyamanywa, 1968 (Tanzania)

Oh, Qué Bueno Es Jesús (Oh, How Good Is Christ the Lord) Dale Grotenhuis, 1985 (Puerto Rico)

Цар воскреслий *(Risen King)* Jonathan Markey, 2015 (Ukraine)

Yessu Jee Utheya (Jesus Is Risen) Nadir Shamir Khan (Pakistan)

EASTER SUNDAY
WORSHIP SERVICE

CALL TO WORSHIP

Good morning church! No, this is a great morning. The greatest day in human history. For generations the church has had a call and response phrase to celebrate the resurrection of Jesus. It begins by proclaiming "Christ is risen!" and the response is "He is risen indeed!" Let's try it: [Say it three times building in excitement each time.]

LEADER:

Christ is risen!

CONGREGATION:

He is risen indeed!

LEADER:

Christ is risen!

CONGREGATION:

He is risen indeed!

LEADER:

Christ is risen!

CONGREGATION:

He is risen indeed!

CHRIST AROSE

Written by Robert Lowry, 1847; Arrangement by Ryan Dahl and Dan Galbraith. © 2008 PraiseCharts

GREAT THINGS

Words and Music by Jonas Myrin and Phil Wickham
© 2018 Capitol CMG Paragon; Son of the Lion; Phil Wickham Music; Simply Global Songs; Sing My Songs

OPENING PRAYER

God, we rejoice for the stone is rolled away and we behold the empty tomb. We rejoice for Scripture has been fulfilled, the sting of death is gone, the victory has been won, and we behold the risen Christ. Father, we rejoice because you have provided the Way. We rejoice because of Jesus and the eternal life he has secured for us. We rejoice because your Spirit has breathed new life into our souls. Amen.

SCRIPTURE PRESENTATION

Luke 24:1–35

CAST:

3 Voices

VOICE 1:

But on the first day of the week,

VOICES 2 & 3:

at early dawn,

VOICE 1:

they went to the tomb, taking the spices they had prepared.

VOICE 2:

And they found the stone rolled away from the tomb,

VOICE 3:

but when they went in

VOICE 2:

they did not find the body of the Lord Jesus. While they were perplexed about this,

VOICES 1 & 3:

behold,

VOICE 2:

two men stood by them in dazzling apparel.

VOICE 1:

And as they were frightened and bowed their faces to the ground, the men said to them,

VOICES 2 & 3:

"Why do you seek the living among the dead? He is not here, but has risen.

VOICE 2:

Remember how he told you, while he was still in Galilee, that the Son of Man must be delivered into the hands of sinful men and be crucified and on the third day rise."

VOICE 1:

And they remembered his words, and returning from the tomb they told all these things to the eleven and to all the rest.

VOICE 3:

Now it was Mary Magdalene and Joanna and Mary the mother of James and the other women with them who told these things to the apostles,

VOICE 2:

but these words seemed to them an idle tale, and they did not believe them.

VOICE 3:

But Peter rose and ran to the tomb; stooping and looking in, he saw the linen cloths by themselves; and he went home marveling at what had happened.

VOICE 1:

That very day two of them were going to a village named Emmaus,

VOICE 3:

about seven miles from Jerusalem,

VOICE 1:

and they were talking with each other about all these things that had happened.

VOICE 2:

While they were talking and discussing together, Jesus himself drew near and went with them.

VOICE 3:

But their eyes were kept from recognizing him.

VOICE 2:

And he said to them,

VOICE 1:

"What is this conversation that you are holding with each other as you walk?"

VOICE 2:

And they stood still, looking sad. Then one of them, named Cleopas, answered him,

VOICE 3:

"Are you the only visitor to Jerusalem who does not know the things that have happened there in these days?"

VOICE 2:

And he said to them,

VOICE 1:

"What things?"

VOICE 2:

And they said to him,

VOICE 3:

"Concerning Jesus of Nazareth, a man who was a prophet mighty in deed and word before God and all the people, and how our chief priests and rulers

delivered him up to be condemned to death, and crucified him. But we had hoped that he was the one to redeem Israel. Yes, and besides all this, it is now the third day since these things happened. Moreover, some women of our company amazed us. They were at the tomb early in the morning, and when they did not find his body, they came back saying that they had even seen a vision of angels, who said that he was alive. Some of those who were with us went to the tomb and found it just as the women had said, but him they did not see."

VOICE 2:

And he said to them,

VOICE 1:

"O foolish ones, and slow of heart to believe all that the prophets have spoken! Was it not necessary that the Christ should suffer these things and enter into his glory?"

VOICE 2:

And beginning with Moses and all the Prophets, he interpreted to them in all the Scriptures the things concerning himself. So they drew near to the village to which they were going. He acted as if he were going farther, but they urged him strongly, saying,

VOICE 3:

"Stay with us, for it is toward evening and the day is now far spent."

VOICE 2:

So he went in to stay with them.

VOICE 1:

When he was at table with them, he took the bread and blessed and broke it and gave it to them.

VOICE 2:

And their eyes were opened, and they recognized him. And he vanished from their sight. They said to each other,

VOICE 3:

"Did not our hearts burn within us while he talked to us on the road, while he opened to us the Scriptures?"

VOICE 2:

And they rose that same hour and returned to Jerusalem. And they found the eleven and those who were with them gathered together, saying,

VOICE 3:

"The Lord has risen indeed, and has appeared to Simon!"

VOICE 1:

Then they told what had happened on the road, and how he was known to them in the breaking of the bread.

CHRIST THE LORD IS RISEN TODAY

Words by Charles Wesley, 1739; Music: EASTER HYMN, 1708
Public Domain

CHRIST OUR HOPE IN LIFE AND DEATH

Words and Music by Keith Getty, Matt Boswell, Jordan Kauflin, Matthew Merker, and Matt Papa
© 2020 Getty Music Publishing, Messenger Hymns, Jordan Kauflin Music, Matthew Merker Music, Getty Music Hymns and Songs, Love Your Enemies Publishing

OFFERING PRAYER

Heavenly Father, on this glorious Easter Sunday, we come before you with hearts brimming with joy and gratitude. We celebrate the victory of your Son, Jesus Christ, over sin and death, and we rejoice in the promise of new life found in his resurrection.

As we gather to proclaim the empty tomb and the triumph of your love, we offer our worship and adoration, giving thanks for the precious gift of salvation through Jesus' sacrifice. On this momentous day, we are reminded of the immeasurable depth of your love for us. We offer our gifts and offerings with hearts overflowing with thankfulness for the hope and eternal life we have through Jesus Christ.

As we celebrate the Resurrection, may the power of the risen Lord transform our lives. May we live as people of hope, shining your light and love to a world in need of healing and redemption. In this Easter season, we seek your guidance to follow in the footsteps of Christ, living lives of compassion, forgiveness, and love towards others.

Bless these offerings, that they may be used to spread the message of Easter hope to all corners of the earth, and to bring comfort and relief to those who are suffering.

In the name of Jesus, our risen Savior, we pray. Amen.

OFFERTORY

REDEEMER

Words and Music by Nicole Mullen
© 2000 Lil'Jas'Music and Curb Wordspring Music

PRAYER OF ILLUMINATION

O Gracious God, as we gather on this momentous Easter Sunday, our hearts are filled with anticipation and joy, seeking the illumination of your divine truth. In the celebration of Christ's resurrection, may your light shine brightly upon us, revealing the profound depth of your love and grace. In the victory over death and sin, may we find hope and assurance of new life, through the resurrection of our Lord and Savior, Jesus Christ.
As we hear the familiar story of the empty tomb, may it resound in our souls with transformative power, stirring us to live as Easter people, filled with faith and hope. Illuminate the corners of our hearts that need healing, and let your light dispel any darkness or doubt as we embrace the promise of redemption and forgiveness. As we gather with joyous hearts and voices, may the message of Easter inspire us to proclaim the good news of Christ's triumph to all the world.

We offer this prayer with gratitude and adoration, in the name of Jesus Christ, our risen Lord, Amen.

SERMON

[If observing the Lord's Supper, continue. If not, proceed to the next congregational song.]

THE LORD'S SUPPER INSTRUCTIONS AND INVITATION

[Instrumental music played or congregational singing.]

THE MYSTERY OF FAITH

And so, in remembrance of these your mighty acts in Jesus Christ, we offer ourselves in praise and thanksgiving as a holy and living sacrifice, in union with Christ's offering for us, as we proclaim the mystery of faith:

CONGREGATION:

Christ has died; Christ is risen; Christ will come again.

GLORIOUS DAY

Words and Music by Kristian Stanfill, Jason Ingram, Jonathan Smith, and Sean Curran
© 2017 KPS 1.0, sixsteps Music, sixsteps Songs, Sounds Of Jericho, Worship Together Music, worshiptogether.com songs, Fellow Ships Music, Hickory Bill Doc, So Essential Tunes

BENEDICTION

May the loving power of God, which raised Jesus to new life, strengthen you in hope, enrich you with his love, and fill you with joy in the faith. Go, in the peace of God, our Father, his risen Son, and the Holy Spirit.

EASTER SUNDAY
SCRIPTURE PRESENTATION

IMMORTAL, INVISIBLE, THE ONLY GOD

1 Timothy 1:1–17

CAST:

4 Voices

VOICE 1:

Listen to these words from the Apostle Paul to his co-worker Timothy:

VOICE 2:

Grace,

VOICE 3:

mercy,

VOICE 4:

and peace

VOICE 3:

from God the Father

VOICE 2:

and Christ Jesus our Lord.

VOICE 1:

As I urged you when I was going to Macedonia, remain at Ephesus so that you may charge certain persons not to teach any different doctrine, nor to devote themselves to myths and endless genealogies, which promote speculations rather than the stewardship from God that is by faith.

VOICE 2:

The aim of our charge is love that issues from a pure heart and a good conscience and a sincere faith.

VOICE 3:

Certain persons, by swerving from these, have wandered away into vain discussion, desiring to be teachers of the law, without understanding either what they are saying or the things about which they make confident assertions.

VOICE 4:

Now we know that the law is good, if one uses it lawfully, understanding this, that the law is not laid down for the just but for the lawless and disobedient, for the ungodly and sinners, for the unholy and profane, for those who strike their fathers and mothers, for murderers, the sexually immoral, men who practice homosexuality, enslavers, liars, perjurers, and whatever else is contrary to sound doctrine, in accordance with the gospel of the glory of the blessed God with which I have been entrusted.

VOICE 1:

I thank him who has given me strength,

ALL:

Christ Jesus our Lord,

VOICE 1:

because he judged me faithful, appointing me to his service, though formerly I was a blasphemer, persecutor, and insolent opponent.

VOICE 2:

But I received mercy because I had acted ignorantly in unbelief, and the grace of our Lord overflowed for me with the faith and love that are in Christ Jesus.

VOICE 3:

The saying is trustworthy and deserving of full acceptance,

VOICE 1:

that Christ Jesus came into the world to save sinners, of whom I am the foremost.

VOICE 2:

of whom I am the foremost.

VOICE 3:

I am the foremost.

VOICE 4:

I'm the foremost.

VOICE 1:

But I received

ALL:

mercy

VOICE 1:

for this reason, that in me, as the foremost, Jesus Christ might display his perfect patience as an example to those who were to believe in him for eternal life.

VOICE 2:

To the King of the ages,

VOICE 3:

immortal,

VOICE 4:

invisible,

VOICE 3:

the only God,

VOICE 2:

be honor and glory forever and ever.

VOICE 1:

Amen.

VOICE 2:

Amen.

VOICE 3:

Amen.

VOICE 4:

Amen.

VOICE 1:

And everyone said . . .

ALL:

Amen.

ASCENSION SUNDAY

OVERVIEW

TIME

Forty days following Easter Sunday—falls on a Thursday. You may decide to celebrate on the Sunday before or Sunday after Ascension Day.

THEMES

The ascension of Jesus to heaven forty days following his resurrection from the dead. Celebrating this event should be a momentous occasion. The ascension represents the climactic and crowning moment of his exaltation, serving as a necessary precursor to his ongoing work through the Spirit and the church. Furthermore, the ascension foreshadows the ultimate event in salvation history: Jesus' personal, physical, and glorious return from heaven.

SPIRITUAL CHALLENGE

Keep one eye to the sky in anticipation of Jesus' return and one eye to those around you being a faithful and true witness for Jesus Christ.

SCRIPTURE

- Old Testament: None
- Psalm: Ps 47; Ps 93
- New Testament: Acts 1:1–11; Eph 1:15–23; Eph 2:4–7; Heb 1:3–4
- Gospel: Luke 24:44–53

SYMBOLS

- Rising dove
- Breaking chains

COLORS
- White
- Gold

ASCENSION SUNDAY
SONG LIST

CONTEMPORARY

Across the Lands Keith Getty and Stuart Townend, 2002

Awesome Is the Lord Most High Chris Tomlin, Jesse Reeves, Cary Pierce, and Jon Abel, 2006

Be Unto Your Name Lynn DeShazo and Gary Sadler, 1998

Before the Throne of God Above Charitie Lees Bancroft and Vicki Cook, 1997

Behold the Lamb Phil Wickham, Kristian Stanfill, and Melodie Malone, 2019

Behold Our God Jonathan Baird, Meghan Baird, Ryan Baird, and Stephen Altrogge, 2011

Christ Be Magnified Cody Carnes, Cory Asbury, and Ethan Hulse, 2019

Glory Honor Power Jeff Pardo, Tiffany Hammer, and Melody Noel, 2021

He Is Exalted Twila Paris, 1985

Here I Am to Worship Tim Hughes, 2000

I See the Lord Chris Falson, 1992

I Will Rise Chris Tomlin, Jesse Reeves, and Louie Giglio, 2008

Lord, I Lift Your Name on High Rick Founds, 1989

Majesty Jack Hayford, 1981

Open the Eyes of My Heart Paul Baloche, 1997

Shout to the Lord Darlene Zschech, 1993

Soon and Very Soon Andrae Crouch, 1971

Such An Awesome God Heath Balltzglier, Mitch Wong, Jonathan Jay, and Johnny Hamilton, 2020

There Is a Higher Throne Keith Getty and Kristyn Getty, 2002

We Fall Down Chris Tomlin, 1998

We Will Glorify Twila Paris, 1982

Worthy You Are Worthy Don Moen, 1986

TRADITIONAL

A Hymn of Glory Let Us Sing The Venerable Bede, 7th century

All Hail the Power of Jesus' Name Edward Perronet, 1780

Alleluia! Sing to Jesus W. Chatterton Dix, 1866

At the Name of Jesus Caroline M. Noel, 1870

Blessing and Honor Horatius Bonar, 1858

Crown Him with Many Crowns Matthew Bridges; George J. Elvey, 1851

Higher Ground Johnson Oatman, Jr., 1898)

Jesus Shall Reign Where'er the Sun Isaac Watts, 1719

Rejoice the Lord Is King Charles Wesley, 1744

PRESENTATIONAL

Jesus Lord Ascend Thy Throne Isaac Watts, 1806; alt. Jered McKenna, 2012

Jesus, My All to Heav'n Has Gone John Cennick, 1743; R. R. Osborne, 1850; arr. Bruce Benedict, 2010

Lord Enthroned in Heavenly Splendor George Hugh Bourne, 1874; add'l chorus by Zac Hicks, 2012

We Believe (Apostle's Creed) Keith Getty, Kristyn Getty, and Stuart Townend, 2016

GLOBAL

Badlan De Takht Te (On the Throne of Clouds) Marqus Fida, 2021 (Pakistan)

El Cielo Canta Alegría (Heaven Is Singing for Joy) Pablo D. Sosa, 1991 (Argentina)

Jesús, Es Mi Rey Soberano (Our King and Our Sovereign, Lord Jesus)
  Vicente Mendoza, 1920 (Mexico)

Thuma Mina (Send Me, Lord) South African Spiritual, 1984 (South
  Africa)

ASCENSION SUNDAY
WORSHIP SERVICE

CALL TO WORSHIP

Last Thursday was Ascension Day [or "this Thursday is," depending on when you are observing the Ascension], the fortieth day after Easter Sunday. An article in Christianity Today online said this:

"The Ascension is often underrated and undervalued by evangelicals. We make a big deal of Christ's coming at Christmas, celebrating with gifts, baked goods, and carols. With solemn services we mourn his horrific death on Good Friday. And with exuberant celebration, we rejoice in his resurrection on Easter Sunday, with glorious services, extravagant bouquets of flowers, Easter eggs, and big hunks of glazed ham. But to Christ's farewell we give very little attention—if any at all."

The book of Hebrews tells us that:
After making purification for sins, he sat down at the right hand of the Majesty on high, having become as much superior to angels as the name he has inherited is more excellent than theirs.
Hebrews 1:3b–4

That's big news! So, let's magnify the name of our Lord Jesus, allowing the words of "Crown Him with Many Crowns" to verbalize the magnificent truth of our ascended and reigning Lord.

CROWN HIM WITH MANY CROWNS

Words by Matthew Bridges, 1851; Music by George J. Elvey, DIADEMATA, 1868
Public Domain

OPENING PRAYER

Jesus, we thank you that our faith is based in the fact that right now in your glorified state you are seated on the throne of the universe, and you are the One who has all authority in heaven and on earth. We praise you, Jesus, the name above all names. We thank you for interceding on our behalf and making a way for us to be in right relationship with God the Father. We accept your call for us to be your witnesses here on earth until you return or call us home. Jesus, in your name we pray, Amen.

SCRIPTURE READING

So when they had come together, they asked him, "Lord, will you at this time restore the kingdom to Israel?" He said to them, "It is not for you to know times or seasons that the Father has fixed by his own authority. But you will receive power when the Holy Spirit has come upon you, and you will be my witnesses in Jerusalem and in all Judea and Samaria, and to the end of the earth." And when he had said these things, as they were looking on, he was lifted up, and a cloud took him out of their sight. And while they were gazing into heaven as he went, behold, two men stood by them in white robes, and said, "Men of Galilee, why do you stand looking into heaven? This Jesus, who was taken up from you into heaven, will come in the same way as you saw him go into heaven."
Acts 1:6–11

A HYMN OF GLORY LET US SING

The Venerable Bede, 7th century; Translated by Benjamin Webb
Public Domain

SCRIPTURE READING

But God, being rich in mercy, because of the great love with which he loved us, even when we were dead in our trespasses, made us alive together with Christ—by grace you have been saved— and raised us up with him and seated us with him in the heavenly places in Christ Jesus, so that in the coming ages he might show the immeasurable riches of his grace in kindness toward us in Christ Jesus.
Ephesians 2:4–7

BEFORE THE THRONE OF GOD ABOVE

Words by Charitie Bancroft; Music by Vicki Cook
© 1997 Sovereign Grace Worship

OFFERING PRAYER

Heavenly Father, on this Ascension Sunday, we come before you with hearts full of reverence and awe. We commemorate the glorious moment when your Son, Jesus Christ, ascended into heaven, triumphantly seated at your right hand. As we contemplate the significance of this day, we offer our worship and praise, acknowledging the majesty and authority of Jesus as the King of Kings and Lord of Lords.

We are grateful for the promise of the Holy Spirit, who was sent to empower and guide us in carrying out the mission entrusted to us by Christ. We offer our gifts and offerings with hearts that are eager to serve you faithfully and fulfill the Great Commission. As we celebrate the ascension of Jesus, may we be reminded of our calling to be ambassadors of Christ's love and grace in the world. Help us to share the good news of salvation with boldness and compassion, knowing that you are with us always.

Bless these offerings, that they may be used to advance your kingdom and bring glory to your name. May they be a tangible expression of our devotion and commitment to your work.

In the name of Jesus, who reigns in glory forever, we pray. Amen.

OFFERTORY

LORD ENTHRONED IN HEAVENLY SPLENDOR

George Hugh Bourne, 1874; Additional chorus by Zac Hicks, 2012
© 2012 Unbudding Fig Music

PRAYER OF ILLUMINATION

God be in our heads and in our understanding. God be in our eyes and in our looking. God be in our mouths and in our speaking. God be in our hearts and in our loving.
—from the *Sarum Primer*, 13th century

SERMON

[If observing the Lord's Supper, continue. If not, proceed to the next congregational song.]

THE LORD'S SUPPER INSTRUCTIONS AND INVITATION

[Instrumental music played or congregational singing.]

THE MYSTERY OF FAITH

And so, in remembrance of these your mighty acts in Jesus Christ, we offer ourselves in praise and thanksgiving as a holy and living sacrifice, in union with Christ's offering for us, as we proclaim the mystery of faith:

CONGREGATION:

Christ has died; Christ is risen; Christ will come again.

THERE IS A HIGHER THRONE

Words and Music by Keith Getty and Kristyn Getty
© 2002 Thankyou Music

BENEDICTION

People of God, let's not just stand here, gazing into heaven as the disciples did after they saw Jesus leave. Instead, let's take up the mission Jesus gave us: to be his witnesses, to tell everyone we meet who Jesus is, and how he has changed us. And may the grace of God, the love of Jesus Christ, and the presence of the Holy Spirit go with us all. Amen.

ASCENSION SUNDAY

SCRIPTURE PRESENTATION

CARRIED UP INTO HEAVEN

Luke 24:44–53 with Acts 1:10–11

CAST:

Narrator
3 Voices
Vocal ensemble (SATB)

NARRATOR:

Jesus said to them,

VOICE 1:

"These are my words that I spoke to you while I was still with you, that everything written about me in the Law of Moses and the Prophets and the Psalms must be fulfilled."

NARRATOR:

Then he opened their minds to understand the Scriptures, and said to them,

VOICE 1:

"Thus it is written, that the Christ should suffer and on the third day rise from the dead, and that repentance for the forgiveness of sins should be proclaimed in his name to all nations, beginning from Jerusalem. You are witnesses of these things. And behold, I am sending the promise of my Father upon you. But stay in the city until you are clothed with power from on high."

NARRATOR:

And he led them out as far as Bethany, and lifting up his hands he blessed them. While he blessed them, he parted from them and was carried up into heaven.

And while they were gazing into heaven as he went, behold, two men stood by them in white robes, and said,

VOICE 2:

"Men of Galilee, why do you stand looking into heaven?

VOICES 2 & 3: (together)

This Jesus, who was taken up from you into heaven,

VOICE 3:

will come in the same way as you saw him go into heaven."

NARRATOR:

And they worshiped Jesus and returned to Jerusalem with great joy, and were continually in the temple blessing God.

VOCAL ENSEMBLE:

[sung in 4 part harmony]
Praise God, from whom all blessings flow
Praise him, all creatures here below
Praise him above, ye heav'nly hosts
Praise Father, Son, and Holy Ghost
Amen.

PRAISE GOD FROM WHOM ALL BLESSINGS FLOW

Written by Thomas Ken, 1674
Public Domain

PENTECOST SUNDAY

OVERVIEW

TIME

Fifty days following Easter Sunday. The eighth Sunday of Easter.

THEMES

Celebrating Pentecost should be a joyous occasion. The observance of this day offers a great opportunity for the utilization of the arts within the worship gathering. The sermon should emphasize the Holy Spirit and the songs should be expressive of the work of the Holy Spirit.

SPIRITUAL CHALLENGE

Live with the power, boldness, and courage you need to accomplish your mission through the Holy Spirit.

SCRIPTURE

- Old Testament: Gen 11:1-9; Num 11:24-30; Ezek 37:1-14
- Psalm: Ps 104:24-34, 35b
- New Testament: Acts 2:1-21; Rom 8:14-17; Rom 8:22-27; 1 Cor 12:3b-13
- Gospel: John 7:37-39; John 14:8-17, (25-27); John 15:26- 27, 16:4b-15; John 20:19-23

SYMBOLS

- Wind
- Fire/Flame
- Dove

COLORS

- Red

PENTECOST SUNDAY
SONG LIST

CONTEMPORARY

All Who Are Thirsty Brenton Brown and Glenn Robertson, 1998

Ancient of Days Gary Sadler and Jamie Harvill, 1992

Awakening Chris Tomlin and Reuben Morgan, 2010

Consuming Fire Tim Hughes, 2002

Create in Me a Clean Heart Keith Green, 1984

Holy Spirit, Living Breath of God Keith Getty and Stuart Townend, 2006

King of Kings Brooke Ligertwood, Jason Ingram, and Scott Ligertwood, 2018

Lift High the Name of Jesus Fionán de Barra, Ed Cash, Keith Getty, and Kristyn Getty, 2013

Light the Fire Again Brian Doerksen, 1994

O Church Arise Keith Getty and Stuart Townend, 2005

Open Our Eyes, Lord Robert Cull, 1976

Open the Eyes of My Heart Paul Baloche, 1997

Refiner's Fire Brian Doerksen, 1990

Shout to the North Martin Smith, 1995

The Power of Your Love Geoff Bullock, 1992

Throne Room Song May Angeles, Ryan Kennedy, Steven Musso, and The Emerging Sound, 2019

TRADITIONAL

Away With Our Fears Charles Wesley, 1749

Come, Holy Spirit, Heavenly Dove Isaac Watts, 1707

Come Thou Fount of Every Blessing Robert Robinson, 1758

Great Is Thy Faithfulness Thomas O. Chisholm, 1923

Holy Spirit, Truth Divine Samuel Longfellow, 1864

Open My Eyes That I May See Clara H. Scott, 1895

Praise, My Soul, the King of Heaven Henry F. Lyte, 1834

Spirit of the Living God Daniel Iverson, 1935

Sweet, Sweet Spirit Doris Akers, 1962

PRESENTATIONAL

Build Your Kingdom Here Chris Llewellyn, Gareth Gilkeson, and William Herron, 2011

Empty Me John Comer and Gene Way, 2003

Fill Me Up Will Reagan, 2008

Fire Kyle Lee, Dwan Hill, Cece Winans, 2021

He Reigns Peter Furler and Steve Tyler, 2003

Holy Spirit Come Bede Benjamin–Korporaal, Nick Herbert, and Patrick Mayberry, 2021

Holy Spirit, Come Wendell Kimbrough, 2009

Send It On Down Geron Davis, 1994

GLOBAL

Come, Holy Spirit The Iona Community, 1988 (Scotland)

Uyai Mose (Come, All You People) Alexander Gondo, 1986 (Zimbabwe)

Wa wa wa Emimimo (Come, O Holy Spirit, Come) Traditional (Nigeria)

Yakanaha Vangeri (Come Holy Spirit/Listen Now for the Gospel) Traditional (Zimbabwe)

PENTECOST SUNDAY
WORSHIP SERVICE

PRAISE TO THE LORD THE ALMIGHTY
Words and Music by Joachim Neander, 1680
Arrangement by Travis Cottrell © 1999 First Hand Revelation Music and van Ness Press

CALL TO WORSHIP
We've gathered to worship and celebrate Pentecost, the day when God first poured out his Spirit on the church, empowering them to be his witnesses across the globe. Today, we give praise to God that his church of more than two billion people has spread throughout the world. On the day of Pentecost, God reversed the curse of Babel. At Babel God confused the people by creating different languages. At Pentecost, God brings unity by giving his people the ability to speak in different languages so that others could understand the saving gospel. Here we see that God is a God for all people, for all nations!

Psalm 96 begins with these words:
Sing to the Lord a new song; sing to the Lord, all the earth.
Sing to the Lord, praise his name; proclaim his salvation day after day.
Declare his glory among the nations, his marvelous deeds among all peoples.
For great is the Lord and most worthy of praise.

"Declare his glory among the nations, his marvelous deeds among all peoples." Let's do that right now. Speak out some of the ways God has blessed you this past week . . .

EXPRESSIONS OF PRAISE FROM THE CONGREGATION
[Invite the congregation to share aloud what they're thankful to God for.]

Robert Robinson wrote this next hymn to pair with his sermon on Pentecost Sunday: "It was a prayer that the Holy Spirit flood into our hearts with his streams of mercy, enabling us to sing God's praises and remain faithful to him." [For more, see Robert J. Morgan's *Then Sings My Soul: 150 of the World's Greatest Hymn Stories*.]

Let's raise our voices and sing "Come Thou Fount of Every Blessing."

COME THOU FOUNT OF EVERY BLESSING
Words by Robert Robinson, 1758; Music: NETTLETON, 1843
Public Domain

SCRIPTURE READING

When the day of Pentecost arrived, they were all together in one place. And suddenly there came from heaven a sound like a mighty rushing wind, and it filled the entire house where they were sitting. And divided tongues as of fire appeared to them and rested on each one of them. And they were all filled with the Holy Spirit and began to speak in other tongues as the Spirit gave them utterance.
Now there were dwelling in Jerusalem Jews, devout men from every nation under heaven. And at this sound the multitude came together, and they were bewildered, because each one was hearing them speak in his own language. And they were amazed and astonished, saying, "Are not all these who are speaking Galileans? And how is it that we hear, each of us in his own native language? . . . we hear them telling in our own tongues the mighty works of God." And all were amazed and perplexed, saying to one another, "What does this mean?" Peter, standing with the eleven, lifted up his voice and addressed them . . . those who received his word were baptized, and there were added that day about three thousand souls.
And they devoted themselves to the apostles' teaching and the fellowship, to the breaking of bread and the prayers. And awe came upon every soul, and many wonders and signs were being done through the apostles. And all who believed were together and had all things in common. And they were selling their possessions and belongings and distributing the proceeds to all, as any had need. And day by day, attending the temple together and breaking bread in their homes, they received their food with glad and generous hearts, praising God and having favor with all the people. And the Lord added to their number day by day those who were being saved.
Acts 2:1–8, 11b–14a, 41–47

HOLY SPIRIT, LIVING BREATH OF GOD

Words and Music by Keith Getty and Stuart Townend
© 2006 Thankyou Music

SCRIPTURE READING IN VARIOUS LANGUAGES

For God so loved the world, that he gave his only Son, that whoever believes in him should not perish but have eternal life. For God did not send his Son into the world to condemn the world, but in order that the world might be saved through him.
John 3:16–17
[Invite people from your congregation to read this Scripture passage in various languages. Be sure to rehearse this before the worship service.]

HOW GREAT IS OUR GOD

Words and Music by Chris Tomlin, Ed Cash, and Jesse Reeves
© 2004 Rising Springs Music; Vamos Publishing; worshiptogether.com songs; Wondrously Made Songs
[If possible, sing this song in various languages selecting languages from within your congregation. See Chris Tomlin's World Edition of this song for inspiration.]

OFFERING PRAYER

Heavenly Father, on this Pentecost Sunday, we come before you with hearts filled with anticipation and reverence. We celebrate the outpouring of your Holy Spirit upon your disciples, empowering them to proclaim the Gospel with boldness and zeal. As we remember the birth of the Church and the transformative work of the Holy Spirit, we offer our worship and praise, acknowledging you as the source of all wisdom, power, and inspiration.

On this special day, we seek a fresh infilling of your Spirit in our lives and in our community of believers. Fill us anew with your presence, that we may be vessels of your love and grace to a world in need. We offer our gifts and offerings, knowing that you have entrusted us with resources to be used for your kingdom's work. May these offerings be used to spread the message of Pentecost, touching hearts and transforming lives.

As we yield to the guidance of your Spirit, may we be emboldened to share the Gospel fearlessly, to serve others selflessly, and to walk in unity and love as one body in Christ.

In the name of Jesus, our Savior, and through the power of the Holy Spirit, we pray. Amen.

OFFERTORY
SWEET, SWEET SPIRIT
Words and Music by Doris Akers
© 1962. Renewed 1990 by Manna Music, Inc.

PRAYER OF ILLUMINATION

Loving God, on this Pentecost Sunday, we gather in your presence with hearts open and eager to receive your divine illumination as we commemorate the outpouring of your Holy Spirit.

As the disciples experienced the rushing wind and tongues of fire, may your Spirit descend upon us with power and grace, igniting a fervent passion for your truth and mission. In the diversity of languages spoken that day, may your message reach the farthest corners of the earth, breaking down barriers and uniting us as one in Christ. As we celebrate the birth of the Church, may your light illuminate the path ahead, empowering us to be bold witnesses of your love and grace.

We offer this prayer with gratitude and expectation, trusting in your unfailing love and guidance, in the name of Jesus Christ, our Savior and Advocate, Amen.

SERMON

[If observing the Lord's Supper, continue. If not, proceed to the next congregational song.]

THE LORD'S SUPPER INSTRUCTIONS AND INVITATION

[Instrumental music played or congregational singing.]

THE MYSTERY OF FAITH

And so, in remembrance of these your mighty acts in Jesus Christ, we offer ourselves in praise and thanksgiving as a holy and living sacrifice, in union with Christ's offering for us, as we proclaim the mystery of faith:

CONGREGATION:

Christ has died; Christ is risen; Christ will come again.

O CHURCH ARISE

Words and Music by Keith Getty and Stuart Townend
© 2005 Thankyou Music

BENEDICTION

May the Holy Spirit's empowering presence, as experienced by the disciples on Pentecost, accompany you on your journey from this place. May his guiding light lead your way, his wisdom ignite your thoughts, and his love overflow in your hearts. Go forth as catalysts of change, sharing the message of Christ's resurrection and the hope it offers to the world. May the blessings of Pentecost rest upon you as you continue to live and serve in the name of the Father, the Son, and the Holy Spirit. Amen.

PENTECOST SUNDAY

SCRIPTURE PRESENTATION

O LORD MY GOD, YOU ARE VERY GREAT!

Psalm 104:1–2, 24, 27–35

CAST:

2 Voices
Group (3–5 voices)

VOICE 1:

Bless the Lord, O my soul!

GROUP:

O Lord my God, you are very great!

VOICE 2:

You are clothed with splendor and majesty, covering yourself with light as with a garment, stretching out the heavens like a tent.

GROUP:

O Lord my God, you are very great!

VOICE 1:

O Lord, how manifold are your works! In wisdom have you made them all; the earth is full of your creatures.

VOICE 2:

These all look to you, to give them their food in due season.

When you give it to them, they gather it up; when you open your hand, they are filled with good things.

VOICE 1:

When you hide your face, they are dismayed; when you take away their breath, they die and return to their dust.

VOICE 2:

When you send forth your Spirit, they are created, and you renew the face of the ground.

GROUP:

O Lord my God, you are very great!

VOICE 1:

May the glory of the Lord endure forever;

VOICE 2:

may the Lord rejoice in his works, who looks on the earth and it trembles, who touches the mountains and they smoke!

VOICE 1:

I will sing to the Lord as long as I live;

VOICE 2:

I will sing praise to my God while I have being.

VOICE 1:

May my meditation be pleasing to him, for I rejoice in the Lord.

VOICE 2:

Let sinners be consumed from the earth, and let the wicked be no more!

GROUP:

Bless the Lord, O my soul! Praise the Lord!

CHAPTER 12

AFTER PENTECOST

PENTECOST MARKS THE BIRTH of the church when the Holy Spirit descended upon the disciples. The season after Pentecost provides an opportunity to bask in God's renewing presence as the church recalls the witness of those who spread the gospel, fostering the growth of Christianity worldwide.

This period between Pentecost and the beginning of Advent is called *Ordinary Time*. In contrast, the period through Advent, Christmas, Epiphany, Lent, and the Easter season ending on Pentecost Sunday is called *Extraordinary Time*.[77] *Extraordinary Time* derives its name from the special significance of its seasons, as it narrates the fullness of God's story throughout this period.

Ordinary Time is not about that which is common, regular, mundane, or boring. The word "ordinary" used here originates from the Latin *ordinalis*, which means numbered as in "ordinal numbers". As opposed to cardinal numbers which indicate quantity (one, two, three, etc.), ordinal numbers indicate position (first, second, third, etc.). Laurence Stookey claims,

> "Ordinary Time" implies no mundaneness, as if more than half the year were dull and unexciting; it refers to the fact that in the original lectionary system the Sundays outside Advent–Christmas and Lent–Easter were simply designated by ordinal numbers: First

---

77. In addition to the seasons of Light and Life, there are two main times that comprise the various seasons of the liturgical year: *Extraordinary Time*, which tells the story of Jesus, and *Ordinary Time*, which tells the story of God's people, the church. *Extraordinary Time* includes the seasons of Advent, Christmas, Epiphany, Lent, Holy Week/ The Great Triduum, and Easter. *Ordinary Time* includes the seasons after Epiphany and Pentecost.

Sunday, Second Sunday, and on through to the Thirty-fourth Sunday.[78]

Ordinary Time is no less important in the Christian year, nor should it be given any less effort in our worship times.

In the Christian year, *Ordinary Time* consists of two distinct parts. The first falls between the feast of Epiphany and Lent, and then continues from Pentecost to Advent. As mentioned, the weeks are numbered, with thirty-four weeks in all.[79] When the second segment of *Ordinary Time* begins, following Pentecost, instead of beginning at week one, the counting continues from where it left off before Lent.

Ordinary Time is the lengthiest season in the Christian year, making it susceptible to being overlooked as unremarkable. However, that is not its intended purpose nor how it can be most advantageous for worshipers. *Ordinary Time* serves as an opportunity for growth, allowing us to deepen our comprehension of Jesus' identity and his desired way of life for us. There is a Sunday-to-Sunday reminder of God's saving event and the salvation history that is now ours.

A few special days celebrated within *Ordinary Time* include Trinity Sunday, All Saints' Day, and Christ the King Sunday. Some Protestant churches also celebrate Reformation Sunday, which is observed the day before All Saints' Day.

TRINITY SUNDAY

Trinity Sunday falls on the first Sunday after Pentecost, and with good reason. At Pentecost, Jesus is proclaimed as both the Messiah and Lord, and God the Father sends the Holy Spirit. The Western church has upheld the tradition of observing Trinity Sunday on the first Sunday after Pentecost since before the year 1000.

Trinity Sunday holds great significance for modern day Christians, as it serves as a vital reminder to fully acknowledge and appreciate the Trinitarian nature of God. In today's culture, where New Age and Islamic beliefs are prevalent, understanding the three in one God—God the Father, God the Son, and God the Holy Spirit—is crucial for the Christian community.

The observance of Trinity Sunday provides an opportunity for worshipers to reflect on and deepen their understanding of the central Christian doctrine of one God in three persons, which is fundamental to the Christian

---

78. Stookey, *Calendar*, 133.

79. *Ordinary Time* may only include thirty-three Sundays, depending on when Easter falls.

faith. Observing Trinity Sunday helps Christians acknowledge and honor the eternal mystery of God's triune nature and the profound relationship between the three persons of the Trinity. Additionally, it serves as a reminder of the unity and diversity within the Godhead, encouraging worshipers to live in unity and love with one another as a reflection of the divine nature.

REFORMATION SUNDAY

Although not officially part of the Christian year calendar, the Protestant Reformation of the sixteenth century left an indelible mark on Christianity. Fueled by a desire to address corruption and abuses within the Roman Catholic church at the time, visionary leaders like Martin Luther and John Calvin spearheaded a transformative movement that led to the emergence of Protestant denominations we know today.

The Reformers were driven by a profound conviction that the church had strayed from the essential, original teachings of Christianity, particularly concerning salvation—how people can find forgiveness of sin through Jesus Christ's death and resurrection and obtain eternal life with God. The Reformation sought to realign Christianity with the original message of Jesus and the early church.

Reformation Sunday is observed on October 31 or the last Sunday of October. The legendary account reports that on October 31, 1517, the priest Martin Luther boldly affixed his protest notice, the *Ninety-five Theses*, to the door of the Castle Church in Wittenberg, Germany. Some believe Luther's *Theses* were sent to his Archbishop rather than being a defiant protest, as they primarily aimed to address certain issues within the church that had obscured the gospel message. Regardless, Luther hoped his *Theses* would initiate acknowledgment and discussion, leading to the church's renewal and bringing the truth about God's forgiveness to people's lives—a hope that has inspired worship renewal for over five centuries.

ALL SAINTS' DAY

All Saints' Day falls on November 1 and is celebrated on the Sunday immediately following or coinciding with that date. For Protestants, observing All Saints' Day serves as an expression of unity and reverence toward the universal Church. Although historically associated with Roman Catholic tradition, All Saints' Day provides an opportunity to remember and honor all Christians, referred to as saints in the Bible (e.g., Rom 8:27; Eph 3:18), emphasizing the shared belief in the communion of saints transcending denominational boundaries.

The recognition and celebration of saints is among the most significant differences in Christian traditions. While Protestants may not have "saints" in the same way as other traditions, Scripture unequivocally states that all believers are saints and should be remembered and honored for their faithfulness to the Lord—both in the past and present. There are numerous individuals who have set an exemplary standard of godly Christian living for us to emulate. Some we know personally, while others are figures we admire from afar, like Billy Graham, Mother Teresa, Martin Luther King Jr., and the Apostle Paul. Nonetheless, this discussion must extend beyond prominent societal figures and encompass the faithful individuals who have made a lasting impact on our lives.

For instance, think of the person who told you about Christ's sacrifice and influenced you toward accepting Christ as your personal Lord and Savior. I imagine you are grateful for that person and the impact they had upon your spiritual life. The Bible talks about a cloud of witnesses that cheer us on in our faith. Throughout the history of the church, All Saints' Day has been set aside to remember and honor those who have set the example of how we should follow Christ. I believe this day is vitally important to our walk with Christ because it reminds us of the enduring legacy of faith and the power of God's grace working through ordinary individuals to bring about extraordinary change in the world. By commemorating the saints of God, we are inspired to follow their example of devotion, selflessness, and perseverance in the face of challenges, encouraging us to deepen our own faith and strive to make a positive impact in our communities and beyond.

The Apostle Paul knew the importance of being an example for others to follow. In 1 Corinthians he says, "Be imitators of me, as I am of Christ" (1 Cor 11:1). Other Scripture passages support the remembrance and honoring of those who have gone before including Ephesians 6:18, Hebrews 12:1, and Revelation 5:8.

Initially the calendars of honoring saints and martyrs varied according to location as local churches honored local saints. However, feast days gradually became more universal. The first reference to a general feast celebrating all saints occurred in the writings of St Ephrem the Syrian (d. AD 373). St. John Chrysostom (d. AD 407) assigned a day to the feast, the first Sunday after Pentecost, where in the Eastern Churches the feast is celebrated to this day. In the West, this date was probably originally used, and then the feast was moved to May 13. The current observance, November 1, probably originates from the time of Pope Gregory III (d. AD 741).

By participating in this observance, we rejoice in celebrating the faithful individuals who have exemplified Christ's teachings and left a profound impact on Christianity and the world. Through this commemoration, we find a moment for reflection and gratitude, acknowledging the spiritual heritage we have inherited. It serves as a reminder that we are part of a larger, timeless Christian family, united in our shared journey of faith with Christ at the center. By observing All Saints' Day, we are prompted to live holy and righteous lives, drawing inspiration from the great cloud of witnesses (Heb 12:1) who encourage and support our present-day faith journey.

CHRIST THE KING SUNDAY

Christ the King Sunday is of modern origin being instituted in 1925. Its observance is of utmost importance for Christians as it serves as a culmination and reminder of Christ's sovereignty and reign over all creation. Falling on the last Sunday before Advent, it marks the completion of the Christian liturgical year. By honoring Christ as King, worshipers reassert their faith in his lordship and contemplate his teachings of love, justice, and compassion. This observance reinforces the centrality of Christ in their lives and worship, fostering a deeper comprehension of their faith and a steadfast commitment to following his example.

It is important to note that the Old Testament knows no distinction between sacred and secular time. Nor did it mark special festival days and seasons to separate them as sacred (extraordinary) from ordinary time. Andrew Hill states that in the Old Testament, "all time is God's gift to humanity (Pss 31:15; 139:16; Isa 60:22), and each season or cycle of time has its appropriate place within the divinely ordered sphere of human experience in time (Eccl 3:1–9; Song 2:12; Hos 10:12). For the ancient Hebrew each day was a special or sacred day because it could be used to fulfill creation's purpose of worshiping and praising God (Pss 34:11; 118:24; Isa 43:7)."[80]

While *Extraordinary Time* focuses on the saving events of the birth, life, death, and resurrection of Christ, the Sundays of *Ordinary Time* not only celebrate those saving events but also encompass the development and continual growth of the church. Deliberately reflecting on the entire story of God during worship profoundly impacts the spiritual formation of worshipers.

---

80. Hill, *Enter His Courts with Praise!*, 94.

INCORPORATING THE SEASON AFTER PENTECOST:

Trinity Sunday

Look through the songs in your church's song database. How many of the songs in your regular rotation at your church mention all three persons of the Trinity—Father, Son, and Holy Spirit? On Trinity Sunday, intentionally plan to sing songs that mention all three persons of the Godhead, as well as incorporating Trinitarian language within the prayers and other worship elements.

Reformation Sunday

Read a question or two from a catechism as part of the service. The New City Catechism, found online, is a good resource if you don't already have one you know and like. Another option is to tell the story of the German reformer Martin Luther—in abbreviated form, of course—to the church family. One potential resource to accomplish this would be the four-minute video "History 101: The Protestant Reformation" by National Geographic found on YouTube.

All Saints' Day

Invite your congregation to write a "Thank You" note to a person who has been a great Christian influence in their life (they should select someone still living). It may be the person who shared the gospel with them, or someone who has discipled them in their Christian walk. Encourage them to send the note to that person. This is a great way to honor those who have set an example of godly living for them to follow.

Christ the King Sunday

In a culture that focuses heavily on the "Jesus is my buddy" mentality, encourage your congregation to consider the kingship of Jesus by developing an art installation at your church and inviting your congregation to create artistic works displaying Jesus Christ as the King of kings. It may be a poem, song, painting, sculpture, etc. Display each of these artistic expressions somewhere at the church where people can see them regularly (i.e. a gallery, hallway, etc.) Since Christ the King Sunday is the Sunday before the season of Advent, which anticipates the coming of the King, you can keep the display up throughout Advent.

TRINITY SUNDAY

OVERVIEW

TIME

The Sunday following Pentecost Sunday.

THEMES

God is triune, comprising one God in three distinct persons—Father, Son, and Holy Spirit.

SPIRITUAL CHALLENGE

Learn to embrace the mystery of God and his unfathomable nature.

SCRIPTURE

- Old Testament: Gen 1:1–2:4a; Prov 8:1–4, 22–31; Isa 6:1–8
- Psalm: Ps 8; Ps 29
- New Testament: Rom 5:1–5; Rom 8:12–17; 2 Cor 13:11–13
- Gospel: Matt 28:16–20; John 3:1–17; John 16:12–15

SYMBOLS

- Trinity symbol

COLORS

- White

TRINITY SUNDAY

SONG LIST

CONTEMPORARY

All Praise to Him Bob Kauflin and Matt Merker, 2017

Father, I Adore You Terrye Coelho, 1972

Father Make Me Holy John Michael Talbot, 1983

Glorify Thy Name Donna Adkins, 1976

Glory to the Father Johnny Markin, 2020

How Great Is Our God Chris Tomlin, Jesse Reeves, and Ed Cash, 2004

King of Kings Brooke Ligertwood, Jason Ingram, and Scott Ligertwood, 2018

Magnificent Trinity Jonathan D. Helser, 2020

O God of Our Salvation Matt Boswell and Michael Bleecker, 2009

Our God Saves Paul Baloche and Brenton Brown, 2007

Praise the Father, Praise the Son Chris Tomlin and Ed Cash, 2008

The Lord Is My Salvation Keith Getty, Kristyn Getty, Jonas Myrin, and Nathan Nockles, 2016

This I Believe (The Creed) Matt Crocker and Ben Fielding, 2014

Wonderful Merciful Savior Dawn Rodgers and Eric Wyse, 1989

TRADITIONAL

All Creatures of Our God and King St. Francis of Assisi, 1225

Ancient of Days, Who Sittest, Throned in Glory William C. Doane, 1886

Come Thou Almighty King Anonymous, 1757

Eternal Father, Strong to Save William Whiting, 1860

God, Our Father, We Adore Thee George W. Frazer and Alfred S. Loizeaux, 1882

Holy, Holy, Holy! Lord God Almighty! Reginald Heber, 1826

O Day of Rest and Gladness Christopher Wordsworth, 1862

O Trinity of Blessed Light Ambrose of Milan, 397; Jason M. Neale, transl., 1852

Praise God From Whom All Blessings Flow Thomas Ken, 1674

PRESENTATIONAL

O God of Our Salvation Matt Boswell, 2012

Only True God Kathryn Scott and Paul Baloche, 2007

Remember Laura Story, 2009

Three In One Mark Altrogge, 2004

Trinity Matt Papa, 2009

Trinity Song Sandra McCracken, 2016

Triune Praise Shai Linne, 2008

We Believe Matthew Hooper, Richie Fike, and Travis Ryan, 2013

We Believe (Apostle's Creed) Keith Getty, Kristyn Getty, and Stuart Townend, 2016

You Are So Good To Me Ben Pasley, Don Chaffer, and Robin D. Pasley, 1999

GLOBAL

Cantai ao Senhor (O Sing to the Lord) Brazilian folk song (Brazil)

Gloria a Dios (Glory to God) Traditional (Peru)

Kar'na Iman (Because of Faith) Budianto Lim and Lidya Siah, 2023 (Indonesia)

Ki Ri Su To No (May the Peace of Christ Be with You) Japanese folk song (Japan)

TUHAN Kami (Our God) Budianto Lim and Lidya Siah, 2023 (Indonesia)

Uyai Mose (Come, All You People) Alexander Gondo, 1986; addt'l stanzas from *With One Voice*, 1995 (Zimbabwe)

TRINITY SUNDAY

WORSHIP SERVICE

HOLY, HOLY, HOLY! LORD GOD ALMIGHTY
Words by Reginald Heber, 1826; Music by John B. Dykes, NICAEA, 1861
Public Domain

We just worshipped "God in three persons," Father, Son, and Holy Spirit. Today in the Christian year is Trinity Sunday—a day to focus our attention on the fact that we worship a God who is three persons, but one God. This is a chief Christian doctrine duplicated by no other religion in the world. An early church catechism question asks, "How many persons are there in God?" Let's say the answer together.

CONGREGATION:

There are three persons in the one true and living God: the Father, the Son, and the Holy Spirit. They are the same in substance, equal in power and glory.

Wrapping our heads around the Trinity—God in three persons—can give us a headache. Eighteenth century preacher John Wesley said . . . "Bring me a worm that can comprehend a man, and then I will show you a man that can comprehend the triune God." As we contemplate the wonder of redemption, the mysteries surrounding the Trinity begin to unfold, revealing the distinct roles each person of the Godhead plays—the various modes of operation in our salvation.

For God so loved the world that he gave his one and only Son, that whoever believes in him shall not perish but have eternal life. For God did not send his Son into the world to condemn the world, but to save the world through him.
John 3:16–17

Let's consider the role of our sanctification by the Holy Spirit by reading responsively from 1 Corinthians 2:

LEADER:

What no eye has seen, what no ear has heard, and what no human mind has conceived – the things God has prepared for those who love him – these are the things God has revealed to us by his Spirit.

CONGREGATION:

The Spirit searches all things, even the deep things of God. For who knows a person's thoughts except their own spirit within them?

LEADER:

In the same way no one knows the thoughts of God except the Spirit of God.

CONGREGATION:

What we have received is not the spirit of the world, but the Spirit who is from God, so that we may understand what God has freely given us.

LEADER:

This is what we speak, not in words taught us by human wisdom but in words taught by the Spirit, explaining spiritual realities with Spirit-taught words.

CONGREGATION:

The person without the Spirit does not accept the things that come from the Spirit of God but considers them foolishness, and cannot understand them because they are discerned only through the Spirit.

LEADER:

The person with the Spirit makes judgments about all things, but such a person is not subject to merely human judgments, for, "Who has known the mind of the Lord so as to instruct him?"

ALL:

But we have the mind of Christ.

COME THOU ALMIGHTY KING

Words: Anonymous; Music by Felice de Giardini, ITALIAN HYMN, 1757
Public Domain

HOW GREAT IS OUR GOD

Words and Music by Chris Tomlin, Jesse Reeves, and Ed Cash
© 2004 sixsteps Music, worshiptogether.com songs, Wondrously Made Songs

OFFERING PRAYER

Eternal and Triune God, on this Trinity Sunday, we gather before you with hearts filled with awe and wonder. We worship you, Father, Son, and Holy Spirit, as one God in three persons, eternally united in perfect love and harmony. As we reflect on the mystery of your divine nature, we offer our worship and praise, acknowledging your greatness and majesty. You are the Creator of all things, the Redeemer of our souls, and the Comforter who guides and sustains us.

On this special day, we seek to deepen our understanding of your triune nature and to draw closer to you in worship and devotion. May our hearts be open to the revelation of your truth and the leading of your Spirit.

We present our gifts and offerings, recognizing that all we have comes from your loving hand. Bless these offerings, and may they be used to further your kingdom and to bring glory to your name. As we celebrate the unity and diversity within the Trinity, may we also embrace the diversity within your church. Help us to love one another as you love us, showing grace and compassion to all, regardless of our differences.

In the name of the Father, the Son, and the Holy Spirit, we pray. Amen.

OFFERTORY

WE BELIEVE (APOSTLE'S CREED)

Words and Music by Keith Getty, Kristyn Getty, and Stuart Townend
© 2016 Thankyou Music, Getty Music Publishing, Townend Songs

PRAYER OF ILLUMINATION

Father, open our hearts and minds by the power of your Holy Spirit, that, as the Scriptures are read and your Son, Jesus Christ, the Word is revealed, we may hear with joy what you say to us today. Amen.

SERMON

[If observing the Lord's Supper, continue. If not, proceed to the next congregational song.]

THE LORD'S SUPPER INSTRUCTIONS AND INVITATION

[Instrumental music played or congregational singing.]

THE MYSTERY OF FAITH

And so, in remembrance of these your mighty acts in Jesus Christ, we offer ourselves in praise and thanksgiving as a holy and living sacrifice, in union with Christ's offering for us, as we proclaim the mystery of faith:

CONGREGATION:

Christ has died; Christ is risen; Christ will come again.

KING OF KINGS

Words and Music by Brooke Ligertwood, Jason Ingram, and Scott Ligertwood
© 2018 Hillsong Music Publishing, Fellow Ships Music, So Essential Tunes

BENEDICTION

As we go from this place, out to the world God loves, let us have these words from the apostle Paul in our hearts, "The grace of the Lord Jesus Christ, and the love of God, and the fellowship of the Holy Spirit be with you all."
2 Corinthians 13:14

TRINITY SUNDAY
SCRIPTURE PRESENTATION

THE MIND OF CHRIST
1 Corinthians 2:9–16

CAST:
3 Voices

VOICE 1:
What no eye has seen,

VOICE 2:
what no ear has heard,

VOICE 3:
and what no human mind has conceived

ALL:
the things God has prepared for those who love him

VOICE 1:
these are the things God has revealed to us by his Spirit.

VOICES 1, 2 & 3:
The Spirit searches all things,

VOICE 2:
even the deep things of God.

VOICE 3:

For who knows a person's thoughts except their own spirit within them?

VOICE 1:

In the same way no one knows the thoughts of God except the Spirit of God.

VOICE 2:

What we have received is not the spirit of the world, but the Spirit who is from God,

VOICE 3:

so that we may understand what God has freely given us.

VOICE 1:

This is what we speak, not in words taught us by human wisdom but in words taught by the Spirit, explaining spiritual realities with Spirit-taught words.

VOICE 2:

The person without the Spirit does not accept the things that come from the Spirit of God but considers them foolishness, and cannot understand them because they are discerned only through the Spirit.

VOICE 3:

The person with the Spirit makes judgments about all things, but such a person is not subject to merely human judgments, for, "Who has known the mind of the Lord so as to instruct him?"

VOICES 1, 2 & 3:

But we have the mind of Christ.

REFORMATION SUNDAY
OVERVIEW

TIME
October 31, or celebrated on the last Sunday of October.

THEMES
Remembering the sixteenth century Protestant Reformation while honoring the transforming life of Jesus Christ and the love given to each of us through his grace.

SPIRITUAL CHALLENGE
Always be reforming according to the Word of God.

SCRIPTURE
- Old Testament: Lev 19:1–2, 15–18; Deut 34:1–12; Job 42:1–6, 10–17; Jer 14:7–10, 19–22; Jer 31:7–9; Joel 2:23–32
- Psalm: Ps 1; Ps 34:1–8; Ps 65; Ps 84:1–7; Ps 90:1–6, 13–17; Ps 126
- New Testament: 1 Thess 2:1–8; 2 Tim 4:6–8, 16–18; Heb 7:23–28
- Gospel: Matt 22:34–46; Mark 10:46–52; Luke 18:9–14

SYMBOLS
- Bible
- Luther seal/Luther rose

COLORS
- Green
- Red

REFORMATION SUNDAY
SONG LIST

CONTEMPORARY

Ancient Words Lynn DeShazo, 2001

By Faith Keith Getty, Kristyn Getty, and Stuart Townend, 2009

Cornerstone Edward Mote, Eric Liljero, Jonas Myrin, Reuben Morgan, and William Bradbury, 2011

Grace Alone Dustin Kensrue, 2013

In Christ Alone Keith Getty and Stuart Townend, 2002

O Great God Bob Kauflin, 2006

Our God Will Go Before Us Keith Getty, Matt Boswell, and Matt Papa, 2023

Reformation Hymn Bob Kauflin and Chris Anderson, 2017

Rock of Ages You Will Stand Brenton Brown and Paul Baloche, 2007

Sola Zac Hicks, 2011

Speak O Lord Keith Getty and Stuart Townend, 2005

There Is One Gospel Jonny Robinson and Rich Thompson, 2022

This I Believe (The Creed) Ben Fielding and Matt Crocker, 2014

We Will Feast in the House of Zion Joshua Moore and Sandra McCracken, 2015

Worthy of It All David Brymer and Ryan Hall, 2012

Your Grace Is Enough Matt Maher, 2003

TRADITIONAL

A Mighty Fortress Is Our God Martin Luther, 1529

All People That on Earth Do Dwell William Kethe, 1650

How Firm A Foundation K. Attributed to Robert Keene and George Keith, 1787

Love Divine, All Loves Excelling Charles Wesley, 1747

May the Mind of Christ, My Savior Kate B. Wilkinson, 1925

My Hope Is Built on Nothing Less Edward Mote, 1834

Not What These Hands Have Done Horatius Bonar, 1864

Now Thank We All Our God Martin Rinkhart, 1636

Praise for Redeeming Love John Newton, 1774

Precious Bible, What A Treasure John Newton, 1774

Sing Praise to God Who Reigns Above Johann Jakob Schütz, 1675

The Church's One Foundation Samuel John Stone, 1866

PRESENTATIONAL

Call On the Name Cody Carnes, Chris Davenport, Aodhan King, Ben Tan, 2023

Rescuer Benjamin Hastings, Bryan Fowler, Chris Llewellyn, and Gareth Gilkeson, 2017

This Is the Gospel Sydney Wilson, Joshua Holiday, Tiffany Hudson, Joel Barnes, 2023

Wholly Yours David Crowder, 2005

GLOBAL

Aus tiefer Not schrei ich zu dir (Out of the Depths I Cry to Thee) Martin Luther, 1524 (Germany)

Ein feste Burg ist unser Gott (A Mighty Fortress Is Our God) Martin Luther, 1529 (Germany)

Erhalt uns, Herr, bei deinem Wort (Lord, Keep Us Steadfast in Thy Word) Martin Luther, 1542 (Germany)

Je te Salue mon Certain Redempteur (I Greet Thee, Who My Sure Redeemer Art) Attributed to John Calvin, 1545 (France)

REFORMATION SUNDAY

WORSHIP SERVICE

The 16th century Protestant Reformation was a game-changer for Christianity. Leaders like Martin Luther and John Calvin, fueled by their concern over the corruption within the Roman Catholic church, ignited a movement that reshaped the entire faith.

These Reformers strongly believed that the church of their era had strayed from the core teachings of Christianity, particularly when it came to the concept of salvation—how people could find forgiveness for their sins through Jesus Christ's death and resurrection, leading to eternal life with God. The Reformation aimed to bring Christianity back to its original message as preached by Jesus and the early church.

The Five Solas are five Latin phrases (or slogans) that emerged during the Reformation to summarize the Reformers' theological convictions about the essentials of Christianity. Throughout our time together today, we'll be looking at each of these Five Solas.

CALL TO WORSHIP

"Let God speak directly to his people through the Scriptures, and let his people respond with grateful songs of praise." Martin Luther

SOLA SCRIPTURA—SCRIPTURE ALONE

[Place each of the Solas on the screen during the introduction to the next worship element.]

Now, as it has always been, the church must only stand upon its sole pillar of authority—the word of God: "All Scripture is breathed out by God and profitable for teaching, for reproof, for correction, and for training in righteousness, that the man of God may be complete, equipped for every good work." (2 Timothy 3:16–17)

HOW FIRM A FOUNDATION

Words and Music by K. Attributed to Robert Keene and George Keith, 1787
Public Domain

SOLA FIDE—FAITH ALONE

The church cannot have an effective voice in the culture if it is merely a people of faith; it must be clear to the world that we are a people of faith in Christ. Let's make a clear declaration of whom we believe in.
[Proceed or utilize the Reformation Sunday Scripture Presentation found immediately after this worship service example.]

THIS I BELIEVE (THE CREED)

Words and Music by Ben Fielding and Matt Crocker
© 2014 Hillsong Music Publishing

SOLA GRATIA—GRACE ALONE

There's a tale of a young soldier in Napoleon's army who committed a serious offense and faced military justice. His mother appeared before the general, pleading for mercy on her son's behalf. Napoleon informed her that the soldier's crime didn't warrant mercy. "That may be true," the mother acknowledged, "but that's precisely why it's called mercy." Napoleon agreed and granted clemency to the young man.

Each one of us may be tempted to rely on our own efforts to stand before God. However, if God's favor towards us depended on our actions, sincerity, or intentions—in essence, anything we've done or might do—we would all be condemned under his judgment. Acknowledging God's sovereign grace not only brings honor to him but also sets us free to respond with joyful gratitude.

PRAYER

Join me in this prayer offered by the German reformer Martin Luther:
"O Lord, we are not worthy to have a glimpse of heaven, and unable with works to redeem ourselves from sin, death, the devil, and hell. For this we rejoice, praise, and thank you, O God, that without price and out of pure

grace You have granted us this boundless blessing in your dear Son through whom You take sin, death, and hell from us, and give to us all that belongs to him."

SOLA CHRISTUS—CHRIST ALONE

[begin music for "In Christ Alone"]
The Scriptures declare that "there is one God, and one mediator between God and mankind, the man Christ Jesus" (1 Timothy 2:5). The Apostle Peter confirms that "there is salvation in no one else, for there is no other name under heaven given to mankind by which we must be saved" (Acts 4:12).

IN CHRIST ALONE

Words and Music by Keith Getty and Stuart Townend
© 2002 Thankyou Music

OFFERING PRAYER

Heavenly Father, on this Reformation Sunday, we come before you with hearts of gratitude and reverence. We thank you for the brave reformers who, guided by your Spirit, sought to restore your Word as the foundation of faith and practice in the Church. As we commemorate this historic day, we offer our worship and praise, acknowledging your faithfulness throughout history in preserving and guiding your people.

We are thankful for the truths rediscovered during the Reformation—salvation by grace through faith, the authority of Scripture, and the priesthood of all believers. These foundational principles have shaped our faith and continue to inspire us to seek a deeper understanding of your Word.

In light of the Reformation's legacy, we present our gifts and offerings. May they be used to further the proclamation of the Gospel and the teaching of your Word, that more hearts may be touched by your truth. As we honor the past, we also look to the future with hope and dedication. Help us, as your Church, to be ever vigilant in discerning your will and remaining faithful to your Word.

In the name of Jesus Christ, our Savior and the cornerstone of our faith, we pray. Amen.

OFFERTORY
SPEAK O LORD
Words and Music by Keith Getty and Stuart Townend
© 2005 Thankyou Music

PRAYER OF ILLUMINATION
Gracious God, on this Reformation Sunday, we come before you with hearts of gratitude, seeking the illumination of your divine truth, as we remember the transformative events of the Protestant Reformation.

As your Spirit moved through faithful reformers, may your light shine upon their courage and conviction, inspiring us to remain steadfast in our faith. In the rediscovery of your word and grace, may your truth resonate deeply within us, drawing us closer to the heart of your Gospel.

As we reflect on the enduring legacy of those who have gone before, may we be reminded of the ongoing need for renewal, and a continuous pursuit of spiritual growth. In the unity of believers, despite differences, may we learn from history and embrace the essential truths, that bind us together as your people.

We offer this prayer with gratitude and humility, trusting in your steadfast love and mercy, in the name of Jesus Christ, our Savior and Redeemer, Amen.

SERMON
[If observing the Lord's Supper, continue. If not, proceed to the next congregational song.]

THE LORD'S SUPPER INSTRUCTIONS AND INVITATION
[Instrumental music played or congregational singing.]

THE MYSTERY OF FAITH
And so, in remembrance of these your mighty acts in Jesus Christ, we offer ourselves in praise and thanksgiving as a holy and living sacrifice, in union with Christ's offering for us, as we proclaim the mystery of faith:

CONGREGATION:
Christ has died; Christ is risen; Christ will come again.

SOLI DEO GLORIA—TO THE GLORY OF GOD ALONE

This is the sola that sums up the other four, giving purpose and meaning to all of them. The entire created order, encompassing the universe, history, humanity, and the plan of salvation, exists for the glory of God. As the Westminster Catechism states, the primary purpose of humanity, or the meaning of life, is to glorify God and enjoy him forever. This timeless truth holds its significance throughout the ages and will endure until the end of time.

WORTHY OF IT ALL

Words and Music by David Brymer and Ryan Hall
© 2012 Forerunner Worship, Common Hymnal Publishing, Innerland, Wayfinder Music

A MIGHTY FORTRESS IS OUR GOD

Words and Music by Martin Luther; chorus by Tommy Walker
This Arr. © 1997 Universal Music—Brentwood Benson Songs

BENEDICTION

(based on Colossians 2:11–12)
As you go from here, remember this:
The same Spirit of God who raised Jesus Christ from the dead, also lives in you, breathing new life and freedom into your hearts and minds. So go from here with joy and confidence, knowing that God is at work within you.

REFORMATION SUNDAY

SCRIPTURE PRESENTATION

THE APOSTLES' CREED WITH THIS I BELIEVE (THE CREED)

Romans 11:33–36

CAST:
4 Voices
Congregation

Instruments play chorus as underscore to readings

CONGREGATION:
I believe in God, the Father almighty, creator of heaven and earth.
I believe in Jesus Christ, his only Son, our Lord,
  who was conceived by the Holy Spirit and born of the virgin Mary.
He suffered under Pontius Pilate, was crucified, died, and was buried;

ALL SING:
Our Father everlasting, the all-creating One, God Almighty.
Through your Holy Spirit, conceiving Christ the Son, Jesus our Savior.
I believe in God our Father, I believe in Christ the Son.
I believe in the Holy Spirit, our God is Three in One.
I believe in the resurrection, that we will rise again.
For I believe in the name of Jesus.

CONGREGATION:
He descended into the deep.
The third day he rose again from the dead.

He ascended to heaven and is seated at the right hand of God the Father almighty.
From there he will come to judge the living and the dead.

ALL SING:

Our Judge and our Defender, suffered and crucified. Forgiveness is in you.
Descended into darkness, you rose in glorious light. Forever seated high.

I believe in God our Father, I believe in Christ the Son.
I believe in the Holy Spirit, our God is Three in One.
I believe in the resurrection, that we will rise again.
For I believe in the name of Jesus.

I believe in you. I believe you rose again.
I believe that Jesus Christ is Lord.

Chorus (2x)

CONGREGATION:

I believe in the Holy Spirit, the holy catholic[81] church, the communion of saints,
the forgiveness of sins, the resurrection of the body, and the life everlasting. Amen.

ALL SING:

I believe in life eternal, I believe in the virgin birth.
I believe in the saints communion and in your holy Church.
I believe in the resurrection when Jesus comes again.
For I believe in the name of Jesus.
I believe in God our Father, I believe in Christ the Son.
I believe in the Holy Spirit, our God is Three in One.
I believe in the resurrection, that we will rise again.
For I believe in the name of Jesus.

VOICE 1:

Oh, the depth of the riches of the wisdom and knowledge of God!

---

81. The term "catholic" (with a lower case "c") does not refer to any specific denomination or group of Christians. The term comes from two Greek words that together mean "throughout the whole." This single word, "catholic," means throughout all time and places and also points to the essential unity or wholeness of the church in Christ.

VOICE 2:

How unsearchable his judgments, and his paths beyond tracing out!

VOICE 3:

"Who has known the mind of the Lord? Or who has been his counselor?"
"Who has ever given to God, that God should repay them?"

VOICE 4:

For from him and through him and for him are all things.

CONGREGATION:

To him be the glory forever! Amen!

THIS I BELIEVE (THE CREED)

Words and Music by Ben Fielding and Matt Crocker
© 2014 Hillsong Music Publishing

ALL SAINTS' SUNDAY

OVERVIEW

TIME

November 1, or celebrated on the Sunday following October 31.

THEMES

This day serves as a special occasion to remember and honor those who have exemplified how we should follow Christ. It prompts us to express gratitude for those who have paved the way—those we have personally known, who shared God's teachings with us, as well as those we have learned about through the pages of Scripture and other sources.

SPIRITUAL CHALLENGE

Inspire others toward holiness by living a life that serves as a spiritual example, just as others have for you.

SCRIPTURE

- Old Testament: Song 3:1–9; Dan 7:1–3, 15–18; Isa 25:6–9
- Psalm: Ps 24; Ps 34:1–10, 22; Ps 149
- New Testament: Eph 1:11–23; Eph 6:18; Heb 12:1; 1 John 3:1–3; Rev 5:8; Rev 7:9–17; Rev 21:1–6a
- Gospel: Mark 12:26–27; Luke 6:20–31; John 11:32–44

SYMBOLS

- Crown
- Sheaf of Wheat

COLORS
- White

ALL SAINTS' SUNDAY
SONG LIST

CONTEMPORARY
All the Saints Join In Tommy Walker, 1998
Ancient Words Lynn DeShazo, 2001
By Faith Keith Getty, Kristyn Getty, and Stuart Townend, 2009
For All the Saints Who've Shown Your Love John Bell, 1996
O Church Arise Keith Getty and Stuart Townend, 2005
One Church Keith Getty and Edward Plumptre, 2001
Pass It On Tommy Walker, 2007
Pass the Promise Kristyn Getty and Sandra McCracken, 2021
Press On Kristyn Getty and Ben Shive, 2022
Shout to the North Martin Smith, 1995
We Will Remember Tommy Walker, 2005

TRADITIONAL
A Mighty Fortress Is Our God Martin Luther, 1529; Frederick Hedge, 1852
Come Let Us Join Our Friends Above Charles Wesley, 1759
Faith Of Our Fathers Frederick W. Faber, 1849
For All the Saints William How, 1864
Great Is Thy Faithfulness Thomas O. Chisholm, 1923
O For A Thousand Tongues Charles Wesley, 1739
Onward Christian Soldiers Sabine Baring-Gould, 1864

When the Saints Go Marching In Negro Spiritual, 19th century

PRESENTATIONAL

Cloud of Witnesses Preston Foster, 2000

Find Us Faithful Jon Mohr, 1987

Let It Be Said of Us Steve Fry, 1994

We Shall Assemble Twila Paris, 1991

You Have Been Good Twila Paris, 1988

GLOBAL

Ein feste Burg ist unser Gott (A Mighty Fortress Is Our God) Martin Luther, 1529 (Germany)

Hamba Nathi (Come, Walk with Us) Traditional (South Africa)

ALL SAINTS' SUNDAY
WORSHIP SERVICE

CALL TO WORSHIP

Hebrews 12:1 states,
Since we are surrounded by so great a cloud of witnesses, let us lay aside every weight and the sin that clings so closely, and let us run with perseverance the race that is set before us.

Take a moment to reflect on the lives of the saints who have gone before us providing us with an excellent example as we follow Christ. Let us remember that great cloud of witnesses, cheering us on in our faith journey.

O FOR A THOUSAND TONGUES

Words by Charles Wesley, 1739; Music by Carl G. Gläser, AZMON, 1828; Adapted by Lowell Mason, 1839
Public Domain
[Consider beginning with this verse: "To God all glory, praise, and love be now and ever given; by saints below and saints above, the Church in earth and heaven."]

OPENING PRAYER

Almighty God, your people of all the ages live and praise you without ceasing. In our communion with you, we have communion with generations past and generations yet unborn. Before your throne we are one with a great multitude which no one could number, and in praising you we join with people from every nation. Grant to your church on earth that as we celebrate the triumph of your saints in glory we may learn from their example and enter with them into the inexpressible joys you have prepared for those who love you, through Jesus Christ our Lord. Amen.

We say in the Apostles' Creed that we believe in the "communion of the saints." Historically, that statement meant the unity of the living and the dead in one community of faith in Christ. In terms that seem perhaps too military to us, the church used to be described as the church militant—the living, still deeply engaged in the great cosmic spiritual battle. Those who are dead in Christ were the church triumphant, now reigning with Christ. This great "cloud of witnesses" surrounds us and cheers us on all through our lives but especially in our worship. Let's join in this creedal statement spoken by followers of Jesus Christ since the fourth century.

THE APOSTLES' CREED

[Invite the congregation to collectively recite the creed. Be aware that this creed affirms, "I believe in the holy catholic church." It's essential to clarify that the term "catholic" in this context does not refer to the Roman Catholic Church, but rather to the universal community of all followers of Christ Jesus. To prevent any confusion among worshipers, you may choose to provide an explanation before reciting the creed. Alternatively, you can replace the words "holy catholic" with the term "universal" in the creed.]

I believe in God the Father Almighty, maker of heaven and earth:
And in Jesus Christ His only Son, our Lord; Who was conceived by the Holy Spirit,
born of the Virgin Mary, suffered under Pontius Pilate,
was crucified, dead, and buried;
He descended into Hades; the third day He rose again from the dead;
He ascended into heaven, and sitteth on the right hand of God, the Father Almighty;
From thence He shall come to judge the quick and the dead.
I believe in the Holy Spirit, the holy catholic church,
the communion of saints, the forgiveness of sins,
the resurrection of the body, and the life everlasting.
Amen.

O CHURCH ARISE

Words and Music by Keith Getty and Stuart Townend
© 2005 Thankyou Music

REMEMBERING WITH GRATITUDE

[This time of worship can be structured in several different ways. Members of the congregation may be invited to give brief expressions or testimonies about people from the congregation, community, or their family who have died during the past year. Another option is to have several people take notes of the "heroes of faith" who have shaped our Christian heritage—these can be personal to the local church community or those among the broader Christian faith—and place them on a wall or display for others to read. To do this effectively, thoughtful planning ahead of time must be done and people should be informed of the opportunity and invited to plan their part in it. Remember, the purpose of a worship service is to worship God. Therefore, you will want to help focus this time on honoring God for those he gave as an example, encouraging our faith and worship.]

Hebrews 10:23-25; begin intro to "For All the Saints"
Let us hold fast the confession of our hope without wavering, for he who promised is faithful. And let us consider how to stir up one another to love and good works, not neglecting to meet together, as is the habit of some, but encouraging one another, and all the more as you see the Day drawing near.

FOR ALL THE SAINTS

Words by William Walsham How, 1864; Music by Ralph Vaughn Williams, SINE NOMINE, 1906
Public Domain

OFFERING PRAYER

Loving and gracious God, on this All Saints' Day, we come before you with hearts of gratitude and remembrance. We thank you for the faithful men and women who have gone before us, shining as examples of your love and grace. As we honor the saints who have lived their lives in service and dedication to you, we offer our worship and praise, acknowledging their influence in shaping our faith and guiding our journey.

On this special day, we seek to be inspired by their commitment to follow you wholeheartedly. May their legacy encourage us to walk in their footsteps, living lives that reflect your love and compassion. We present our gifts and offerings, knowing that you have called us to be good stewards of all that you have entrusted to us. Bless these offerings, and may they be used to support the ministry of your Church and to extend your love to those in need.

As we remember the saints who have passed on, we also celebrate the living members of your Church, each one uniquely gifted to serve you and others. Help us to be a united and loving community, supporting and encouraging one another in faith.

In the name of Jesus, who is the source of our salvation and the ultimate example of a holy life, we pray. Amen.

OFFERTORY

HOLY, HOLY, HOLY! LORD GOD ALMIGHTY!

Words by Reginald Heber, 1826; Music by John B. Dykes, NICAEA, 1861
Public Domain

PRAYER OF ILLUMINATION

Heavenly Father, on this All Saints' Sunday, we gather in your presence, with hearts filled with reverence and gratitude, seeking the illumination of your divine truth. As we remember and honor the lives of the saints who have gone before us, may your light shine upon their faithful witness, inspiring us to follow their example of unwavering devotion.

In this moment before the sermon, we humbly seek your wisdom, to comprehend the significance of this special day, and the eternal bond we share with the communion of saints. As we reflect on the lives of those who have finished their earthly race, may their legacy inspire us to run our own race with endurance, fixing our eyes on Jesus, the author, and perfecter of our faith. As we celebrate the unity of the church, both visible and invisible, may we be reminded of the unbreakable bond of love, that transcends time and unites us in Christ.

We offer this prayer with thanksgiving and hope, trusting in your unfailing love and grace, in the name of Jesus Christ, the author of life, Amen.

SERMON

[If observing the Lord's Supper, continue. If not, proceed to the next congregational song.]

THE LORD'S SUPPER INSTRUCTIONS AND INVITATION

[Instrumental music played or congregational singing.]

THE MYSTERY OF FAITH

And so, in remembrance of these your mighty acts in Jesus Christ, we offer ourselves in praise and thanksgiving as a holy and living sacrifice, in union with Christ's offering for us, as we proclaim the mystery of faith:

CONGREGATION:

Christ has died; Christ is risen; Christ will come again.

COME, LET US JOIN OUR FRIENDS ABOVE

Sung to the tune of "Come People of the Risen King"
Words by Charles Wesley, 1759; Music by Keith Getty and Stuart Townend
© 2007 Thankyou Music

BENEDICTION

As we go from this place, let's remember to join with the writer of the book of Hebrews in acknowledging and honoring those who have gone before us, setting an example for us to follow in the faith:

Therefore, since we are surrounded by so great a cloud of witnesses, let us also lay aside every weight, and sin which clings so closely, and let us run with endurance the race that is set before us, looking to Jesus, the founder and perfecter of our faith, who for the joy that was set before him endured the cross, despising the shame, and is seated at the right hand of the throne of God. Consider him who endured from sinners such hostility against himself, so that you may not grow weary or fainthearted.
Hebrews 12:1–3

ALL SAINTS' SUNDAY
SCRIPTURE PRESENTATION

BY FAITH

Portions of Hebrews 11:1–12:2

CAST:

11 Voices
Congregation sings hymn verses

VOICE 1:

Now faith is the assurance of things hoped for, the conviction of things not seen. For by it the people of old received their commendation. By faith we understand that the universe was created by the word of God, so that what is seen was not made out of things that are visible.

HYMN VERSE 1:

By faith we see the hand of God in the light of creation's grand design
In the lives of those who prove His faithfulness who walk by faith and not by sight

VOICE 2:

By faith Abel offered to God a more acceptable sacrifice than Cain, through which he was commended as righteous.

VOICE 3:

By faith Enoch was taken up so that he should not see death, and he was not found, because God had taken him.

VOICE 4:

By faith Noah, being warned by God concerning events as yet unseen, in reverent fear constructed an ark for the saving of his household.

VOICE 5:

By faith Abraham obeyed when he was called to go out to a place that he was to receive as an inheritance. And he went out, not knowing where he was going. By faith he went to live in the land of promise, as in a foreign land, living in tents with Isaac and Jacob, heirs with him of the same promise. For he was looking forward to the city that has foundations, whose designer and builder is God.

HYMN VERSE 2:

By faith our fathers roamed the earth with the pow'r of His promise in their hearts
Of a holy city built by God's own hand, a place where peace and justice reign

VOICE 6:

By faith Sarah herself received power to conceive, even when she was past the age, since she considered him faithful who had promised.

VOICE 5:

By faith Abraham, when he was tested, offered up Isaac, and he who had received the promises was in the act of offering up his only son, of whom it was said, "Through Isaac shall your offspring be named."

VOICE 7:

By faith Isaac invoked future blessings on Jacob and Esau.

VOICE 8:

By faith Jacob, when dying, blessed each of the sons of Joseph, bowing in worship over the head of his staff.

HYMN VERSE 3:

By faith the prophets saw a day when the longed-for Messiah would appear
With the pow'r to break the chains of sin and death and rise triumphant from the grave

VOICE 9:

By faith Joseph, at the end of his life, made mention of the exodus of the Israelites and gave directions concerning his bones.

VOICE 10:

By faith Moses chose rather to be mistreated with the people of God than to enjoy the fleeting pleasures of sin.

VOICE 11:

By faith Rahab the prostitute did not perish with those who were disobedient, because she had given a friendly welcome to the spies.

HYMN VERSE 4:

By faith the church was called to go in the pow'r of the Spirit to the lost
To deliver captives and to preach good news in ev'ry corner of the earth

VOICE 1:

And what more shall we say? For time would fail to tell of Gideon, Barak, Samson, Jephthah, of David and Samuel and the prophets—who through faith

VOICE 2:

conquered kingdoms,

VOICE 3:

enforced justice,

VOICE 4:

obtained promises,

VOICE 5:

stopped the mouths of lions,

VOICE 6:

quenched the power of fire,

VOICE 7:

escaped the edge of the sword,

VOICE 8:

were made strong out of weakness,

VOICE 9:

became mighty in war,

VOICE 10:

put foreign armies to flight.

VOICE 11:

Women received back their dead by resurrection.

VOICE 2:

Some were tortured, refusing to accept release, so that they might rise again to a better life.

VOICE 3:

Others suffered mocking and flogging, and even chains and imprisonment.

VOICE 4:

They were stoned, they were sawn in two, they were killed with the sword.

VOICE 5:

They went about in skins of sheep and goats,

VOICES 6, 7, & 8:

destitute, afflicted, mistreated—

VOICE 9:

of whom the world was not worthy—

VOICE 10:

wandering about in deserts and mountains, and in dens and caves of the earth.

VOICE 11:

And all these, though commended through their faith, did not receive what was promised, since God had provided something better for us, that apart from us they should not be made perfect.

HYMN VERSE 5:

By faith the mountain shall be moved and the pow'r of the gospel shall prevail
For we know in Christ all things are possible, for all who call upon His name

VOICE 1:

Therefore, since we are surrounded by so great a cloud of witnesses, let us also lay aside every weight, and sin which clings so closely, and let us run with endurance the race that is set before us, looking to Jesus, the founder and perfecter of our faith, who for the joy that was set before him endured the cross, despising the shame, and is seated at the right hand of the throne of God.

CHORUS:

We will stand as children of the promise
We will fix our eyes on Him our soul's reward
Till the race is finished and the work is done
We'll walk by faith and not by sight

BY FAITH

Words and Music by Keith Getty, Kristyn Getty, and Stuart Townend
© 2009 Thankyou Music; Getty Music Publishing

CHRIST THE KING SUNDAY
OVERVIEW

TIME

The last Sunday of the Christian year; the Sunday before the first Sunday of Advent.

THEMES

The Feast of Christ the King celebrates Christ's messianic kingship and sovereign rule over all creation. This day reminds the church of the authority of Christ over all aspects of our lives. Christ the King Sunday has an eschatological element pointing to the end of time when the kingdom of Jesus will be established in all its fullness to the ends of the earth. It leads into Advent when the church anticipates Christ's second coming.

SPIRITUAL CHALLENGE

Resolve to give Christ the central place in your life.

SCRIPTURE

- Old Testament: 2 Sam 23:1–7; Ezek 34:11–16, 20–24; Dan 7:9–10, 13–14; Jer 23:1–6
- Psalm: Ps 93:1–2, 5; Ps 95:1–7a; Ps 100; Ps 132:1–12, (13–18)
- New Testament: Eph 1:15–23; Col 1:11–20; 1 Tim 1:17; Rev 1:4b–8; Rev 19:6
- Gospel: Matt 25:31–46; Matt 27:11; Luke 23:33–43; John 18:33–37

SYMBOLS

- Cross
- Crown

COLORS
- White
- Gold

CHRIST THE KING SUNDAY

SONG LIST

CONTEMPORARY

All Hail the King of Heaven Matt Boswell and Matt Papa, 2021

Ancient of Days Michael Farren, Jesse Reeves, Jonny Robinson, and Rich Thompson, 2018

Before the Throne of God Above Charitie Lees Bancroft and Vicki Cook, 1997

Christ Be Magnified Cory Asbury, Cody Carnes, and Ethan Hulse, 2019

Christ Our Glory David Zimmer and Nathan Stiff, 2019

Glory to God Forever Steve Fee and Vicki Beeching, 2009

God the Uncreated One (King Forevermore) Aaron Keyes and Pete James, 2016

He Is Exalted Twila Paris, 1985

Here I Am to Worship Tim Hughes, 2001

Here Is Our King David Crowder, 2005

How Great Is Our God Chris Tomlin, Jesse Reeves, and Ed Cash, 2004

Lift High the Name of Jesus Keith Getty, Kristyn Getty, Fionán De Barra, and Ed Cash, 2013

Lord, I Lift Your Name on High Rick Founds, 1989

King of Glory Todd Dulaney, 2017

King of Glory Brett Younker, Hank Bentley, Jason Ingram, Kristian Stanfill, and Matt Maher, 2019

King of Heaven Paul Baloche and Jason Ingram, 2010

King of Kings Brooke Ligertwood, Jason Ingram, and Scott Ligertwood, 2019

King of My Heart John Mark McMillan and Sarah McMillan, 2015

Majesty Jack Hayford, 1981

My God My King David Leonard and Leslie Jordan, 2013

Only King Forever Steven Furtick, Chris Brown, Wade Joye, and Mack Brock, 2013

Praise the King Corey Voss, Michael Bryce Jr., Michael Farren, and Dustin Smith, 2014

Resurrecting Chris Brown, Mack Brock, Matthews Ntlele, Steven Furtick, and Wade Joye, 2015

Sing to the King Billy J. Foote and Charles S. Horne, 2003

The King In All His Beauty Matt Boswell and Matt Papa, 2015

This Kingdom Geoff Bullock, 1995

Turn Your Eyes George Romanacce, Kevin Winebarger, Nathan Stiff, and Nic Trout, 2019

Unto the King Geron Davis, 2006

We Bow Down Twila Paris, 1984

We Declare That the Kingdom of God Is Here Graham Kendrick, 1986

We Will Glorify Twila Paris, 1982

TRADITIONAL

All Hail the Pow'r of Jesus' Name Edward Perronet, 1780

Alleluia Sing to Jesus W. Chatterton Dix, 1866

At the Name of Jesus Caroline M. Noel, 1870

Be Thou My Vision Mary E. Byrne, transl., 8th century; Eleanor H. Hull, versifier

Come, Christians, Join to Sing Christian H. Bateman, 1843

Come Thou Almighty King Anonymous, 1757

Crown Him with Many Crowns Matthew Bridges, 1851; George Elvey

Hail to the Lord's Anointed James Montgomery, 1821

Jesus Shall Reign Where'er the Sun Isaac Watts, 1719

O Worship the King Robert Grant, 1833

Praise, My Soul, the King of Heaven Henry Francis Lyte, 1834

Rejoice the Lord Is King Charles Wesley, 1744

The King Shall Come When Morning Dawns John Brownlie, 1907

PRESENTATIONAL

God and King Sandi Patty, 2013

How Great Is Your Faithfulness Matt Redman, 2009

Jesus King of Angels Fernando Ortega, 1998

Meekness and Majesty Graham Kendrick, 1986

Psalm 24 (The King of Glory) Keith Getty, Kristyn Getty, Ed Cash, and Chris Tomlin, 2016

We Shall Behold Him Dottie Rambo, 1980

GLOBAL

Mohot O Ashchorjo (Magnificent and Wonderful) David Roy, 2022 (Bangladesh)

Te Exaltaré Mi Dios, Mi Rey Casiodoro Cárdenas, 1975 (Ecuador)

Yesu Azali Awa (Jesus Christ Is With Us) Traditional (Democratic Republic of the Congo)

CHRIST THE KING SUNDAY
WORSHIP SERVICE

Today in the Christian year calendar is a special day called Christ the King Sunday. It is a day to honor and glorify Jesus as King of our lives . . . and King of this world. This is an important day because we too often relegate Jesus to buddy status. And though he can be considered our friend, we must rightfully acknowledge him as King of kings and Lord of lords.

In a sermon preached on September 13, 1857, the great English preacher Charles Spurgeon said,

> "If I had a tale to tell you this day, of some king, who, out of love to a fair maiden, left his kingdom and became a peasant like herself, you would stand and wonder, and would listen to the charming tale; but when I tell of God concealing his dignity to become our Savior, our hearts are scarcely touched. We know the tale so well; we have heard it so often. And unfortunately, some of us tell it so badly that we cannot expect that you would be as interested in it as the subject demands. But surely, as it is said of some great works of architecture, that though they are seen every morning, there is always something fresh to wonder at; so, we may say of Christ, that though we saw him every day, we should always see fresh reason to love, and wonder, and adore."

Let's say 2 Corinthians 8:9 together . . .

CONGREGATION:

For you know the grace of our Lord Jesus Christ, that though he was rich, yet for your sakes he became poor, so that you through his poverty might become rich.

Let us guard against allowing this wonderful story to become old and stale. Instead, this morning, let us lift our hearts and voices in praise of Jesus, the King.

CROWN HIM WITH MANY CROWNS

Words by Matthew Bridges, 1851; Music by George Elvey, DIADEMATA, 1868
Public Domain

As we spend time in the gospels, we learn many things about Jesus' life and the reason he came to earth and the salvation we find only through him. Then, in the letters of the apostle Paul, we understand more of Christ's nature and are instructed on how to respond.

Your attitude should be the same as that of Christ Jesus: Who, being in very nature God, did not consider equality with God something to be grasped, but made himself nothing, taking the very nature of a servant, being made in human likeness.

And being found in appearance as a man, he humbled himself and became obedient to death—even death on a cross! Therefore God exalted him to the highest place and gave him the name that is above every name, that at the name of Jesus every knee should bow, in heaven and on earth and under the earth, and every tongue confess that Jesus Christ is Lord, to the glory of God the Father.
Philippians 2:5–11

HE IS EXALTED

Words and Music by Twila Paris
© 1985 by StraightWay Music and Mountain Spring Music

PRAISE THE KING

Words and Music by Corey Voss, Dustin Smith, Michael Bryce Jr., and Michael Farren
© 2014 Centricity Music Publishing, CentricSongs, Integrity's Alleluia! Music, Integrity's Praise! Music

Descending from his heavenly throne, Jesus entered the world he formed and offered himself as the ultimate sacrifice. In doing so, he solidified his triumph over the rule of sin and darkness. Yet this victory isn't something he keeps to himself; He graciously imparts it to all who acknowledge him as their Lord.

The kingdom and the dominion and the greatness of the kingdoms under the whole heaven shall be given to the people of the saints of the Most High; his kingdom shall be an everlasting kingdom, and all dominions shall serve and obey him.
Daniel 7:27

OFFERING PRAYER

Almighty God, on this Christ the King Sunday, we come before you with hearts filled with reverence and adoration. We lift our voices in praise, proclaiming Jesus Christ as the King of Kings and Lord of Lords, reigning in power and glory. As we honor the authority of Christ over all creation, we offer our worship and thanksgiving, acknowledging that every aspect of our lives belongs to you. You are the source of all goodness, and it is by your grace that we have received all that we have.

On this special day, we seek to align our hearts and minds with the will of our King. May our offerings be a reflection of our devotion and commitment to follow Christ's teachings and spread his love to the world. We present our gifts with joyful hearts, knowing that through them, we participate in your kingdom work. Bless these offerings, and may they be used to advance your gospel and bring transformation to the lives of others.

As we celebrate Christ's sovereignty, we also remember his humility and sacrificial love. Help us to serve others with the same selflessness and compassion, becoming living witnesses of Christ's reign.

In the name of Jesus Christ, our King and Savior, we pray. Amen.

OFFERTORY

ANCIENT OF DAYS

Words and Music by Jonny Robinson, Rich Thompson, Michael Farren, and Jesse Reeves
© 2018 CityALight Music, Farren Love And War Publishing, Integrity's Alleluia! Music, BEC Worship, WriterWrong Music

PRAYER OF ILLUMINATION

Eternal God, on this Christ the King Sunday, we come before you with hearts uplifted, seeking the illumination of your divine truth, as we celebrate the majestic reign of your Son, Jesus Christ. In this moment before the sermon, we bow in reverence, inviting your Spirit to guide our understanding, may your light shine upon the profound mystery of Christ's kingship. As we reflect on his sovereignty and authority, may your truth resonate deeply within us, empowering us to live in obedience to his teachings.

As we acknowledge Jesus as the King of kings, may his love and compassion transform our hearts, inspiring us to serve one another with humility. Amid the challenges of the world, may the message of Christ the King give us hope, assuring us that he holds all things in his hands. As we look forward to his glorious return, may we be found faithful and vigilant, proclaiming his kingdom to the ends of the earth.

We offer this prayer with gratitude and devotion, in the name of Jesus Christ, our Savior and King, Amen.

SERMON

[If observing the Lord's Supper, continue. If not, proceed to the next congregational song.]

THE LORD'S SUPPER INSTRUCTIONS AND INVITATION

[Instrumental music played or congregational singing.]

THE MYSTERY OF FAITH

And so, in remembrance of these your mighty acts in Jesus Christ, we offer ourselves in praise and thanksgiving as a holy and living sacrifice, in union with Christ's offering for us, as we proclaim the mystery of faith:

CONGREGATION:

Christ has died; Christ is risen; Christ will come again.

LIFT HIGH THE NAME OF JESUS

Words and Music by Keith Getty, Kristyn Getty, Fionán De Barra, and Ed Cash

© 2013 Getty Music Publishing, Alletrop Music, Fionán De Barra

BENEDICTION

Our life's mission goes beyond simply recognizing Jesus Christ as our Lord and King. It's about making his kingdom a reality here and now, impacting those around us with both our words and actions. Let's emulate his way of living: selflessly, lovingly, and in service to others. May the blessings of Almighty God rest upon you as you embrace this calling. Now, go in peace, ready to shape his kingdom through your love and service.

CHRIST THE KING SUNDAY
SCRIPTURE PRESENTATION

THE KING OF GLORY

Psalm 24

CAST:

1 Voice
Group (3–5 voices)
Congregation

VOICE 1:

The earth is the Lord's and the fullness thereof, the world and those who dwell therein, for he has founded it upon the seas and established it upon the rivers.

GROUP:

Who shall ascend the hill of the Lord?
And who shall stand in his holy place?

CONGREGATION:

He who has clean hands and a pure heart, who does not lift up his soul to what is false and does not swear deceitfully.

VOICE 1:

He will receive blessing from the Lord and righteousness from the God of his salvation. Such is the generation of those who seek him, who seek the face of the God of Jacob.

CONGREGATION:

Lift up your heads, O gates!
And be lifted up, O ancient doors, that the King of glory may come in.

GROUP:

Who is this King of glory?

CONGREGATION:

The Lord, strong and mighty, the Lord, mighty in battle!

VOICE 1:

Lift up your heads, O gates!
And lift them up, O ancient doors, that the King of glory may come in.

GROUP:

Who is this King of glory?

ALL:

The Lord of hosts,
he is the King of glory!

CONCLUSION

THE OBSERVANCE OF THE Christian year helps develop a life lived in the pattern of the birth, life, death, resurrection, and ultimate return of Christ. It enjoys biblical sanction, historical staying power, and contemporary relevance.[82] Following the Christian year encourages the formation of our spiritual lives and brings unity to the church—not only unity with one another, but unity with Christ. We are heartened by the Apostle Paul's directive for us to "be eager to maintain the unity of the Spirit in the bond of peace" (Eph 4:3) with the ultimate aim of glorifying God. In the celebrations of the seasons of the Christian year, the unity of the church is on display, and a watching world joins in some level of participation in worship. Observing sacred time within the church does not mean the worshiper gets special access to God. As we have seen, the seasons of the Christian year provide opportunities for greater attention and devotion, but not necessarily greater proximity to the divine.

In the epilogue of his book devoted to forming spirituality through the Christian year, Robert Webber states,

> *Finally, the rhythm of the Christian year, particularly that of the extraordinary season from Advent to Pentecost, would guide the Christian through a variety of times and emotions. As we have seen:*
>
> *Advent is a time to wait.*
>
> *Christmas is a time to rejoice.*
>
> *Epiphany is a time to witness.*
>
> *Lent is a time for repentance and renewal.*
>
> *The Great Triduum is a time to express the resurrected life.*

---

82. Webber, *Ancient-Future Time*, 22.

After Pentecost is a time to study and evangelize.

Of course, we are to do all these Christian practices all the time. But a rule of thumb is that specific time set aside for each facilitates and empowers our Christian experience at all times.[83]

When we participate in corporate worship as a church, we join in one accord fulfilling the main purpose of the Christian year—to relive the major events in Jesus' life in real time. The keeping of sacred time enables the church to recall the story of God on a consistent basis throughout the year resulting in the deepening of theological perspectives, spiritually formative worship, and increased vitality within the congregation.

The Christian year calendar stands as a valuable tradition offering a holistic and meaningful approach to worship, spiritual formation, and communal identity. Rooted in history, focused on Christ, and promoting unity, this calendar encourages believers to engage deeply with the foundational events of the Christian faith. By embracing the Christian year, churches can cultivate a vibrant and transformative worship experience, fostering a deeper understanding of the gospel and a closer relationship with God and one another.

---

83. Webber, *Ancient-Future Time*, 180.

POSTSCRIPT

As I MENTIONED EARLIER, I grew up in a small conservative Baptist church. In that denomination, the worship format didn't include a formal "liturgical" style, and my church was no exception. When I began attending university for my undergraduate studies, I met someone who, by God's design, would become my wife. She was raised in a Lutheran church. Her worship background was foundationally "liturgical." Early on in our relationship, she could see how at times, my understanding of corporate congregational worship could be narrow because of my upbringing. My liturgical understanding was woefully limited.

Today, we are both amazed at how open I am to liturgy . . . not just open to it but drawn to it. Although I know there's much more to learn and experience, I am deeply thankful for the profound impact that worship education and my worship experiences have had on my life. I urge you to embrace the possibilities of how God might work in your life through the use of sacred time in your worship, whether through traditional or contemporary practices. Perhaps one day, like me, you'll look back and be astonished by the growth in your understanding and appreciation of sacred time in your worship. May God bless you on your journey.

SUGGESTED RESOURCES FOR LEARNING MORE ABOUT THE CHRISTIAN YEAR

Bradshaw, Paul F., and Maxwell E. Johnson. *The Origins of Feasts, Fasts and Seasons in Early Christianity*. Collegeville: The Liturgical Press, 2011.

Johnson, Maxwell E. *Between Memory and Hope: Readings on the Liturgical Year*. Collegeville: The Liturgical Press, 2000.

Webber, Robert E. *Ancient-Future Time: Forming Spirituality Through the Christian Year*. Grand Rapids: Baker Books, 2004.

White, James F. *Introduction to Christian Worship*. Nashville: Abingdon Press, 2000.

For more worship service examples and Scripture presentations visit worshipquest.net/resources

ABOUT THE ARTWORK

I am honored to have the artwork of Minna Lim included in this book. Minna is an interior designer with a Bachelor of Arts and certification in painting and print-making from Virginia Commonwealth University and University of California, Los Angeles. She currently resides in Southern California with her husband and two dogs and attends Calvary Baptist Church in Huntington Beach.

Here are the artist's remarks about each piece:

COVER ART

Artist's expression of Psalm 1:1 and Revelation 22 with Jesus Christ portrayed as the "Blessed Man whose leaves do not wither" and the "Healer of the Nations and Tree of Life" in Revelation 22.

SEASONS OF LIGHT ART

Artist's expression of John 1:1–5 and James 1:17 and the seasons of light expressed through the Trinity that breaks every chain and shines brighter in the darkness.

SEASONS OF LIFE ART

Artist's expression of the Tree of Life and the first and second Eden found in Genesis 3 and Revelation 22 with theological focus towards Jesus Christ as the Word of God that flows from the throne as High King of Heaven.

BIBLIOGRAPHY

Adam, Adolf. *The Liturgical Year: Its History and Its Meaning After the Reform of the Liturgy.* Collegeville: The Liturgical Press, 1981.
Aniol, Scott. *Worship in Song: A Biblical Approach to Music and Worship.* Winona Lake: BMH, 2009.
Brooks, Steven D. *The Week that Changed the World: Daily Reflections for Holy Week.* Bloomington: Westbow, 2021.
———. *Worship Formation: A Call to Embrace Christian Growth in Each Element of the Worship Service.* Eugene, OR: Wipf & Stock, 2020.
———. *Worship Quest: An Exploration of Worship Leadership.* Eugene, OR: Wipf & Stock, 2015.
Butler, Dom Cuthbert, ed. *Saint Benedict's Rule for Monasteries.* Translated by Leonard J. Doyle. Collegeville: The Liturgical Press, 1948.
Chan, Francis. "Why Are They Leaving?" *Worship Leader Magazine* (September 2008) 22.
Dawn, Marva J. *How Shall We Worship? Biblical Guidelines for the Worship Wars.* Wheaton: Tyndale, 2003.
Donaldson, James, trans. *Apostolic Constitutions, VII, 23 (c. 375) ANF, VII,* 469.
Duchesne, Louis. *Christian Worship: Its Origin and Evolution.* London: Society for Promoting Christian Knowledge, 1904.
Dues, Greg. *Catholic Customs and Traditions: A Popular Guide.* New London: Twenty-Third Publications, 2000.
Durham, John I. *Exodus.* Vol. 3, *Word Biblical Commentary.* Waco: Word, 1987.
Easton, Burton S. *The Apostolic Tradition of Hippolytus.* Hamden: Archon, 1962.
Edersheim, Alfred. *The Temple: Its Ministry and Services.* Peabody: Hendrickson, 1994.
Flannery, Austin P., ed. "The Constitution on the Sacred Liturgy," no. 106, in *Documents of Vatican II.* 29–30.
Gross, Bobby. *Living the Christian Year: Time to Inhabit the Story of God.* Downers Grove: InterVarsity, 2009.
Hartley, John E. *Leviticus.* Vol. 4, *Word Biblical Commentary.* Dallas: Word, 1992.
Hickman, Hoyt L., et al. *The New Handbook of the Christian Year: Based on the Revised Common Lectionary.* Nashville: Abingdon, 1992.
Hill, Andrew E. *Enter His Courts with Praise!: Old Testament Worship for the New Testament Church.* Grand Rapids: Baker, 1997.
Hustad, Donald P. *Jubilate II: Church Music in Worship and Renewal.* Carol Stream: Hope, 1993.
Martin, Ralph P. *The Worship of God: Some Theological, Pastoral, and Practical Reflections.* Grand Rapids: Eerdmans, 1982.

McKnight, Scot. *Praying with the Church: Following Jesus Daily, Hourly, Today.* Brewster: Paraclete, 2006.

Moody, Dale. *Spirit of the Living God: What the Bible Says about the Spirit.* Nashville: Broadman, 1976.

Munger, Robert Boyd. *My Heart, Christ's Home.* Downers Grove: InterVarsity, 1986.

Pratt, Waldo S. "The Liturgical Responsibilities of Non-Liturgical Churches." *The American Journal of Theology* 5 (1901) 641–65.

Richardson, Cyril. *Early Christian Fathers.* Philadelphia: Westminster, 1953.

Searle, Mark. "Sunday: The Heart of the Liturgical Year." In *Between Memory and Hope: Readings on the Liturgical Year*, edited by Maxwell E. Johnson, 59–76. Collegeville: The Liturgical Press, 2000.

Stookey, Laurence H. *Calendar: Christ's Time for the Church.* Nashville: Abingdon, 1996.

Taft, Robert F. *Beyond East and West: Problems in Liturgical Understanding.* Rome: Pontifical Oriental Institute, 1997.

Talley, Thomas J. *The Origins of the Liturgical Year.* Collegeville: The Liturgical Press, 1986.

Tertullian, *De baptismo* 19.2; ET from Cantalamessa, 91.

Torrance, Thomas. *Conflict and Agreement in the Church.* Eugene, OR: Wipf & Stock, 1996.

Von Allmen, J. J. *Worship: Its Theology and Practice.* London: Lutterworth, 1965.

Wainwright, Geoffrey. "Beginning with Easter." *The Reformed Journal* 38 (1988) 13–17.

Webber, Robert E. *Ancient-Future Time: Forming Spirituality Through the Christian Year.* Grand Rapids: Baker, 2004.

———. *Ancient-Future Worship: Proclaiming and Enacting God's Narrative.* Grand Rapids: Baker, 2008.

———. *The Divine Embrace: Recovering the Passionate Spiritual Life.* Grand Rapids: Baker, 2006.

White, James F. *Introduction to Christian Worship.* 1980. Reprint, Nashville: Abingdon, 2000.

www.ingramcontent.com/pod-product-compliance
Lightning Source LLC
Chambersburg PA
CBHW050618300426
44112CB00012B/1563